Christ, Church, and World

Christ, Church, and World

Bonhoeffer and Lutheran Ecclesiology after Christendom

Theodore J. Hopkins

LEXINGTON BOOKS/FORTRESS ACADEMIC
Lanham • Boulder • New York • London

Published by Lexington Books/Fortress Academic
Lexington Books is an imprint of The Rowman & Littlefield Publishing Group, Inc.
4501 Forbes Boulevard, Suite 200, Lanham, Maryland 20706
www.rowman.com

86-90 Paul Street, London EC2A 4NE, United Kingdom

Copyright © 2021 by The Rowman & Littlefield Publishing Group, Inc.

All rights reserved. No part of this book may be reproduced in any form or by any electronic or mechanical means, including information storage and retrieval systems, without written permission from the publisher, except by a reviewer who may quote passages in a review.

British Library Cataloging in Publication Information Available

Library of Congress Cataloging-in-Publication Data

Names: Hopkins, Theodore J., author.
Title: Christ, church, and world: Bonhoeffer and Lutheran ecclesiology after Christendom / Theodore J. Hopkins.
Description: Lanham: Lexington Books/Fortress Academic, [2021] | Includes bibliographical references and index.
Summary: "In this book, Theodore J. Hopkins utilizes the work of Dietrich Bonhoeffer to navigate the relationship between the church and the world in the emerging post-Christian context. Following Bonhoeffer's Christology, Hopkins situates the church within the story of Jesus to be formed by him for his mission of witness and service in the world"—Provided by publisher.
Identifiers: LCCN 2021034083 (print) | LCCN 2021034084 (ebook) | ISBN 9781978708587 (cloth) | ISBN 9781978708600 (paperback) | ISBN 9781978708594 (epub)
Subjects: LCSH: Church. | Bonhoeffer, Dietrich, 1906–1945. | Jesus Christ—Person and offices. | Lutheran Church—Doctrines.
Classification: LCC BV600.3 .H665 2021 (print) | LCC BV600.3 (ebook) | DDC 262.001/7—dc23
LC record available at https://lccn.loc.gov/2021034083
LC ebook record available at https://lccn.loc.gov/2021034084

Contents

Preface	vii
Acknowledgments	xiii
Abbreviations	xvii
Introduction: The Hermeneutical Task of Ecclesiology after Christendom	1
1 Logics of Lutheran Ecclesiology and the Necessity of Christology	17
2 Dietrich Bonhoeffer's Christology in Ecclesiological Perspective	43
3 Christ-Church-World: The Christological Center of the Church-World Relation	69
4 Jesus Christ, Lord and Servant: A Storied Ecclesiology for Post-Christendom	105
Conclusion	147
Bibliography	155
Subject Index	175
Scripture Index	179
About the Author	181

Preface

A theology that cannot be preached, believed, and lived is worthless. Hence, Stanley Hauerwas has rightly approached the task of theology as teaching Christians "how to speak Christian."[1] How do Christians "speak Christian" with regard to the identity and mission of the church? How do Christians "live Christian" in the same? This book intends to address these questions not merely to think about the church, but to use ecclesial thought-forms to proclaim the gospel and live faithfully in community.[2]

The cultural context of post–Christian North America is part of what makes this project necessary. North American Christianity is dominated by an individualistic framework that almost always says "I" and rarely says "we."[3] Although individualism is decried so frequently among theologians that such criticism may appear trite and pedantic, I am convinced of the myopia of the Christian imagination. Christians speak about themselves and their families in their native tongue, but few have learned to envision and confess the church as a dynamic part of God's own mission in Christ through the Spirit. For many of us, Christianity is about "me and Jesus," and the church has almost nothing to do with it. At best, the church helps me in my individual walk of faith, but it often seems ambivalent to fulfilling my religious needs and aspirations.[4]

I suspect that theologians, we systematic theologians most of all, have reinforced this conclusion. Sometimes, we have been so involved in denominationally centric questions with regard to the church, that what matters most—the church's connection to the triune God and the world to which it is called to participate in God's mission—has been overshadowed by intramural affairs. For instance, traditional Lutheran ecclesiologies—such as those that employ the loci method[5]—have primarily focused upon the work of the professionals (ministry), the rules about who is allowed to preach, teach, and commune (fellowship), and how institutions should relate to one another (ecumenism), usually in contradistinction from other confessional viewpoints.[6] These are important institutional questions, to be clear, but they do not help much in cultivating God's mission in concrete congregations. Instead, these things are abstract to people in the pews, and as such reinforce the idea that Christianity is an individual matter of faith and spirituality, fulfilling religious needs. If ecclesiology is so irrelevant, perhaps so is the church.

In the Lutheran tradition, individualism looms large—for example, the history of pietism—including in my own conservative American branch of Lutheranism called The Lutheran Church—Missouri Synod (LCMS). What the LCMS does well is proclaim the gospel of Jesus Christ for individual sinners—the forgiveness of sins delivered to a person in Word and sacrament from Jesus himself through his Spirit. This is good, right, and salutary! Too often, though, LCMS preachers and even official statements make congregations irrelevant to social or ethical issues except insofar as churches play the games of partisan politics: lobbying and voting. The result is that Christians have little language or vision about how to address and work in the public realm as a *Christian* community, and politics fills the void. Hence, in the LCMS the church is imagined mostly as a denominational structure, a bastion of social conservativism, or as the place where those essential "me and Jesus" moments occur. Preaching is directed at individuals, for individuals, and about individuals, and rarely does it concern the formation of the community in its identity, life together, and mission. Who should be surprised that few Christians are equipped to see Christ, church, and world together in the dynamic of Jesus' identity and mission? Propositions about the church are not enough; the church needs to be re-imagined, which begins with language in the pulpit, classroom, and Christian homes.[7]

At some level, this task is hardly new. Michael Gorman argues, "Already in the first Christian century the apostle Paul wanted communities he addressed not merely to *believe* the gospel but to *become* the gospel, and in so doing to participate in the very life and mission of God."[8] Similarly, my task is to help the church *confess* the gospel by learning to speak Christ, church, and world together, and begin to participate in the life and mission of God by reimagining the world as God's own and embodying the gospel accordingly.[9] At the minimum, when Christianity is perceived to be about me and not we, Christians have not yet learned to "speak Christian" about the church. This is something conservative Lutherans—and I suspect many more American Christians—still need to learn. Although I situate my work within the Lutheran tradition and my emphasis on preaching is *reformatorisch*, my reading of Reformed and Roman Catholic theology suggests that the church more broadly needs this kind of training to "speak Christian," especially concerning the relationship of the church and the world. After all, following the Augsburg Confession, the foundational confession of Lutheran theology, a Lutheran ecclesiology can never be merely Lutheran. If Lutheran theology does not speak to the church catholic, it has lost its way. As such, I hope my engagement with Lutheran theology will also aid other Christians in engaging in their traditions to proclaim the church in relationship to Christ and the world.

In this project, I use Dietrich Bonhoeffer extensively to establish a Christology that recognizes the church and the world as part and parcel of the story of Christ Jesus. To be clear, this is not a historical project, trying to establish something new about Bonhoeffer in his context. Bonhoeffer is a vital resource because his "*Christological* conception of the God-world relation makes him a particularly important thinker for the future direction of any theology that wants to address our current intellectual climate."[10] Bonhoeffer's Christology affirms God's transcendence, God's encounter with humanity *ab extra* as the justifying God, while situating the Christian life in a concrete, historical community in the world. History is not obliterated by theology, but opened up for recognizing God's own presence within it in Christ and by the Spirit.[11] Further, Bonhoeffer grounds and affirms the dialectical relationship of the church and the world Christologically, bringing together Christ, church, and world in the dynamic relation of God's story, known in the Holy Scripture.[12] In so doing, Bonhoeffer's Christology supports both the unity of and the distinction between the church and the world. My examination of Bonhoeffer illuminates the Christological logic that undergirds the tensions across the Berlin theologian's corpus concerning the church-world relation.

Christians must learn to say Christ, church, and world within the dynamic of Jesus' mission in the world. The church is known in and through Christ; the world is known in and through Christ; and Christ is the Lord and Servant who was sent by the Father, empowered by the Spirit, redeemed the world with his own blood, and calls his church to bear witness by the Spirit to that redemption in word and deed. In seeing the church always in and through Jesus, I believe that the church and its relationship to the world can be reimagined not as part of the individualistic story of America but as part of the story of God. Such a project will not be completed by writing a book, but by being preached, taught, and envisioned by a church who begins to see and live "Jesus and *us*" rather than just "me and Jesus." Only then will this project truly come to fruition.

Lent 2021

NOTES

1. Stanley Hauerwas, *The Work of Theology* (Grand Rapids, MI: Eerdmans, 2015), 111.

2. Compare Eva Harasta, "The Responsibility of Doctrine: Bonhoeffer's Ecclesiological Hermeneutics of Dogmatic Theology," *Theology Today* 71, no. 1 (2014): 24.

3. Carl R. Trueman, *The Rise and Triumph of the Modern Self: Cultural Amnesia, Expressive Individualism, and the Road to Sexual Revolution* (Wheaton, IL: Crossway, 2020), 25: Expressive individualism "is the very essence of the culture of which we are all a part. To put it bluntly, we are all expressive individuals now." See also the excellent work of Charles Taylor: *Sources of the Self: The Making of the Modern Identity* (Cambridge, MA: Harvard University Press, 1989); and *A Secular Age* (Cambridge, MA: Belknap Press of Harvard University Press, 2007).

4. Mark Sayers, *Disappearing Church: From Cultural Relevance to Gospel Resilience* (Chicago: Moody Publishers, 2016), 19–21, observes the rise of atheist "churches" where the community is not about Jesus at all, but a place to gather for connection and self-fulfillment in an alienating world. Such a community is certainly less pious than the "me and Jesus" mentality, but it does share a similar instrumental notion of the church.

5. For example, see Kurt E. Marquart, *The Church and Her Fellowship, Ministry, and Governance*, vol. 9 of Confessional Lutheran Dogmatics, ed. Robert D. Preus (St. Louis: Luther Academy, 1990).

6. Compare Risto Saarinen, "Lutheran Ecclesiology," in *The Routledge Companion to the Christian Church*, ed. Gerard Mannion and Lewis S. Mudge (New York: Routledge, 2008), 173:

> One historical problem of Lutheran ecclesiology is that most confessional formulations express a criticism that, in turn, forces Lutherans to steer their course among a variety of real and imagined enemies. Confessional Lutherans often know what the church should not be, but they are less aware of what the church actually is.

7. Compare William James Jennings, "The Desire of the Church," in *The Community of the Word: Toward an Evangelical Ecclesiology,* ed. Mark Husbands and Daniel J. Treier (Downers Grove, IL: Intervarsity, 2005), 249: We need "cleansing images, holy icons that focus our attention and begin to destroy the formation of distorted desire through false and unholy images."

8. Michael J. Gorman, *Becoming the Gospel: Paul, Participation and Mission* (Grand Rapids, MI: Eerdmans, 2015), 2.

9. I am suggesting that learning to confess, speaking Christian, is central to being the church. I explore my notion of confession in a recent editorial: Theodore J. Hopkins, "Theology Is for Confession," *Concordia Theological Journal* 6, no. 1 (2018): 7–9.

10. Jens Zimmermann, "Suffering with the World: The Continuing Relevance of Dietrich Bonhoeffer's Theology," in *Dietrich Bonhoeffer Jahrbuch 3: 2007/2008*, ed. Clifford J. Green, et al. (Gütersloh: Gütersloher Verlagshaus, 2008), 313. Emphasis original.

11. Compare Zimmermann, "Suffering with the World," 314.

12. On the importance of Bonhoeffer's Christology for hermeneutics, see Derek W. Taylor, *Reading Scripture as the Church: Dietrich Bonhoeffer's Hermeneutic of Discipleship* (Downers Grove, IL: IVP, 2020); Jens Zimmermann, "Reading the Book of the Church: Bonhoeffer's Christological Hermeneutics," *Modern Theology* 28, no. 4 (2012): 764–80; and Zimmermann, "Suffering with the World," 311–37.

Acknowledgments

"One becomes 'a whole person' not all by oneself but only together with others."[1] It is not possible for me to acknowledge all of the people who have been part of the process of this text. I feel obligated to the professors of Christ College at Valparaiso University, especially Profs. Visser, Hoffman, and Creech, who taught me to interrogate texts and authors and to be interrogated in turn. At Concordia Seminary, St. Louis, Joel Okamoto taught me to question every theological assumption in order that the reality of the story of God in Christ would criticize, ground, and enable all theological thought-forms. His guidance also led me to fall in love with the work of Gerhard Forde, who still has a profound impact on my thought. In my graduate studies at Concordia Seminary, my friend and colleague Rick Serina helped me understand the landscape of twentieth-century ecumenism, challenged me to recognize the depth of Lutheranism's catholicity, and encouraged me to read the great Karl Barth, who became my second love in theology. I have yet to find anyone—except Luther himself—who can speak with the systematic aptitude, biblical erudition, and evangelical force of Barth. Working with my mentor and friend Bob Kolb and professor Joel Biermann, I began to read Dietrich Bonhoeffer near the end of my graduate studies because of Bonhoeffer's affinity with Barth. Bonhoeffer's corpus lacks the breadth and depth of Barth's, but sacramentally and arguably Christologically (i.e., *lutherisch*) Bonhoeffer is superior. Over the last ten years, Bonhoeffer has become a friend, and I have spent more time reading him than in conversation with almost anyone else, except my wife and children. I have learned much from these friends and professors, and from the authors and works they opened for me. That I am me because of them is truer than I can imagine. In that vein, to all the above and below I acknowledge a debt of gratitude, and I give them my thanks.

Although this book has long roots, the most significant research took place during the summer and fall semesters of 2019. I received a generous study grant from a Concordia Intramural Research Grant. With the generous support from the administration of Concordia University Wisconsin/Ann Arbor, especially from our Vice Provost Dr. Leah Dvorak and the chair of the CIRG committee Dr. Beth Buckley, I was able to explore and analyze the structure of Bonhoeffer's thought, the surface of which I had only been skimming in years prior. During this semester, I gave a presentation on Bonhoeffer's hermeneutics for the Theological Symposium at Concordia Seminary, St. Louis, and I was invited by Rev. Tony Sikora to give three presentations on Bonhoeffer as part of a theological conference at Hope Lutheran Church in Holt, MI. The research for these four presentations demanded that I engage Bonhoeffer deeply and extensively, which helped me understand how his Christological logic permeates his work outside of the Christology lectures. I hope the attendees learned as much from me as I learned in preparing the lectures.

I am blessed to have great colleagues at Concordia University, Ann Arbor. Phil Penhallegon is now at Concordia Seminary, St. Louis, yet he remains a dear friend who continually provides meaningful encouragement; Charles Schulz is my favorite Platonist who reminds me of the importance of Church Fathers, and Scott Yakimow has compelled me to think more sharply about theological method, especially with regard to a pragmatic approach to theology. Scott also has given me the honor of reading parts of this book and discussing its structure and logic with me; I can only hope to reciprocate this honor in the future.

My students across the years, at Concordia Seminary, St. Louis, Lutheran High School South in St. Louis, and especially Concordia University, Ann Arbor, deserve my thanks for forming me into a better teacher and illuminating how theology matters daily. I sincerely hope that my students in senior seminar have become better writers and thinkers under my tutelage because I know that mentoring their projects has improved my writing and thinking. In my last round of editing, I found myself criticizing my work in the same way I do theirs: "If it does not support the thesis, cut it out." As they know, this is easier advice to hear than to heed.

I also want to thank those who supported me throughout the project's development. Thank you to my friend Mark Koschmann who chatted with me regularly about the project in its earliest phases, usually over libations. Mark is a great companion on this adventure of the ministry of the gospel. Bob Kolb has been a true friend and mentor throughout the process of this book. Bob not only connected me to Fortress Academic and encouraged me that this was a valuable project, but he also read and commented upon the book, improving it significantly. I hope that my formulations honor his input.

Charles Arand, Joel Biermann, Erik Herrmann, and Joel Okamoto also provided valuable insights as they read early drafts of the chapters. Additionally, I want to thank Neil Elliott and the Fortress Academic team at Lexington Books, including my anonymous peer reviewer, for all of their support and constructive criticism of the project, even through the challenges of the COVID-19 pandemic.

Finally, my wife Beth not only gives me a picture of God's faithfulness by her trustworthiness and loyalty, but she also willingly read a draft of this work to help me with copy-editing. Since theology is hardly her first love, she proved herself to be a far better wife than I deserve. It is to her that I dedicate this book. Our children, Thomas and Emma, are joys as they show me the goodness of creation in this fallen world. My parents too, Dean and Sofia, have never ceased to be supportive.

Of course, the customary caveat applies: all the errors of commission and omission that are present in this book belong to me alone. May it provide even a syllable in the on-going conversation of theology, all to the glory of God: Father, Son, and Holy Spirit.

NOTE

1. DBWE 8, 278.

Abbreviations

DBWE 1   Bonhoeffer, Dietrich. *Sanctorum Communio: A Theological Study of the Sociology of the Church.* Edited by Clifford J. Green. Vol. 1 of *Dietrich Bonhoeffer Works English Edition.* Minneapolis: Fortress, 1998.
DBWE 2   Bonhoeffer, Dietrich. *Act and Being: Transcendental Philosophy and Ontology in Systematic Theology.* Edited by Wayne Whitson Floyd, Jr. Vol. 2 of *Dietrich Bonhoeffer Works English Edition.* Minneapolis: Fortress, 1996.
DBWE 3   Bonhoeffer, Dietrich. *Creation and Fall: A Theological Exposition of Genesis 1–3.* Edited by John W. de Gruchy. Vol. 3 of *Dietrich Bonhoeffer Works English Edition.* Minneapolis: Fortress, 1997.
DBWE 4   Bonhoeffer, Dietrich. *Discipleship.* Edited by Geffrey B. Kelly and John D. Godsey. Vol. 4 of *Dietrich Bonhoeffer Works English Edition.* Minneapolis: Fortress, 2001.
DBWE 5   Bonhoeffer, Dietrich. *Life Together and Prayerbook of the Bible.* Edited by Geffrey B. Kelly. Vol. 5 of *Dietrich Bonhoeffer Works English Edition.* Minneapolis: Fortress, 1996.
DBWE 6   Bonhoeffer, Dietrich. *Ethics.* Edited by Clifford J. Green. Vol. 6 of *Dietrich Bonhoeffer Works English Edition.* Minneapolis: Fortress, 2005.
DBWE 8   Bonhoeffer, Dietrich. *Letters and Papers from Prison.* Edited by John W. de Gruchy. Vol. 8 of *Dietrich Bonhoeffer Works English Edition.* Minneapolis: Fortress, 2009.
DBWE 10 Bonhoeffer, Dietrich. *Barcelona, Berlin, New York: 1928–1931.* Edited by Clifford J. Green. Vol. 10 of

	Dietrich Bonhoeffer Works English Edition. Minneapolis: Fortress, 2008.
DBWE 11	Bonhoeffer, Dietrich. *Ecumenical, Academic and Pastoral Work: 1931–1932*. Edited by Victoria J. Barnett, Mark S. Brocker, and Michael B. Lukens. Vol. 11 of *Dietrich Bonhoeffer Works English Edition*. Minneapolis: Fortress, 2012.
DBWE 12	Bonhoeffer, Dietrich. *Berlin: 1932–1933*. Edited by Larry L. Rasmussen. Vol. 12 of *Dietrich Bonhoeffer Works English Edition*. Minneapolis: Fortress, 2009.
DBWE 14	Bonhoeffer, Dietrich. *Theological Education at Finkenwalde: 1935–37*. Edited by H. Gaylon Barker and Mark S. Brocker. Vol. 14 of *Dietrich Bonhoeffer Works English Edition*. Minneapolis: Fortress Press, 2013.
DBWE 15	Bonhoeffer, Dietrich. *Theological Education Underground: 1937–1940*. Edited by Victoria J. Barnett. Vol. 15 of *Dietrich Bonhoeffer Works English Edition*. Minneapolis: Fortress, 2012.
DBWE 16	Bonhoeffer, Dietrich. *Conspiracy and Imprisonment: 1940-1945*. Edited by Mark S. Brocker. Vol. 16 of *Dietrich Bonhoeffer Works English Edition*. Minneapolis: Fortress, 2006.

Introduction

The Hermeneutical Task of Ecclesiology after Christendom

Once there was no ecclesiology.[1] According to Wolfhart Pannenberg, "The church did not form a separate theme in the systematic presentation of Christian doctrine until the 15th century."[2] Before that time, the church was not something to explain but something to be experienced. The church was the community and context in which worship, preaching, the Sacraments, Bible reading, and works of love took place. Martin Luther's *Smalcald Articles* of the sixteenth century reflects this earlier notion of the church: "A seven-year-old child knows what the church is: holy believers and 'the little sheep who hear the voice of their shepherd.'"[3] The church might be understood best without systematic ecclesiology, Luther insinuates. The church is simply the people gathered around the Word of God and the Sacraments who hear the voice of the Lord. The key to the church's life is not in explaining its nature but in receiving Christ by the Word and living in him. In such an understanding of the church, a systematic explanation of this gathering could detract from the centrality of the church that lives in Christ and in the world.

In the early church, not a single Latin or Greek church father developed a systematic understanding of the church.[4] Even Augustine, who is foundational to the ecclesiological reflections of Radical Orthodoxy,[5] never wrote a systematic presentation on the church. In *On Christian Doctrine*, Augustine speaks of the church in scriptural terms as the bride and body of Christ, but he does not set forth the nature of the church in a formal or comprehensive fashion. Augustine mentions the church in connection to Christ's reconciliation, Christian sanctification or unity in love, and the office of the keys, but Augustine offers no sustained reflection on the church's being.[6] *City of God* too is not a comprehensive, systematic ecclesiology, but a reflection upon the church's relationship to God and what that means for its life in the world. Before the ecclesial crisis of the late middle ages culminated in the Protestant

Reformation in the West, the church simply *was* the context for theology and the Christian faith without forming a separate dogmatic topic. In the language of twentieth-century German Lutheran theologian Dietrich Bonhoeffer, the church was the "presupposition" for theology instead of a theme of systematic thought.[7]

During the sixteenth century, however, *de ecclesia* became a standard chapter in dogmatic presentations. What sparked the revolution from understanding the church as a presupposition of theology to conceptualizing it as a separate topic in theological reflection? In short, an ecclesial crisis necessitated a new focus on the nature of the church. According to historian Scott Hendrix, this ecclesial crisis began with the Spiritual Franciscans and the Waldensians in the thirteenth century as the "quest for the *vera ecclesia*."[8] Eventually, the church—as well as larger European society—entered a new reality of division and confessionalization that concluded the era of Reformation and corresponded to an explosion of ecclesiology.[9]

In the late medieval quagmire of ecclesial division and church authority, questions such as "Whose leader?", "Which church?", and "What confession?" became as natural as "Which god?" was to the ancient Israelites. The church could no longer be assumed as a presupposition "in the age of conciliarism and after the experiences of the Western schism and the papal captivity in Avignon."[10] The Protestant Reformation only exacerbated this ecclesial crisis, requiring ecclesiology to be a dogmatic topic that places one Christian confession against another, but distancing ecclesiology from reflection upon the church's fundamental relationships, especially its relationship to the world.

THE CONTEMPORARY ECCLESIOLOGICAL TURN

The social and ecclesiastical crises of Christendom during the late medieval period provoked a turn in which ecclesiology became a standard topic of systematic theology for the first time, although it was just one topic among many.[11] In the subsequent period of confessionalization across Europe, the primary theological focus was grace and justification, individual salvation, stemming from the Reformation debates of the sixteenth century. Because of this, some Lutherans pushed ecclesiology to the back of dogmatics, almost as an appendix to systematic theology, clearly subordinated to the individual appropriation of salvation.[12]

Recently, theology has taken another ecclesiological turn, making ecclesiology come into focus as a fundamental theological task.[13] In the twentieth century, ecumenism inspired many ecclesiologies, most notably *communio* ecclesiology, that sought to bring together Orthodox, Roman Catholic, and

Protestant visions of the church under one heading: the communion of the triune God and the church's participation in that communion.[14] Although communion ecclesiology is alive and well,[15] the ecumenical task appears to have lost its fire, and ecclesiology has begun to consider more deeply the church's place in and relationship to the emerging post-Christian world.[16] Instead of being one topic among many in dogmatics, ecclesiology has become "the normative study" of communities.[17] As a normative study, ecclesiology is "fundamental to Christian theological reflection as such" since it "concerns the nature of the social space which makes language about God, and therefore faith itself, possible."[18] In this way, Mannion and Mudge consider the church primarily as a context for theological reflection and the Christian life rather than an object of investigation. How did this change take place?

When Karl Barth spurned the theological trajectory of Protestant liberalism, including the thought of theological giants like Adolf von Harnack, Barth charted a new path that presumed the church was something more than a topic of systematic investigation. Karl Barth named his second attempt at a systematic theology *Church Dogmatics*. The title *Church Dogmatics* indicates that dogmatics is not religious *Wissenschaft*, academic scholarship of religion; dogmatics is subordinate to the Word of God and to the proclamation of the church that results in faith.[19] Barth argues that the church cannot merely be a topic of theology since theology happens in the church. Theology does not only talk about the church, but the community of faith also makes theology intelligible. At a minimum, the relationship between theology and the church is more complex than the topical method suggests.

Following the theological direction of Karl Barth—with significant influence from the philosopher Ludwig Wittgenstein and sociologist Clifford Geertz—the Lutheran ecumenist George Lindbeck articulated an understanding of Christianity which places the church at the center. In his influential book *The Nature of Doctrine*, Lindbeck's ecumenical endeavors propelled him to advocate a "postliberal" theory of religion different from two common models.[20] The two common models for understanding religion are the cognitive model, which privileges propositional, cognitive truth-claims about reality as the heart of religion, and the "experiential-expressive" model, which emphasizes the interior and personal side of religion so that church doctrines are "noninformative and nondiscursive symbols of inner feelings, attitudes, or existential orientations."[21] As an alternative to these two models, *Nature of Doctrine* proposes a "cultural-linguistic" model that understands religions "as comprehensive interpretive schemes, usually embodied in myths or narratives and heavily ritualized, which structure human experience and understanding of self and world."[22] In other words, for Lindbeck, religion is a comprehensive hermeneutic—like culture and language—that interprets all reality so that its adherents understand the world they live in based on the stories they tell, the language they employ, and the rituals they practice in community with others. Hence, Lindbeck audaciously claims that "for those who are steeped in [the canonical writings of religious communities], no world is more real than the ones they create. A scriptural world is thus able to absorb the universe."[23]

Although *Nature of Doctrine* appears more sociological and philosophical in orientation, it has extensive theological roots in ecclesiology. Lindbeck himself recognizes the need for rethinking the church as a language and culture because of the post-Christian context.[24] In a post-Christian culture, the survival of the Christian faith depends on Christians being rooted in church-communities in which the story of the Scriptures is imagined as the story of the world and the practices of the church are more basic than the cultural practices of production and consumption.[25] In short, for Lindbeck, the "plausibility structures" of Christianity in society at large—Christendom—have eroded, which means that the church must be a community in which the Christian faith is plausible again.[26] Although ecumenism was a driving factor for Lindbeck's theory of religion, the final chapter of *Nature of Doctrine* discusses the postliberal focus on intratextuality—letting the text and its story "absorb the world" rather than the world absorb the text—in light of the decline of the Christian heritage in the West.[27] Lindbeck asserts, "Western culture is now at an intermediate stage, however, where socialization is ineffective, catechesis impossible, and translation [of Christian language and culture into culturally dominant forms] a tempting alternative."[28] The church is in an "awkward" position vis-à-vis North American society, having been in power but now in the midst of losing it.[29]

The details of Lindbeck's ecclesiology are unimportant here;[30] the point is to see ecclesiology at the heart of Lindbeck's theological proposal, and recognize how the proposal's intelligibility is dependent upon the emerging post-Christian context, the nature of the world as Lindbeck understands it. Ecclesiology remains under the radar of *Nature of Doctrine* except at a few crucial points, yet the whole proposal presumes an ecclesiology: the church is a "community identified by and participating in a common language, the basis of which is the story of Jesus Christ."[31] Since Lindbeck believes that the church is this sort of community,[32] *Nature of Doctrine* functions both as a sociological and philosophical defense of this ecclesiology from the standpoint of the theory of religion and as a substantive argument for its implications—particularly the centrality of catechesis and the importance of Christian formation.[33] Just as one learns a language by immersion into its forms and use, so Christians must be immersed in the language and stories of the Bible and church practices that "socialize [church] members into coherent and comprehensive religious outlooks and forms of life."[34]

Lindbeck's proposal thus places the church in a central position, elevating ecclesiology from a mere topic within a theological system. The church is inseparable from understanding Christianity's central message and living the Christian life.[35] In response to the changing church-world dynamic, Lindbeck argues that the church needs to cultivate its own story and way of life in order to survive in a post-Christian environment.[36] Hence, ecclesiology is not merely a topic to be understood but an urgent task to support the church's life in the emerging post-Christian world.[37]

LUTHERAN ECCLESIOLOGY AT THE END OF CHRISTENDOM

Although the central insight of Lutheran ecclesiology is that the church is a creature of God's Word,[38] Lutheran ecclesiology has rarely integrated the necessary hermeneutical task to navigate the church-world relationship after Christendom.[39] On one side, Lutheran theology has been heavily invested in the ecumenical conversations of the twentieth century, and the post-Christendom situation has been a secondary consideration.[40] Even when the changing culture is recognized, prominent Lutheran theologians like Robert Jenson have highlighted the scandal of the divided church, and confessed the one, holy, catholic, and apostolic church in relationship with the triune God.[41] The visible church that gathers in the divine service around the Word of God and the Eucharist, participating in the divine life, comes to the fore,[42] but the church's relationship with the world outside of this gathering is not as clear.[43] Instead of regarding also Christ's relationship with the world and the church's relationship with the world as central matters for ecclesiology, questions of structure and authority dominate. The church is rightly understood as a visible community in relationship to the Lord that forms Christians in virtue and practice, but the church's relationship with the world remains unmoored outside of worship.

On the other side, Lutheran theologians like Oswald Bayer have focused on the doctrine of justification, describing the church's being and life as a creature of God's Word.[44] The church's relationship with God through the Word takes center stage since God comes to sinners through preaching and the Sacraments to create faith and bring them into the people of God. The church is understood theologically from its origin, but its visible life in relationship to the world takes a back seat, outside of the means of grace. Although this ecclesiology rightly prioritizes the Word and work of God, the Word is understood primarily as preaching that encounters and converts individuals, emphasizing individual hearing, conversion, and vocation.[45] The church-world relationship arises primarily from the work of Christian individuals in the world, displacing social justice from the church's mission as a community and fragmenting the community outside of the Word and Sacraments.[46] Although the ecclesiology of the Word stresses the constitutive nature of God's Word, the Word functions primarily individually rather than hermeneutically to shape the church's life in the world and form Christians into this ecclesial life.

Further complicating the church's relationship with the world in contemporary Lutheran ecclesiology is the specific nature of post-Christendom. The North American Christian church has operated with privilege and power from the inception of the American colonies. While no Christian denomination was officially established as an arm of the state throughout America, the Christian church nonetheless acted like it was "the only show in town."[47] The truth of the church was the truth of politics—the truth period—and the church expected society to get in line.[48] Although the Christian church is losing that privilege as the synthesis of Christian religion and politics disintegrates, the church continues to operate vis-à-vis the world according to the Christendom model of power.[49] James Davison Hunter has shown how the language and logic of politics has influenced the way that Christians interact with the world in contemporary North America.[50] Christians on both the right and the left fight culture wars at the ballot box and lobby political parties while believing these partisan political battles are constitutive of the church's mission.[51] The problem is not only that Christians have succumbed to the will of power as a technique of mission, but also that Christians can hardly imagine the church as a community with its own identity and logic for working in the world.[52] The church-world relation shaped by partisan politics is distorted and even unhinged from the gospel of Jesus that creates the church and fashions it into his cruciform mission.

When the church manages to remove itself from partisan politics, the problem of the church-world relationship persists. The church in North America has been instrumentalized as a religious good in the marketplace, helpful for some individuals, but not integral to the hard truths of the real world.[53] Many Christians, for instance, treat their faith as a "private whim or caprice,"[54] something they choose to practice because of "just feeling right."[55] Accordingly, Christian Smith and Melinda Lundquist Denton's landmark research on the religious lives of American teens found that many young people identify as Christian but their predominant faith has more in common with a "parasitic faith" Smith calls "Moralistic Therapeutic Deism."[56] At the heart of moralistic therapeutic deism is the idea that God is a "Divine Butler or Cosmic Therapist," at an individual's beck and call, ready to assist.[57] In this frame, the church is at most the butler's house where people expect to receive the fulfillment of their religious needs.[58] Such a church may not succumb to the powerplays of partisan politics, but it has been warped into an instrument of individual self-help.[59]

My point is that the church-world relationship stands in a precarious position in post-Christendom, and Lutheran ecclesiology has rarely offered a hermeneutical framework to situate the church's relationship to the world. The church is known in its relationship to God in Lutheran ecclesiology, but the descriptions tend to focus on the church in its perfection rather than the messiness of its concrete life in the world.[60] The church is the eucharistic communion where it embodies the communion of the Triune God, as in Jenson, or the church is God coming to it through Word and Sacrament, as in Bayer. In both cases, the emphasis falls on the church in its ideal form, and Lutheran ecclesiology gives little direction for congregational life in the world beyond the divine service. To be clear, my point is not that the church needs to be understood sociologically rather than theologically.[61] Rather, the church and the world are rightly known in the story of the triune God, revealed in Jesus Christ, and the specifics of this story should shape concrete congregational life in the world. This story not only defines the church, but it also gives the church ears to hear the Scriptures and be molded into Christ's cruciform mission vis-à-vis the world. It is this hermeneutical task that is so necessary for Lutheran ecclesiology after Christendom.

THE ARGUMENT

Although I am critical of the Lutheran ecclesiology of the Word for failing to establish the visible community and shape congregational mission outside of Sunday morning, this project is not a rejection of the enterprise. With the Lutheran ecclesiology of the Word, I confess that the Word and the Word alone creates faith, draws people into God's church, and makes congregations participants in the mission of the Triune God.[62] I intend to repair Lutheran ecclesiology of the Word by recognizing the Word that creates and forms the church first and primarily as the crucified and living Lord who makes himself present by his Spirit through preaching and the Sacraments—in which he is also the basic content. In this way, the story of God in Christ is confessed as the church's narrative identity that forms its life together and its mission. In other words, I locate the church primarily in Christology in order that the story of God in Christ calls congregations to repentance, faith, and obedience to Jesus in the world. Dietrich Bonhoeffer's Christology connects Christ, church, and world in the story of God, providing a framework for a hermeneutical ecclesiology that recognizes the church as a creature of the Word, the world as a recipient of Christ's work, and congregations as participants in Christ's cruciform mission. Bonhoeffer's Christology thus situates church and world in the story of God in Christ, drawing the church to follow Christ's mission faithfully in the changing world that is post-Christendom.

Central to my work is the Christ-church-world triad: the church's relationship to Christ, the world's relationship to Christ, and the church's relationship to the world.[63] Instead of identifying the church in itself, the church is understood within the Christ-church-world triad with Christology functioning as the animating center of all three relationships. If ecclesiology is about the interrelations of Christ, church, and world, as I argue, propositions (and polemics) are necessary to describe the actors and delimit the relationships, but the hermeneutical task is the more important one in the post-Christian milieu. Ecclesiology needs to provide a vision of the church and the world in Christ Jesus so that concrete congregations learn to imagine their place in Christ and the world,[64] and read, preach, and teach the Bible to be formed into the mission of the crucified one in the emerging post-Christian world.[65] Stated differently, a hermeneutical ecclesiology informs preaching and teaching, which in turn forms Christians to imagine the church in relationship to Christ and the world and follow his mission.[66] A hermeneutical ecclesiology that follows Bonhoeffer's Christology will be theological—rooted in the story of God in Christ—concrete—preached, taught, and lived in local congregations—and missional—focused on the church-world relationship.[67]

THE OUTLINE

Chapter 1 investigates the logic of two types of Lutheran ecclesiology, showing how both fall short of the needed hermeneutical task. I first examine the Lutheran ecclesiology of the Word. This understanding of the church confesses the assembly of believers as the creation of the justifying Word of God, but the church as a concrete community, formed for and called to discipleship and witness, is sidelined in favor of the sermon. The ecclesiology of the Word prioritizes the stories of individual Christians encountered by God's Word, but does little to cultivate the community of the church into discipleship and mission. Next, I explore Reinhard Hütter's ecclesiology, which recognizes the church as a visible community that forms Christians as the people of God. Hütter's project grounds the visible, public character of the church through an account of core church practices that participate in the work of the Holy Spirit. Although Hütter's account avoids the Scylla of individualism and invisibility, his ecclesiology falls into the Charybdis of ecclesial introspection, directing congregations inward to their own status quo rather than outward to Christ.

To avoid such introspection but retain an emphasis on the visible community, I turn to Dietrich Bonhoeffer's Christology in chapter 2. Focusing on Bonhoeffer's 1933 Christology lectures, I present the logic of Bonhoeffer's Christology that binds Christ, church, and world in one story. Bonhoeffer's

Christology confesses Jesus as the transcendent Lord who is also the humiliated one. He is graspable in his church in the Word, and he is the center of the world's ontology. Bonhoeffer's Christology establishes church and world independently in the story of Jesus, directing the church outward to Christ in repentance and faith and to the world in Christ's mission.

Chapter 3 expounds the Christ-church-world triad. On the basis of Bonhoeffer's Christology, I argue for a dialectical relationship of "dynamic tension" between Christ and the church[68] in which Christ is both present in the church and for the church in the gospel and the Sacraments, and Christ is outside of the church and against it in calling it to repentance and obedience. Bonhoeffer's hermeneutic of Scripture enacts this dialectic so that the church attends to the living voice of God in the Word, is called to repentance by the Word, and is molded for its cruciform mission, following Jesus. Turning to the church-world relationship, I examine Bonhoeffer's apparent oscillation in his corpus between a strong distinction between church and world during the Finkenwalde period and the unity of church and world in his later writings. Using the logic of his Christology, both perspectives are affirmed dialectically. The church is distinct from the world as the community in which Christ is present by his promise, *and* the church is in full solidarity with the world in the one story of Jesus Christ. The church's engagement with and mission in the world must be shaped not only by the Christ-church relation but also by the Christ-world relation.

In the fourth chapter, I offer two narrative readings of Scripture that enact the dialectics of the Christ-church-world triad, showing how the story of Christ molds concrete communities for faith and mission. I tell two stories of Jesus, Christ the Lord and Christ the Servant, that identify the church in Christ and bring the church into his mission in the world. The narrative of the Lord Jesus emphasizes the identity of the church that belongs to Jesus and is called to listen to him. In the story of the Lord Jesus, the church is distinct from the world so that the church is bound to Christ and brought into his mission, just as Dietrich Bonhoeffer does in *Discipleship*. On the other side of the dialectic, the story of Christ the servant is just as necessary for the church after Christendom. Christ came to be the suffering servant, and he gives the church his cruciform mission. In this account, the church embodies Christ's solidarity with the world, not making power plays or demands from above but working from below, with and for others, as Bonhoeffer's *Letters and Papers from Prison* and *Ethics* portray.

Through preaching and teaching both of these stories of Jesus in Christian congregations, the Lord calls his people to repentance by the Word, grants them their identity in the gospel, gives them eyes to see the world as God's own, and sends them out in obedience to his mission in and with the world. Such is the purpose of Bonhoeffer's theology and this book: not merely faithful thinking but faithful teaching and preaching that makes space for congregations and Christians to be formed into the likeness of Christ by the Spirit.

NOTES

1. I am playing on John Milbank's: "Once there was no 'secular.'" Milbank, *Theology and Social Theory: Beyond Secular Reason*, 2nd ed. (Malden, MA: Blackwell, 2006), 9.

2. Wolfhart Pannenberg, *Systematic Theology*, vol. 3, trans. Geoffrey W. Bromiley (Grand Rapids, MI: Eerdmans, 1997), 21.

3. Robert Kolb and Timothy J. Wengert, eds., *The Book of Concord: The Confessions of the Evangelical Lutheran Church* (Minneapolis: Fortress, 2000), 324–25.

4. Pannenberg, *Systematic Theology*, 3:21.

5. See James K.A. Smith, *Introducing Radical Orthodoxy: Mapping a Post-Secular Theology* (Grand Rapids, MI: Baker Academic, 2004).

6. Augustine, *On Christian Teaching*, trans. R.P.H. Green (New York: Oxford University Press, 1999), 15–16.

7. DBWE 11, 283.

8. Scott Hendrix, "In Quest for the Vera Ecclesia: The Crisis of Medieval Ecclesiology," *Viator* 7 (1976): 347–78.

9. Hendrix, "In Quest," 347, argues that the new focus on ecclesiology does not originate with the Protestant Reformation, which is "the concluding phase of the late medieval quest" to come to grips with the ecclesial and social crises of the time. See also R. Van Caenegem, "Government, Law and Society," in *The Cambridge History of Medieval Political Thought, c. 350–c. 1450*, ed. J.H. Burns (Cambridge: Cambridge University Press, 1988), 185–95, for the beginning of the modern European nation state as a key context for understanding the anxieties of the time. On the reformatory milieu of the late middle ages, see Steven Ozment, *The Age of Reform (1250–1550): An Intellectual and Religious History of Late Medieval and Reformation Europe* (New Haven: Yale University Press, 1980).

10. Pannenberg, *Systematic Theology*, 3:22.

11. Pannenberg, *Systematic Theology*, 3:21–24.

12. Pannenberg, *Systematic Theology*, 3:23–24. Heinrich Schmid's compendium of Lutheran Orthodoxy is a good example. The only topic that comes after ecclesiology is eschatology, which has its own history of reemerging as a central category in twentieth-century theology. See Heinrich Schmid, *The Doctrinal Theology of the Evangelical Lutheran Church*, 3rd ed., trans. Charles A. Hay and Henry E. Jacobs (Minneapolis: Augsburg, 1899).

13. Compare Gerard Mannion and Lewis S. Mudge, *The Routledge Companion to the Christian Church* (New York: Routledge, 2008), 1. Already in the early nineteenth century, the German Lutheran Theodor Kliefoth recognized the emergence of ecclesiology as an essential task: "Thus, at the least we must recognize that investigations

into the being, emergence, growth, and completion of the church are already taking a dominant place in our dogmatic activity and . . . [dogmatics in our time period] will have its specific task in the doctrine of the church." Theodor Kliefoth, *Einleitung in die Dogmengeschichte* (Parchim: D.C. Hinstorff, 1839), 98–99. My translation. I am obliged to Shawn Barnett for this reference.

14. For a Roman Catholic vision that sees a diversity of approaches in *communio* ecclesiology, see Dennis M. Doyle, *Communion Ecclesiology* (Maryknoll, NY: Orbis, 2000). Doyle points out that Cardinal Ratzinger names communion ecclesiology as the "one basic ecclesiology," which necessitates Doyle's own recognition of the diversity of approaches within communion ecclesiology (pp. 1–5). John D. Zizioulas offers an orthodox vision in *Being as Communion: Studies in Personhood and the Church* (Crestwood, NY: St. Vladimir's Seminary Press, 1985). Miroslav Volf articulates a protestant vision in *After Our Likeness: The Church as the Image of the Trinity* (Grand Rapids, MI: Eerdmans, 1998). For Lutherans appropriating this approach, see Heinrich Holze, ed., *The Church as Communion: Lutheran Contributions to Ecclesiology* (Geneva: Lutheran World Federation, 1997).

15. Criticism of communion ecclesiology has been offered by, for example, Nicholas M. Healy, "Communion Ecclesiology: A Cautionary Note," *Pro Ecclesia* 4, no. 4 (Fall 1995): 442–53; and Healy, "Ecclesiology and Communion," *Perspectives in Religious Studies* 31, no. 3 (Fall 2004): 273–90. Joseph Mangina confirms its importance but with an important amendment: "The Cross-Shaped Church: A Pauline Amendment to the Ecclesiology of *Koinōnia*," in *Critical Issues in Ecclesiology: Essays in Honor of Carl E. Braaten*, ed. Alberto L. García and Susan K. Wood (Grand Rapids, MI: Eerdmans, 2011), 68–87. For my project, the ecumenical context of communion ecclesiology limits its usefulness because communion ecclesiology tends to be abstract from congregational life. Compare Healy's criticism of "blueprint ecclesiologies," in Nicholas M. Healy, *Church, World and the Christian Life: Practical-Prophetic Ecclesiology* (Cambridge: Cambridge University Press, 2001), 25–51.

16. Most significant theologically are those ecclesiologies connected to post-liberalism and radical orthodoxy. For instance, George Lindbeck and the so-called "Yale School" have been influential. See Paul J. DeHart, *The Trial of the Witnesses: The Rise and Decline of Postliberal Theology* (Malden, MA: Blackwell, 2006), 41–53, for a short history of the so-called "Yale School" and some of the conversations that came from the work of Lindbeck and Hans Frei, especially. Other important figures in this discussion include Reinhard Hütter, *Suffering Divine Things: Theology as Church Practice*, trans. Doug Stott (Grand Rapids, MI: Eerdmans, 2000); William T. Cavanaugh, *Migrations of the Holy: God, State, and the Political Meaning of the Church* (Grand Rapids, MI: Eerdmans, 2011); and James K. A. Smith, *Imagining the Kingdom: How Worship Works*, vol. 2 of Cultural Liturgies (Grand Rapids, MI: Baker Academic, 2013), as well as the other volumes of Smith's Cultural Liturgies series. I would be remiss not to name Stanley Hauerwas too, who is almost a school in himself. Recently, see Stanley Hauerwas, *The Work of Theology* (Grand Rapids, MI: Eerdmans, 2015), 32–52. Among his older stuff that has been influential, see *Community of Character: Toward a Constructive Christian Social Ethic* (Notre Dame: Notre Dame University Press, 1981). In addition, the Gospel and Our Culture

Network has produced many missiological and ecclesiological reflections that recognize this post-Christian situation in North America. For example, see Darrell L. Guder, *The Continuing Conversion of the Church* (Grand Rapids, MI: Eerdmans, 2000). Many popular works also acknowledge this change, such as Rod Dreher, *The Benedict Option: A Strategy for Christians in a Post-Christian Nation* (New York: Sentinel, 2017); and David E. Fitch, *Faithful Presence: Seven Disciplines that Shape the Church for Mission* (Downers Grove, IL: IVP Books, 2016).

17. Mannion and Mudge, *Routledge Companion to the Christian Church*, 3.
18. Mannion and Mudge, *Routledge Companion to the Christian Church*, 3.
19. Karl Barth, *Church Dogmatics*, vol. 1, part 1, ed. G.W. Bromiley and T.F. Torrance (1936; reprint, Peabody, MA: Hendrickson, 2010), 1–25.
20. George A. Lindbeck, *The Nature of Doctrine: Religion and Theology in a Postliberal Age* (Philadelphia: Westminster, 1984), 135n.1. Postliberal is the term Lindbeck prefers for his project.
21. Lindbeck, *Nature of Doctrine*, 16.
22. Lindbeck, *Nature of Doctrine*, 32.
23. Lindbeck, *Nature of Doctrine*, 117.
24. DeHart, *Trial of the Witnesses*, 58–62.
25. Compare George A. Lindbeck, "The Sectarian Future of the Church," in *The God Experience*, ed. J.P. Whelan (New York: Newman, 1971), 230: Without "social support" in the larger society, Lindbeck argues that Christians will need to "gather together in small, cohesive, mutually supporting groups."
26. On plausibility structures, see Peter L. Berger, *Facing Up to Modernity: Excursions in Society, Politics, and Religion* (New York: Basic Books, 1977), 173–74.
27. Lindbeck, *Nature of Doctrine*, 118.
28. Lindbeck, *Nature of Doctrine*, 133.
29. Lindbeck, *Nature of Doctrine*, 134.
30. See George A. Lindbeck, *The Church in a Postliberal Age*, ed. James J. Buckley (Grand Rapids, MI: Eerdmans, 2002).
31. DeHart, *Trial of the Witnesses*, 154–55.
32. DeHart, *Trial of the Witnesses*, 60–62. DeHart notes how Lindbeck's understanding of the church in *Nature of Doctrine* is already present in outline in his work written a decade earlier.
33. Lindbeck, *Nature of Doctrine*, 104–8 for Lindbeck's summary in defense of his theory. See pp. 112–35 for the importance of catechesis and formation. Famously, Lindbeck opines, "Religious communities are likely to be practically relevant in the long run to the degree that they do not first ask what is either practical or relevant, but instead concentrate on their own intratextual outlooks and forms of life" (p. 128).
34. Lindbeck, *Nature of Doctrine*, 126.
35. The theological interpretation of Scripture "school" recognizes the integration of hermeneutics and ecclesiology. For instance, James K.A. Smith concludes his book on interpretation: "Our hermeneutics of Scripture will require, first and foremost, an ecclesiology." *The Fall of Interpretation: Philosophical Foundations for a Creational Hermeneutics*, 2nd ed. (Grand Rapids, MI: Baker Academic, 2012),

221. Recently, Derek Taylor has used Bonhoeffer toward this end, though working more through hermeneutics than ecclesiology: Derek W. Taylor, *Reading Scripture as the Church: Dietrich Bonhoeffer's Hermeneutic of Discipleship* (Downers Grove, IL: IVP, 2020). Unfortunately, Taylor's book arrived toward the end of my writing journey, and I do not engage with it as much as it deserves.

36. To be fair, Lindbeck does not say that the church needs to do so *only or primarily* to survive. In his own words, those of postliberal inclinations "will argue for intratextuality on both religious and nonreligious grounds: the integrity of the faith demands it, and the vitality of Western societies may well depend in the long run on the culture-forming power of the biblical outlook in its intratextual, untranslatable specificity." Lindbeck, *Nature of Doctrine*, 134.

37. Compare Gerard Mannion, "Postmodern Ecclesiologies," in *The Routledge Companion to the Christian Church*, ed. Gerard Mannion and Lewis S. Mudge (New York: Routledge, 2008), 132: the major questions for a postmodern ecclesiology regard "the relationship between the church and the world, and the ecclesial attitudes and practices which relate to, shape and reflect this." See also in the field of missiology, George R. Hunsberger, "Proposals for a Missional Hermeneutic: Mapping a Conversation," *Missiology: An International Review* 39, no. 3 (2011): 309–21.

38. Even those Lutherans who depict the church as more than this still say this. For example, Robert Jenson, *Systematic Theology*, vol. 2 (Oxford: Oxford University Press, 1999), 207. Reinhard Hütter too asserts that the church suffers God's activity, even as Hütter claims the church as a locus of the Spirit's work. On the pathic nature of the church, see Hütter, *Suffering Diving Things*, 69–93.

39. Cheryl Peterson is an exception by offering a reading of Acts to understand the church in the movement of the Spirit, focusing on the church's identity and mission after Christendom. Cheryl M. Peterson, *Who Is the Church? An Ecclesiology for the Twenty-first Century* (Minneapolis: Fortress, 2013).

40. For example, Carl E. Braaten, *Mother Church: Ecclesiology and Ecumenism* (Minneapolis: Fortress, 1998); Holze, ed., *Church as Communion*; Hütter, *Suffering Divine Things*; and Ola Tjørhom, *Visible Church—Visible Unity: Ecumenical Ecclesiology and "The Great Tradition of the Church"* (Collegeville, MN: Liturgical Press, 2004), though it was published shortly after Tjørhom became Roman Catholic. Even Hinlicky's recognition of the post-Christian situation focuses more on the divided church than the problem of mission without power or privilege: Paul R. Hinlicky, *Beloved Community: Critical Dogmatics After Christendom* (Grand Rapids, MI: Eerdmans, 2015).

41. Jenson, *Systematic Theology*, 2:189–288.

42. For example, Jenson, *Systematic Theology*, 2:207, rightly states,

> Thus the church is a creature of the gospel not only in the sense that she comes into being as those who have heard and therefore must tell this message but also in the sense that its speaking within her shapes her as the specific polity she is.

43. Compare Peterson, *Who Is the Church*, 75: "It is unclear . . . how this communion lives out its identity as the body of Christ apart from the altar."

44. Oswald Bayer, *Theology the Lutheran Way*, trans. and ed. Jeffrey G. Silcock and Mark C. Mattes (Grand Rapids, MI: Eerdmans, 2007); Bayer, *Martin Luther's Theology: A Contemporary Interpretation*, trans. Thomas H. Trapp (Grand Rapids, MI: Eerdmans, 2008). For more discussions of this ecclesiology, see chapter 1.

45. Peterson, *Who Is the Church*, 52: An ecclesiology of the Word "puts the focus more on the event of the word than on the community created by that event. This can lead to an overly narrow focus on the individual hearing of the word."

46. Hence, the lack of a role of the church as a community in some protestant missiology. For instance, see Greg Finke, *Joining Jesus on his Mission: How to be an Everyday Missionary* (Elgin, IL: Tenth Power, 2014).

47. Stanley Hauerwas and William H. Willimon, *Resident Aliens: Life in the Christian Colony* (Nashville, TN: Abingdon, 1989), 16. On the *de facto* nature of the Christendom establishment, see Douglas John Hall, *The End of Christendom and the Future of Christianity* (Valley Forge, PA: Trinity Press International, 1997), 29.

48. Oliver O'Donovan, *The Desire of the Nations: Rediscovering the Roots of Political Theology* (Cambridge: Cambridge University Press, 1996), 195: Christendom was "an era in which the truth of Christianity was taken to be a truth of secular politics."

49. See Hall, *End of Christendom*.

50. James Davison Hunter, *To Change the World: The Irony, Tragedy, and Possibility of Christianity in the Late Modern World* (Oxford: Oxford University Press, 2010).

51. Hunter, *To Change the World*, 111–49. See also Mark Chaves, *American Religion: Contemporary Trends*, 2nd ed. (Princeton, NJ: Princeton University Press, 2017), 101–16, which shows increasing political polarization between religious and nonreligious people, data that correlates well with Hunter's analysis.

52. Hunter, *To Change the World*, 103: "the state has increasingly become the incarnation of the public weal. Its laws, policies, and procedures have become the predominant framework by which we understand collective life, its members, its leading organizations, its problems, and its issues." Compare William T. Cavanaugh, *Theopolitical Imagination* (London: T&T Clark, 2002), 3: "Too often the modern Christian theological imagination has got lost in the stories that sustain modern politics."

53. Robert Wuthnow, *America and the Challenges of Religious Diversity* (Princeton, NJ: Princeton University Press, 2005), 254, notes that even Christian pastors tend to treat other religions superficially, as an "ethnic custom," "little more than ethnic food and dress," without dealing with the truth claims of the religion, thereby reinforcing this notion of religion as a matter of individual choice and not truth. To understand the pervasive nature of therapy in North America, see Eva Illouz, *Saving the Modern Soul: Therapy, Emotions, and the Culture of Self-Help* (Berkeley, CA: University of California Press, 2008); Eva S. Moskowitz, *In Therapy We Trust: America's Obsession with Self-Fulfillment* (Baltimore: Johns Hopkins University Press, 2001); and Robert N. Bellah et al., *Habits of the Heart: Individualism and Commitment in American Life*, Updated ed. (Berkeley, CA: University of California Press, 1996).

54. Karl Marx, "The Jewish Question," in *Karl Marx: Early Writings*, trans. T.B. Bottomore (New York: McGraw-Hill, 1964), 15: Religion "is now only the abstract avowal of an individual folly, a private whim or caprice. The infinite fragmentation of religion in North America, for example, already gives it the *external* form of a strictly private affair." Emphasis original.

55. Wuthnow, *America and the Challenges of Religious Diversity*, 165–66: "The ground on which decisions are made increasingly takes the form, as expressed in people's comments, of 'just feeling right.'" Wuthnow is speaking about "Christian exclusivists" who still treat their faith like a good of the religious marketplace.

56. Christian Smith with Melinda Lundquist Denton, *Soul Searching: The Religious and Spiritual Lives of American Teenagers* (Oxford: Oxford University Press, 2005), 166:

> This religious creed appears to operate as a parasitic faith. It cannot sustain its own integral, independent life; rather it must attach itself like an incubus to established historical religious traditions, feeding on their doctrines and sensibilities, and expanding by mutating their theological substance to resemble its own distinctive image.

57. Smith, *Soul Searching*, 165.

58. See Philip D. Kenneson and James L. Street, *Selling Out the Church: The Dangers of Church Marketing* (Nashville, TN: Abingdon, 1997), 63–83, and John W. Wright, *Telling God's Story: Narrative Preaching for Christian Formation* (Downers Grove, IL: Intervarsity, 2007), 10–11.

59. Darrell L. Guder, "Missional Hermeneutics: The Missional Vocation of the Congregation—and How Scripture Shapes That Calling," *Mission Focus: Annual Review* 15 (2007): 134, argues that this is a remnant of Christendom. When the state became the primary actor, the church became a servant to citizens of the state. Guder summarizes, "The congregation that meets the needs of its members and provides all their religious ministrations betrays the ongoing influence of the Christendom legacy."

60. See Healy, *Church, World and the Christian Life*, 25–51, for criticism of ecclesiologies that focus on the ideal form of the church.

61. Gary D. Badcock, *The House Where God Lives: Renewing the Doctrine of the Church for Today* (Grand Rapids, MI: Eerdmans, 2009) is right to insist that ecclesiology must be theological, rooted in the identity and work of the triune God (pp. 24–26), even though Badcock's criticisms of Nicholas Healy's practical-prophetic ecclesiology miss the mark (pp. 1–7).

62. In this way, justification remains a "*discrimen*" of theology, but does not function as the animating center. On justification as a *discrimen*, see Mark C. Mattes, *The Role of Justification in Contemporary Theology* (Grand Rapids, MI: Eerdmans, 2004), 11: justification is "the critical point that shapes other doctrines and church practices."

63. Derek Taylor identifies the church as characterized by four "identity-defining relationships": 1) with Christ; 2) with the church's own history and tradition; 3) with a concrete, local community; and 4) with the world (*Reading Scripture as the Church*, 14). While all four relationships are undoubtedly important, for a church that

confesses the ancient Creeds, the second relationship is deeply interrelated with the first and fourth, confessing Christ and the world within a certain confessional account. The third relationship is also essential, but it flows out of the story of Christ.

64. I use the language of the imagination in the same sense as James K.A. Smith, *Imagining the Kingdom*, 16–17: "By 'imagination' here I don't mean something merely inventive or fantastic . . . nor do I have in mind some romantic sense of Creator-like 'invention' or merely an act of 'pretense,' whereby we imagine something that is a fiction . . . . I mean it more as a quasi-faculty whereby we construe the world on a precognitive level, on a register that is fundamentally *aesthetic* precisely because it is so closely tied to the *body*." Emphases original.

65. This is hermeneutical primarily by shaping the nature of reality—ontology—but it also offers a framework for reading the Scriptures ecclesiologically—interpretation of texts. These are two of the categories mentioned by Simone Sinn, "Hermeneutics and Ecclesiology," in *The Routledge Companion to the Christian Church*, ed. Gerard Mannion and Lewis S. Mudge (New York: Routledge, 2008), 576. I was reminded of Sinn's work by Taylor, *Reading Scripture as the Church*, 10.

66. I do not believe that ecclesiology itself does the formation, but preaching, catechesis, scriptural study, and the witness of service shape the Christian imagination. Ecclesiology functions in service of such ministry. Nicholas Healy stresses this practical nature of ecclesiology: *Church, World, and the Christian Life*.

67. Compare Michael J. Gorman, *Becoming the Gospel: Paul, Participation and Mission* (Grand Rapids, MI: Eerdmans, 2015), 2: "Already in the first Christian century the apostle Paul wanted communities he addressed not merely to *believe* the gospel but to *become* the gospel, and in so doing to participate in the very life and mission of God."

68. Fleming Rutledge, *The Crucifixion: Understanding the Death of Jesus Christ* (Grand Rapids, MI: Eerdmans, 2015), 31–33. What Rutledge says about tensions in understanding the crucifixion applies to the Christ-church-world triad too: "There is no midpoint compromise between paradoxical affirmations; the way ahead is found *in the tension itself*" (p. 33).

Chapter 1

Logics of Lutheran Ecclesiology and the Necessity of Christology

Lutheran ecclesiology is a conundrum. Whether Lutherans are merely "ecclesiologically challenged," as Charles Arand submits, or they do not even have an ecclesiology, according to a common trope,[1] Lutheran theology has struggled to establish a robust ecclesiology. Lutheran theology vacillates between affirming the Word and sacraments as the foundation of the church—not merely epistemic markers[2]—and valuing the visible, concrete community that exists beyond preaching, baptizing, forgiving, and eating. Lutheran theology seems unable to establish both desiderata at the same time. Hence, Risto Saarinen asserts that Lutherans are better at ruling out definitions of the church than describing what the church should be. Lutheran theology rightly rejects institutionalism that locates a human hierarchy at the heart of the church, and it properly refutes enthusiasm that mandates an internal enlightening by the Spirit to make the church.[3] Nevertheless, "confessional Lutherans often know what the church should not be, but they are less aware of what the church actually is."[4]

Lutheran ecclesiology, as I see it, exists primarily in two modes. In the first, the logic of justification structures the Lutheran ecclesiology of the Word, which decisively shows what the church is not. The church is not primarily a human institution, nor is it created by human whims, decisions, or feelings. Rather, the church is created by God encountering people in his Word, creating faith in the heart, and calling his people to respond to his work in sanctified lives in the church and in the world.[5] This Word of God ecclesiology rightly confesses the centrality of God and his work to create the church, but the logic of performative speech disconnects justification from its proper context in the story of God. In the logic of performative speech acts, the individual is prioritized as the recipient of God's Word, and the church is more of a collection of justified individuals than it is a real community with a corporate story, mission, and life together. The other mode of Lutheran ecclesiology has tried to correct this individualizing tendency by describing the church as a visible community constituted by its participation in the triune God, usually in the sacraments or church practices.[6] As exemplified in Reinhard Hütter's *Suffering Divine Things*, the church is a visible community of practices and people that has its own way of life, rooted in the communion and work of God. This ecclesiology eliminates the problem of individualism, but its logic produces an introspective church rather than a church that is oriented outward to Christ, ready to hear the Word of repentance and faith and be formed into Jesus and his mission.

THE LUTHERAN ECCLESIOLOGY OF THE WORD

"The church is the assembly of saints in which the gospel is taught purely and the sacraments are administered rightly."[7] This definition from Philip Melanchthon in the 1530 *Confessio Augustana* stands at the heart of the ecclesiology of the Word in the Lutheran tradition. The Word of God—in its oral, written, and sacramental forms—constitutes the church as well as faith which hears and receives the Word. In one phrase, the church is "the creature of the Word."[8] This position reaches back to the Lutheran Confessions and Luther to articulate the meaning of the church, and it finds broad support in a variety of Lutheran theologians across North America and Europe.[9]

Although he is best known as a Luther scholar, Robert Kolb is an important advocate for this ecclesiology, and his work indicates its basic features.[10] In an essay on the ecclesiology of the Lutheran Confessions, Kolb argues that "the church lives as God's community from his Word," as God speaks anew his Word that brings life in its many forms.[11] "Lutheran ecclesiology always proceeds from Luther's and Melanchthon's understanding of God's Word and what it does as his instrument for creating his universe and re-creating his human creatures who have fallen into sin."[12] Although this has become a familiar Lutheran position, it was revolutionary in Luther's day. The church as a creature of God's Word was diametrically opposed to two alternative notions of the church: first, the Roman Catholic hierarchy as the substance of the church and, second, the church as the arbiter of sacred rituals. In the first, Rome had argued that only the Pope could properly interpret Scripture, and thus without the Pope the church had no sure foundation. The reformers, however, believed that the Scriptures interpret themselves, making God's Word itself the foundation of the church. More clearly stated, the reformers taught that the Holy Spirit drives Christ home through the Scriptures apart from an authoritative magisterium, and this living voice of God creates and sustains his church.[13] In the second case, Luther's revolutionary move, for

Kolb, was to move from a ritual-based religion to a religion of the Word. In the popular late medieval understanding, the church was the institution in which sacred rituals were enacted to appease God.[14] The church was the keeper and the authoritative performer of these sacred rituals. Luther, however, argued that the church was constituted by God speaking his Word to human beings, not by humans striving to God through religious rites or deeds. God descends to his people through the words of a preacher and gives the promise of the forgiveness of sins, the gospel, within the church.

The church, therefore, is not defined by human actions, whether as the authoritative keeper of sacred rituals or as a voluntary society of like-minded people. Instead, the church belongs to God and is defined by his action. God creates the church by his Word and the waters of baptism, and he sustains it by the same preaching of the good news of forgiveness in Jesus. God himself is at work to justify sinners through the proclamation of the gospel, and this preaching is how God creates, sustains, and calls his church to be his people and to live in his kingdom. Without God's Word that justifies sinners and makes them his own, there is no church. Hence, the reformation dictum states, the church stands or falls on the doctrine of justification. Kolb summarizes, "The justifying action of the Savior Jesus Christ, his work through the Holy Spirit using God's Word, and, in a derived sense, the new obedience of the faithful constitute the church."[15] Charles Evanson, accordingly, schematizes the crucial ecclesiological relationships of Lutheran theology as Christ→Gospel→Church: Christ's atoning sacrifice for sin is proclaimed through the gospel that creates the church.[16]

Through the logic of justification, the Lutheran ecclesiology of the Word correctly locates the church outside of itself in the Word and work of God. The church's identity is *extra se*, produced by God's own Word of forgiveness of sins in Jesus Christ delivered through preaching and the sacraments by the Spirit. This logic accords with a biblical understanding of God's relationship with his people. Abraham was a wandering Aramean, but he was chosen by God through a promise to be a blessing to the world.[17] God saved his people Israel from Egypt not because they were great in number but because of his own love and promise.[18] Jesus echoes the same idea to his apostles in the New Testament: "You did not choose me, but I chose you and appointed you."[19] The logic of justification follows this scriptural perspective of God's relationship with his people. Human beings are lost in their trespasses and sins, not merely separated from God but rebels against God, unable and unwilling to save themselves. To these ungodly sinners, God descends in grace, bringing forgiveness through the death and resurrection of his Son, and the Holy Spirit creates faith in the hearts of the ungodly to believe the promise and become part of the assembly of believers. In this dynamic of God's Word that is proclaimed and the faith that believes the Word, the church is not only created but also sustained. The church lives always in God and God's Word, oriented away from itself to the promise of the gospel, from which the church's obedient life follows.

In addition to the orientation to God *extra ecclesiam*, another positive characteristic of the Lutheran ecclesiology of the Word is its emphasis on concrete preaching and administration of the sacraments. In the Lutheran ecclesiology of the Word, the church is not a static institution but the dynamic of God's own delivery of the promise. The dynamic of preaching takes center stage in the notion of God's Word as a performative speech act, a deed that is accomplished by speaking.[20] Oswald Bayer argues that God's *promissio* is a "performative statement," which means that it "actually constitutes a reality; it does not affirm something as if it exists already, but presents it for the first time."[21] For Bayer, a promise does not merely describe reality, like a constative speech act does; it generates reality, producing something new. God's promise creates *ex nihilo* just as his Word did in the beginning. Bayer maps this understanding of God's promise onto the Christian life, which is "the receptive life," the *vita passiva*. What properly characterizes humanity before God is not doing—the *vita activa*—or thinking—the *vita contemplativa*—but receiving, even suffering, God's Word.[22]

The same logic of God's performative Word characterizes Bayer's understanding of the church: "Everything that makes the church the church is contained in the 'Word': the *preaching* of the gospel, its visible and tangible form in the *sacrament*, and the *Holy Spirit* by the gospel, whose office is to sanctify."[23] The church cannot determine itself from within but only in its receptivity to the God who speaks all things into existence.[24] The church is thus constructed by God's promise delivered to sinners through preaching, sustained by the Word and the sacraments, and sanctified by the Spirit through the same. The key to the church is the Word as it encounters God's people in concrete congregations so that they hear, feel, taste, and believe the gospel.

The Logic of Performative Speech Acts in the Lutheran Ecclesiology of the Word

Lutheran theology explicitly defines the human being and the church on the basis of the Word of God,[25] but the logic of performative speech acts, prevalent in the Lutheran ecclesiology of the Word, places an undue emphasis on the effect of the speech over its content.[26] Even when God is confessed to be the Father who sent the Son in the Spirit to reconcile all things to himself, the logic of performative speech acts prioritizes the Word's impact upon individuals over the corporate story and mission of the church. The content of the gospel's story, then, moves into a secondary position, leaving the church vulnerable to a therapeutic or instrumental understanding. Focused on the logic of performative speech acts, the Lutheran ecclesiology of the Word describes the church almost exclusively as preaching and hearing, losing sight of the visible community, and individual vocation becomes the primary driver of congregational mission in the world, as we will see in exploring Oswald Bayer and Steven Paulson on the church.

For Bayer, God "accomplishes the hard work of translation . . . giving himself completely to the world," even to death upon a cross,[27] and this divine action establishes the gospel story as the proper context in which to interpret God's living voice. Despite this explicit recognition, Bayer's logic tends to retreat from the story of God in Christ to the way that human beings experience God's Word in the present, stressing how individuals are encountered by God's Word.[28] In *Theology the Lutheran Way* and *Martin Luther's Theology*, Bayer makes God's conversation with his creatures concrete in three life settings in which God encounters "me."[29] First, the law accuses me of sin and delivers me to death; second, God speaks for me in the gospel that Christ has taken my death and my judgment for me; third, God assaults me in "incomprehensible, crushing hiddenness."[30] In short, the three primary ways God encounters human beings with the Word are the law that kills, the gospel that gives life, and the inconsolable terror of incomprehensible evil. Bayer specifies the ways that God's Word encounters individuals; the Word accuses, forgives, and terrifies human beings. When God's Word is interpreted according to this logic, the primary account is the individual story of conversion or existential angst on account of God's hiddenness. The church is important for preaching this Word of God that kills sinners and makes them alive through the promise, but the corporate identity and mission of the community is secondary at best.[31] Moreover, when the story of the individual becomes primary, preaching is construed as therapeutic, making the purpose of the Word to make people feel better about their guilt or shame and serve their individual stories.[32]

To be clear, Bayer has a more robust understanding of God's Word than this narrow sense of performative speech acts, recognizing the Word as "the true universal community of communication, the community of the justified sinner, among their fellow creatures—as well as the authority that creates this community."[33] Yet, when the performative nature of speech acts is emphasized over the content of the gospel, the story that shapes the church is primarily a story of individual encounters with the Word. Reinhard Hütter agrees that the logic of performative speech acts is ecclesiologically problematic in Oswald Bayer's theology.[34] According to Hütter, Bayer's stark distinction between constative and performative speech renders him unable to identify a doctrine of the gospel "that is both antecedent to and distinct from the performance of the *promissio*."[35] In other words, when the logic of performative speech is disconnected from the content of the gospel story, Bayer makes it possible for the church to proclaim God's promise without the doctrinal and ecclesial contexts that make sense of this divine Word. Bayer abstracts the promise of God from the church, its creeds, and the story of the Scriptures.[36] Hütter may not sufficiently acknowledge how Bayer locates God's performative speech within an account of the incarnation of the Son of God,[37] but Hütter is still right about the ecclesiological deficit resulting from the logic of performative speech acts.[38] Performative speech hardly needs content; without stress upon the content of the gospel, the performative Word can convict and promise, accuse and acquit, and be intelligible within an individual's experience rather than the story of God in Christ. Hence, in the logic of performative speech acts, the church can be intelligible as little more than the place in which relevant preaching encounters individuals.

Steven Paulson further illustrates the problems of the logic of preaching in the Lutheran ecclesiology of the Word. In his book *Lutheran Theology* Paulson expounds his understanding of the church in the chapter "The Fruit of Faith."[39] Since faith comes by hearing, and the church is the product of such hearing in faith, preaching and justification dominate Paulson's understanding of the church: "The preached Word makes the church, which word is solely authorized by the law and promises of Scripture."[40] Thus, the church is not the papacy, nor an institution; it is an assembly of people who hear the Word of God. Paulson takes this emphasis on proclamation to its logical conclusion: the church is constituted by and exists primarily in preaching and hearing. Accordingly, in another essay Paulson defines his "notion of church" almost exclusively in terms of the preached Word: "The Holy Spirit works anew all that is needed by bringing Christ to his sinners by the preaching office."[41]

As Paulson describes the marks of the church, proclamation eclipses any other sign of God's presence among his people.

> Signs of true church are therefore all acts of preaching: sermons that distinguish law and gospel, baptism, Lord's Supper, Absolution, the calling of a public minister from among the Royal priesthood, and suffering for the gospel—the exact opposite of any sign of glory or power in the world.[42]

Paulson names six of Luther's marks of the church from his 1539 treatise, "On the Councils and the Church," but conspicuously absent are the church's visible, public marks of prayer and acts of love for the neighbor.[43] These visible marks are further from the center of the church's identity,[44] but they are still important markers of Christ's church. In Paulson, though, the logic of preaching as a performative speech act that magnifies God's wrath and delivers God's promise of forgiveness has overcome the life of the church outside of individual absolution.⁴⁵ The church is defined by preaching and known by preaching, making its story primarily the one enacted by preaching to individuals: conversion from unbelief to faith through the Spirit and the fruits of faith.

The problem of Paulson's notion of church intensifies in his understanding of social ethics. Paulson places his social ethics within the context of general society:

> The fruit of love for the neighbor comes in the unromantic form of a call (*vocatio*) into an office (*vocation*) that organizes life in opposition to the forces of destruction. Love is born by children honoring parents, spouses being faithful, not murdering our enemies or coveting, and so on (Romans 13:9), and—least romantic of all—by being subject to the governing authorities (Romans 13:1). Institutions are the way God gets good works done by sinners, and the way love happens.⁴⁶

For Paulson, the Christian life becomes visible primarily in secular society as individuals inhabit institutions and live out their vocations according to natural law.⁴⁷ The church is largely hidden while the family, government, and work are the visible contexts for life in the world.⁴⁸ Although Paulson's concerns for disembodiment and Christian triumphalism are valid—and God is certainly at work outside of the church—Paulson's social ethics make the most sense inside of Christendom. The family, honor, marriage, faithfulness, enemies, and the government, for Paulson, are clear and obvious realities. He never explains these in detail nor locates them within the Christian story.⁴⁹ Because of this assumption, Paulson places the Christian in society to love others but without the story of God in Christ structuring the gathering of Christians in community or its visible participation in Christ's mission in the world outside of proclamation. Because no concrete biblical or ecclesiastical context is given in which social ethics can take root, Paulson's social ethics can only gain their intelligibility within a political frame.⁵⁰ Paulson's notion of vocation enables *individual* Christians to live their faith in the world, but the church as a community hardly connects with the world outside of Sunday worship.

Justification and Ecclesiology

The Lutheran ecclesiology of the Word insists upon justification as the Word of God that creates the church and provides its animating center. The church is known by its origin in the proclamation of law and gospel, and the same Word of God defines the church's mission and life together. Considering how the Lutheran ecclesiology of the Word shies away from describing the visible community of the church and is open to a therapeutic understanding of the church, the doctrine of justification itself needs to be scrutinized.

Stanley Hauerwas and William Willimon contend that Reformation theology was wrong in making justification by faith the theological center, calling it a "profound mistake."[51] For Willimon and Hauerwas, justification by faith establishes "essentially individualistic accounts of salvation that [have been] combined with liberal political theory to produce an outrageously accommodated church."[52] Rejecting justification by faith as an individualistic story of salvation, Hauerwas and Willimon focus on the church, claiming that participation in the church is itself salvation. For them, there is no such thing as salvation which is "somehow *extra* political," that is, outside the church as a political, social, and visible community.[53] Inverting the traditional Lutheran mantra, Hauerwas and Willimon suggest that the church is the community on which justification stands or falls. In another essay, Hauerwas clarifies that salvation is not prior to the church but salvation is incorporation into the church-community and its practices:

> Salvation, then, is best understood not as being accepted no matter what we have done, but rather as our material embodiment in the habits and practices of a people that makes possible a way of life that is otherwise impossible. That is why we are not saved in spite of our sin, but we are saved precisely through practices of confession, forgiveness and reconciliation.[54]

According to my analysis of the Lutheran ecclesiology of the Word, Hauerwas' critique has merit. The Lutheran ecclesiology of the Word emphasizes the preaching event as God's creation of his church, understanding God's encounter with people according to the logic of performative speech acts. This logic prioritizes the impact of God's Word upon individuals over the story of the church. Although the ecclesiology of the Word does not have to result in an individualistic account of salvation,[55] the challenges of post-Christendom make individualism a clear and present danger. Unless justification and preaching are contextualized clearly within a scriptural account of the identity and mission of God, the logic of proclamatory preaching is too easily conscripted into the story of religious therapy, in which the church's mission is to make people feel better about their individual pursuits of well-being.

Hauerwas' solution, however, inverts Lutheran theology's understanding of the gospel and the church. Instead of the gospel creating the church, Hauerwas suggests that the church makes the gospel possible. While the Lutheran ecclesiology of the Word can be represented schematically as Christ→Gospel→Church, Hauerwas' account flips gospel and church:

Christ→Church→Gospel. Because of the centrality of the doctrine of the church in Hauerwas' thought, Nicholas Healy contends that Hauerwas' theology is "founded upon, and governed by, a single locus—in his case, the church."[56] Healy's criticism is overstated,[57] but it points to a clear problem from the perspective of the Reformation. For Lutheran theology, justification cannot in any way be subject to the doctrine of the church. The church is *God's* church, not a work of human hands. The church does not make the gospel possible; the gospel makes the church. God's Word always calls from the outside, and *God* creates the church as his people to do his mission of proclaiming the gospel and serving his world. In this way, the doctrine of justification demands that God always has priority over the church,[58] and the church is to be oriented to him *extra se*.

Although this book will not follow Hauerwas' direction, his challenge to the relationship between the church and the doctrine of justification illumines the problem in Lutheran ecclesiology: What theological account can hold together the church's concrete, visible life as a community with a confession of God standing outside of the church, creating it by his Word, and calling it into his mission? The doctrine of justification understood according to the logic of performative speech seems unable to hold both together. As we have seen, the Lutheran ecclesiology of the Word rightly orients the church to God and his Word, ready to hear God speak and live by every Word that comes from his mouth. The logic of performative speech, however, prioritizes the impact of the Word upon individuals over the community's story and mission. As such, the concrete community of people that confesses the faith together, obeys God together, and lives out its Christian witness in the gospel by word and deed becomes tangential both to personal faith and the individual Christian life in society. The church is in danger of becoming an instrument to the story of individuals coming to faith.[59] Hence, the Lutheran ecclesiology of the Word has failed to function hermeneutically to shape the preaching and teaching necessary for the life of the church after Christendom.

Some, however, would challenge one of the premises on which the prior paragraph is built. They would argue that the visible life of the church is not only tangential to the church's center, but must remain so in order that God's work of salvation retains its privileged place.[60] Such critics correctly point out that the church, according to the reformers, is not about outward appearances but saving faith in the heart,[61] which means that the church is hidden and even, in a sense, invisible.[62] My point, however, is not that the church's identity requires certain visible forms, nor am I arguing that the church is constituted by an ecclesial brand of social ethics. The church's identity is given by God and received by faith—hidden in Christ who gives himself in the external Word and sacraments—and the church's life and mission are also given in Jesus by the Spirit. Accordingly, the church must be continually oriented toward God and his Word, turned toward God to receive its life and mission from him, as affirmed by the Lutheran ecclesiology of the Word. At the same time, however, the cultural context has shifted significantly since the Reformation. The late medieval church put an emphasis on outward works over faith in the heart, but the therapeutic and political contexts shape Christians to either spiritualize or politicize their faith.[63] In other words, the problem today is not that outward works are the center of the church, but North American Christians have drunk deeply from the wells of Western culture and cannot imagine the life and work of the church in the gospel.[64] For example, Christian faith is often privatized so that the church has little to do with public life, except in the form of partisan politics.[65] To overcome the politicization and privatization of the church, ecclesiology must not only foster the proclamation of the forgiveness of sins, as the Lutheran ecclesiology of the Word rightly does, but also the preaching and teaching of the story of God that shapes the life of faith lived in the visible community.

THE SPIRIT AND THE VISIBLE COMMUNITY OF THE CHURCH: HÜTTER'S LUTHERAN ECCLESIOLOGY OF THE THIRD ARTICLE

A number of Lutheran theologians have offered ecclesiologies that move beyond the Lutheran ecclesiology of the Word to establish and emphasize the visible community of the church. Many of these were developed in ecumenical discourse leading up to and after the Second Vatican Council,[66] and the ecumenical conversation remains important for a number of recent ecclesiologies within the Lutheran tradition that emphasize the visible church.[67] These do not deny the importance of proclamation or the Word, but they seek to understand the church not from the logic of performative speech but in relationship to the triune God.

Considering Luther's own connections of Word, Spirit, and church in his catechisms, it is not surprising that some Lutherans have grounded ecclesiology in pneumatology.[68] In doing so, these ecclesiologies confess the church as a visible community inhabited by the Spirit while retaining an emphasis on God's work through the external Word. We will see, however, that pneumatology, without substantial Christology, lacks the resources to bring the church to repent for its complicity in sin and form its common life and mission in light of the story of God. Unless the Spirit is not only confessed but described as the Spirit of the Son, sent by the Father to reconcile the world to the Father through the Son, the Spirit will be concretized either in the church, leading to ecclesial introspection, or in the world, leading to cultural captivity.[69]

Reinhard Hütter's ecclesiology shows both the potential and the problems of a pneumatological ecclesiology. As part of the turn to church practices, Hütter's ideas are wide-spread and his work has been influential.[70] In addition, Hütter offers what I believe is one of the most persuasive Lutheran accounts of the church as a public community for post-Christendom.[71] In agreement with the Lutheran ecclesiology of the Word, Hütter recognizes the church's preaching and the sacraments as the very work of God the Spirit, but Hütter takes it a step further to confess the church as "the public of the Holy Spirit."[72] In this way, the church is understood to be a visible community in and through which God speaks and works.

Christian faith today is experienced in two contexts, Hütter acknowledges, "on the one hand, in the context of the split in Western Christendom, and on the other with regard to a modernity that understands itself to be post-Christian."[73] Hütter argues that both contexts have pushed modern Protestantism to make the church into a "private interest group," with the American project providing coherence and meaning for the church.[74] Religion and faith are understood as "essentially private gnosis," prioritizing the spiritual well-being of individuals and instrumentalizing the Protestant church.[75] Even those who react against modernity, such as in biblical fundamentalism, tend to make the church irrelevant to public life by submitting to a modern American understanding of reality and playing its game.[76] In Protestantism as a whole, Hütter concludes, "the church as a genuine 'public' is lost."[77]

Hütter establishes the church as a public by connecting pneumatology to the core practices and doctrine of the church. For Hütter, core practices and doctrine are essential to the church's character as a public of the Holy Spirit. On one level, practices and doctrine are built into his definition of a public so the constitutive nature of practices and doctrines is essentially tautological.[78] Hütter goes beyond this definition based upon the Greek polis, however, arguing that the church participates in the Holy Spirit and the salvific mission of God precisely through its core practices and doctrine. In his own words, the church is "the soteriological locus of God's actions, as a space constituted by specific core practices and church doctrine. These practices . . . participate in the being of the Spirit as the latter's work in the Spirit's mission of the triune God's economy of salvation."[79] Hütter acknowledges the visible, core practices and doctrinal teachings of the church as the Holy Spirit's work in the world today.

To be clear, Hütter never simply identifies the church with the third person of the Trinity. Hütter follows Oswald Bayer in asserting the church as pathic, suffering—passively receiving—the work of God, thus placing the church in its proper position as a receiver of God's action. At the same time, Hütter faults Bayer for separating God's promise that is suffered from the content of the promise, especially as confessed in church doctrine.[80] Hütter's ecclesiology develops further as he criticizes Karl Barth for a Christological ecclesiology with a deficient pneumatology, which does not distinguish between the mission of Christ and the mission of the Spirit.[81] According to Hütter, the relationship between the Spirit and the church is "far from clear" in Barth's theology, resulting in an ecclesiology that tends toward privatization.[82] Barth's dialectical approach does not allow the Holy Spirit to "tie itself" to confessions of faith or dogma[83] but tends to interiorize and concretize the Spirit inside the believer.[84]

To clarify the relationship between the Spirit and the church, Hütter gives an account of church practices and doctrine, directed toward God's economy of salvation, through which "the Holy Spirit's work becomes public, is announced and interpreted."[85] The Spirit's work becomes concrete in the core practices of the church and church doctrine. In fact, doctrine and church practices *are* the Spirit's work as they testify to God's economy of salvation and contribute to discipleship and Christian formation.[86] The true actor of the church's practices and doctrine is the Holy Spirit, not human beings.

The church is *the public of the Holy Spirit*, both as its core practices actualize the salvific mission of Christ in the Spirit and as its practice of theology constitutes a public, communal activity.[87] The church's *koinonia* is grounded in the *koinonia* of the triune God because "the triune God has bound his communion to the ecclesiastical *koinonia*."[88] The church is not merely called by God to take part in God's mission, but the church is "the actualizing agent of the salvific-economic mission of Christ and of the Holy Spirit."[89] For Hütter, the church's doctrine, practices, formation of believers, and teaching office have been brought into the mission of God. When the church acts in preaching, authoritative teaching, and core practices as part of its communion with the triune God, the Holy Spirit is acting to save and form God's people.[90]

By incorporating the church into the person and work of the Holy Spirit, Hütter establishes the church as a visible, public community *of God*. The church's work of teaching, preaching, formation, and mission are located pneumatologically, incorporating the visible life of the Christian community in God's own mission. In one way, Hütter has provided a forward stride from the Lutheran ecclesiology of the Word. Whereas the Lutheran ecclesiology of the Word prioritized preaching and hearing to such a degree that the church's public life could be disregarded theologically, the myriad of the church's visible practices are grounded in God's economy in Hütter's ecclesiology. Moreover, his ecclesiology recognizes the importance of justification, in which the church is the pathic receiver of the work of the Spirit.

Hütter, Pneumatological Ecclesiology, and the Problem of Introspection

Despite this advance on the Lutheran ecclesiology of the Word, Hütter's pneumatological account suffers from a fatal flaw: ecclesial introspection. Hütter claims that the church remains "strictly separate from the Holy Spirit" in his ecclesiology since it stands continually as a receiver of the Holy Spirit's work and "is thus pathically determined by the Spirit's poiesis."[91] This limit on the relationship between the Spirit and the church, however, is largely formal, creating a problematic circularity. The church is supposed to be determined as the receiver of the Spirit's work, but the Spirit's work is primarily the core practices, doctrines, and teaching office of the church.[92] In fact, Hütter contends that the core practices of the church "subsist enhypostatically in the Spirit."[93] Using this Christological terminology, Hütter argues that the visible, human work of these constitutive core practices inheres in the mission of the Spirit and "through them the Holy Spirit performs its economic mission."[94] Although I agree that the Spirit has made preaching and the sacraments part of the Spirit's salvific work to bring Christ to sinners and form them into the likeness of Jesus, Hütter's ecclesiology determines the economic mission of the Spirit primarily by the work of the church and the church by the work of the Spirit. Hütter confesses the Spirit to be the Spirit of the Father who sent the Son into the flesh, but the story of the divine economy hardly animates his understanding of the Spirit's work or the identity and mission of the church.

By describing a church that functions in consonance with the Spirit, Hütter's church is essentially an ideal institution, giving little rationale to confess the sinfulness of the church and work to reform its mission and practices in the world.[95] What shapes the church ultimately is not an account of the story of the triune God—which would require Christology—but an idealized version of the church's own practices and institutional structures, which are regarded as the work of the Spirit.[96] The result is a problematic introspection in which the church is directed to its own status quo rather than outward to the story of God in Christ. In spite of his claim to the contrary, then, Hütter *is* in danger of reifying the salvific-economic mission of the triune God in the church's core practices, binding doctrine, and the authoritative teaching office of the bishop.

This ecclesial introspection is particularly problematic after Christendom. Christians, especially conservative Christians, often see themselves and their churches as holy sanctuaries standing over-against a wicked and debased culture,[97] making them easy prey for partisan power games and political narratives.[98] Hütter's ecclesiology does not have the resources to interrogate congregations and reform them according to the Word of God when their mission reflects partisan politics. Even worse, Hütter's notion of the church as a public of the Spirit positions the church as not only distinct from the world but even privileged within it as the community that God deigned to make part of his own economic-salvific mission.[99] Congregations need to repent for their complicity in partisan power-plays and hear God's Word that calls them to a new sense of God's mission in the world, but Hütter's ecclesiology points the church primarily to an idealized version of itself.

What Hütter's ecclesiology needs is a concrete account of the Spirit that does not depend upon the church. As Miroslav Volf and Maurice Lee acknowledge, in the Holy Scriptures, "a certain elusiveness" surrounds the Spirit, as the Spirit reveals himself by the prophets, in the Son, and in the life of the church.[100] Pneumatology, therefore, has no concrete story other than the history of God with Israel and the church, the center of which is Jesus Christ. Pneumatology without substantial Christology is too abstract to prevent the church from "sacred inflation," overidentifying its own structure and acts with God, or becoming "de-sacralized" as another human project in this age.[101]

Hütter's work suggests two options to concretize the Spirit outside of the church: God's *koinonia* or God's *oeconomia*, the common life of the three divine persons or the salvific mission of the Father through the Son by the Spirit. Although communion ecclesiology's use of the former points toward it as an excellent option,[102] Trinitarian theology does not provide the concretions necessary to ground the church and its life.[103] As Kathryn Tanner explains, the relations among the divine persons are just too different from human relations. The ambiguity of the connection between the Trinity and human relations requires theologians to argue on non-scriptural, non-theological grounds for the shape of ecclesial social ethics.[104] Karen Kilby summarizes how theologians have used perichoresis, which designates the relation among the divine persons, in this problematic way:

> First, a concept, perichoresis, is used to name what is not understood, to name whatever it is that makes the three Persons one. Secondly, the concept is filled out rather suggestively with notions borrowed from our own experience of relationships and relatedness. And, then, finally, it is presented as an exciting resource Christian theology has to offer the wider world in its reflections upon relationships and relatedness.[105]

Tanner's point is that God's own *koinonia* with the Son and the Spirit quickly turns into an interpretation of human experience unless the Trinity is understood in the biblical account of Jesus Christ.[106] The church ends up rooted in its own life or practices, or in philosophical or sociological theory.

In order for the church to have concrete content to shape its life together and God's mission in the world, ecclesiology needs to be grounded in the divine economy,[107] which requires Christology.[108] Even Volf and Lee, advocates for the importance of pneumatology in ecclesiology, admit that the Spirit functions more formally than materially, "guard[ing] a certain kind of relation between Christ and the church."[109] For Volf and Lee, the relation of the Spirit and the church depends upon the relations of Christ and the church and Christ and the Spirit.[110] On its own, then, pneumatology is too abstract and formal to ground the church's identity and purpose. The Spirit who makes the church and works through it must be known as the Spirit who conceived Jesus of Nazareth, was sent upon him, was borne by him, and was sent by him and the Father upon the church. Only in the story of God's salvation, which is centered in the person and work of Jesus, can ecclesiology offer a vision of the church to combat the crises of the age and form congregations for God's mission, while recognizing its identity in the Word and work of God *extra se*.

CONCLUSION: THE NECESSITY OF CHRISTOLOGY

Christology provides concrete biblical content in the person and ministry of Jesus that reveals the identity of the triune God in the economy of salvation, and can form the church, its mission, and its politics according to God's own mission.[111] Robert Jenson states it simply: Christ's "one life establishes in the first place what it is to be God and what it is to be creature."[112] Jesus is the heart of Holy Scripture, as he both reveals God's identity and how human beings live as God's creatures.[113] Paul writes in Colossians: the Son "is the image of the invisible God" (1:15), the one who reveals the Father's heart, his intentions, and will. John echoes the same idea: "No one has ever seen God; the only God, who is at the Father's side, he has made him known" (John 1:18). Jesus himself states in the same Gospel: "Whoever has seen me has seen the Father" (14:9). Jesus, the eternal Son and Word become flesh, reveals the Father, and he does so precisely as a human being. Jesus reveals the reality of human life as the faithful creature and at the same time reveals the heart and identity of the Father as the one eternally in the Father's bosom. If Christians know God and themselves rightly in Jesus, ecclesiology too ought to point primarily and most centrally to the Christ. In Tanner's words, "Christ is the key . . . to what God is doing everywhere. Christ clarifies and specifies the nature, aim, and trustworthiness of all God's dealings with us because Christ is where those dealings with us come to ultimate fruition."[114] God ultimately relates to humanity in Christ, which means that ecclesiology—and theology in general—must keep Christ Jesus at the center of its reflections if it is to be rooted in the doctrine of God.[115]

My point is not that the pneumatology or justification is irrelevant to ecclesiology, but the Spirit who creates, calls, and transforms the church through the Word of justification, has to be known as the Spirit *of Jesus*, the Spirit who worked in the life and ministry of Jesus from incarnation through resurrection, before being breathed upon his apostles by Jesus.[116] Christology, then, must take center stage in the story by which the church is formed and in which the church lives.

The logic of performative speech is too easily co-opted by private religiosity, leaving the church as an institution of religious therapy that plays little role in the world outside of partisan power games. Pneumatology without Christology is concretized in the existing institution of the church or in the culture, focusing the church on itself in unhealthy introspection or sacralizing some portion of the world. In Christology, however, the church receives its identity within the economy of God, oriented outside of itself to its Lord, and comes to understand its life in the world according to the story of Christ rather than any American narrative like politics or therapy. In Christology, church and world find their true foundation and unity.

NOTES

1. Charles P. Arand, "What Are Ecclesiologically Challenged Lutherans To Do? Starting Points for a Lutheran Ecclesiology," *Concordia Journal* 34 (2008): 157–71. On the trope, consider the pin that Lutheran theologian Gerhard Forde proudly bore: "This man has no ecclesiology." Of course, the pin overstates the case. Forde's understanding of the proclamation of the Word *is* his ecclesiology. For analysis of Forde's ecclesiology, see Cheryl M. Peterson, *Who Is the Church? An Ecclesiology for the Twenty-first Century* (Minneapolis: Fortress, 2013), 45–48.

2. Risto Saarinen, "Lutheran Ecclesiology," in *The Routledge Companion to the Christian Church*, ed. Gerard Mannion and Lewis S. Mudge (New York: Routledge, 2008), 172.

3. Saarinen, "Lutheran Ecclesiology," 170.

4. Saarinen, "Lutheran Ecclesiology," 173.

5. Compare Arand, "Ecclesiologically Challenged Lutherans," 163–65.

6. Miroslav Volf has a helpful discussion of the opposition that often arises between individual forgiveness and a corporate understanding of the church in communion ecclesiology, even if his notion of faith makes the human being too active vis-à-vis God, at least for a Lutheran: *After Our Likeness: The Church as the Image of the Trinity* (Grand Rapids, MI: Eerdmans, 1998), 159–89.

7. CA VII; Robert Kolb and Timothy J. Wengert, eds., *The Book of Concord: The Confessions of the Evangelical Lutheran Church* (Minneapolis: Fortress, 2000), 43.

8. Christoph Schwöbel, "The Creature of the Word: Recovering the Ecclesiology of the Reformers," in *On Being the Church: Essays on the Christian Community*, ed. Colin E. Gunton and Daniel W. Hardy (Edinburgh: T&T Clark, 1989), 110–55.

9. For example, see Oswald Bayer, *Theology the Lutheran Way*, trans. and ed. Jeffrey G. Silcock and Mark C. Mattes (Grand Rapids, MI: Eerdmans, 2007); Bayer, *Martin Luther's Theology: A Contemporary Interpretation*, trans. Thomas H. Trapp (Grand Rapids, MI: Eerdmans, 2008); Gerhard O. Forde, *Theology Is for Proclamation* (Minneapolis: Fortress, 1990); Robert Kolb, "The Sheep and the Voice of the Shepherd: The Ecclesiology of the Lutheran Confessional Writings," *Concordia Journal* 36 (2010): 324–41; and Steven D. Paulson, *Lutheran Theology* (London: T&T Clark, 2011). The Reformed tradition makes similar assertions about the church. For example, see Schwöbel, "Creature of the Word," 110–55; Michael S. Horton, *People and Place: A Covenant Ecclesiology* (Louisville, KY: Westminster John Knox Press, 2008), 37–71; and John Webster, *Word and Church: Essays in Christian Dogmatics*, Cornerstones (London: Bloomsbury T&T Clark, 2016), 228–29. The Word of God ecclesiology shares some features with what Avery Dulles calls the "herald model" of the church: *Models of the Church*, expanded ed. (New York: Image Books, 2002), 68–80.

10. Although Kolb follows the general direction of the Lutheran ecclesiology of the Word, he focuses more on the life of the church than many. Robert Kolb, *The Christian Faith: A Lutheran Exposition* (Saint Louis: Concordia, 1993), 261–68.

11. Kolb, "The Sheep and the Voice of the Shepherd," 337.

12. Kolb, "The Sheep and the Voice of the Shepherd," 325.

13. Kolb, "The Sheep and the Voice of the Shepherd," 325–36. On this understanding of the Lutheran dictum *Scriptura sacra sui ipsius interpres*, see Gerhard O. Forde, *A More Radical Gospel: Essays on Eschatology, Authority, Atonement, and Ecumenism*, ed. Mark C. Mattes and Steven D. Paulson (Grand Rapids, MI: Eerdmans, 2004), 68–74. Compare in the Reformed tradition a similar theme using *sola scriptura* in Horton, *People and Place*, 72–98.

14. Kolb, "The Sheep and the Voice of the Shepherd," 328–30.

15. Kolb, "The Sheep and the Voice of the Shepherd," 331.

16. Charles J. Evanson, "Center and Periphery in Lutheran Ecclesiology," *Concordia Theological Quarterly* 68 (2004): 239.

17. Gen. 12:13.

18. Deut. 7:7–8: "It was not because you were more in number than any other people that the Lord set his love on you and chose you, for you were the fewest of all peoples, but it is because the Lord loves you and is keeping the oath that he swore to your fathers."

19. John 15:16. Unless otherwise noted, all Scripture quotations are from the ESV® Bible (The Holy Bible, English Standard Version®), copyright © 2001 by Crossway, a publishing ministry of Good News Publishers. Used by permission. All rights reserved.

20. On speech acts, see J. L. Austin, *How to Do Things with Words*, 2nd ed. (Oxford: Clarendon Press, 1975).

21. Bayer, *Martin Luther's Theology*, 51.
22. On the "receptive life," see Bayer, *Theology the Lutheran Way*, 21–27.
23. Bayer, *Martin Luther's Theology*, 257. Emphases original.
24. Compare Oswald Bayer, "Hermeneutical Theology," *Scottish Journal of Theology* 56, no. 2 (2003): 135: "It is necessary to take our starting point as the word, understood as the promise which encounters us, and not as the self-understanding of faith; it is necessary to define the human being who receives according to God who speaks and not proceed the other way around."
25. Bayer, "Hermeneutical Theology," 135. See prior footnote.
26. Hütter, *Suffering Divine Things*, 82–83.
27. Bayer, "Hermeneutical Theology," 131.
28. Even in "Hermeneutical Theology," which is quite theocentric, see p. 140. Bayer hints at God's communication of salvation to humanity in a similar logic. God's communication of salvation seems to come down to the perlocutionary effect of the Word. This section is more concrete with regard to humanity's place in God's story than the story of Christ. For reference, here are Bayer's own words: "Corresponding to this rupture in time, God befalls us in his wrath, in which he convicts us of sin, differently than he meets us in forgiving love, different again than his forbearance, in which he preserves the old world towards his future, all the more different is he however when we encounter his terrifying hiddenness, in which he—impenetrably to us—brings about life and death, all in all." Notice the way that Bayer highlights God's Word affecting *us*.
29. Bayer, *Theology the Lutheran Way*, 102–6. Bayer begins with three contexts but adds a fourth context later—the "grace of preservation" of the first use of the law (p. 106), which is subordinate in importance to the other three. See also Bayer, *Martin Luther's Theology*, 41–42, and "Hermeneutical Theology," 140.
30. Bayer, *Theology the Lutheran Way*, 102.
31. Oswald Bayer, *Living by Faith: Justification and Sanctification*, trans. Geoffrey W. Bromiley (Grand Rapids, MI: Eerdmans, 2003), is striking in how little it says about the church though it is mentioned as an estate through which sanctification happens (60–61). To be fair, the book emphasizes "the eschatological removal of the terrible hiddenness of God and God's righteousness" (xiv), but the emphasis drives home my point. Justification in the logic of performative speech concerns itself with individual conversion to such a degree that the church is devalued.
32. On therapeutic preaching, see John W. Wright, *Telling God's Story: Narrative Preaching for Christian Formation* (Downers Grove, IL: Intervarsity, 2007).
33. Bayer, "Hermeneutical Theology," 138.
34. Hütter, *Suffering Divine Things*, 82–83.
35. Hütter, *Suffering Divine Things*, 82.
36. Hütter, *Suffering Divine Things*, 89–90.
37. Bayer, "Hermeneutical Theology," 138–41, identifies the incarnation as central to understanding God's communication even though it does hint toward an emphasis on individual experience of the Word.
38. For related criticism of Bayer (largely on the doctrine of God and the law/gospel distinction—which is closely related to God's speech acts), see Christine

Helmer, *The Trinity and Martin Luther: A Study on the Relationship Between Genre, Language and the Trinity in Luther's Works (1523–1546)* (Mainz: Verlag Philipp Von Zabern, 1999), 148–49; and Paul R. Hinlicky, *Luther and the Beloved Community: A Path for Christian Theology after Christendom* (Grand Rapids, MI: Eerdmans, 2010), 122–30.

39. Paulson, *Lutheran Theology*, 228–43.

40. Paulson, *Lutheran Theology*, 238.

41. Paulson, "Do Lutherans Need a New Ecclesiology," 233. Paulson does refer to the church as "public and communal" two sentences prior, but his focus is clearly upon the preaching office by which God creates the church.

42. Paulson, *Lutheran Theology*, 239.

43. Martin Luther, "On the Councils and the Church," in vol. 41 of *Luther's Works* (Philadelphia: Fortress, 1966), 148–67.

44. Luther says acts of love and works of the second table of the Decalogue "cannot be regarded as reliable." Luther, "On the Councils and the Church," 167.

45. Peterson, *Who Is the Church*, 48, identifies a similar problem with Forde's proclamation ecclesiology, which shares much with Paulson's approach. Compare Joel D. Biermann, *A Case for Character: Toward a Lutheran Virtue Ethics* (Minneapolis: Fortress, 2014), 115–18, who recognizes that a reductive view of law and gospel (law/gospel polarity) is problematic for positive descriptions of the Christian life.

46. Paulson, *Lutheran Theology*, 245.

47. This may be the result of what David Yeago has noticed with regard to Lutheranism speaking of the gospel as a word that comforts but is "without positive content." With no positive content to shape the church, the church and the Christian life will be shaped by society. David S. Yeago, "Sacramental Lutheranism at the End of the Modern Age," *Lutheran Forum* 34, no. 4 (Christmass 2000): 12.

48. The story of the city of Magdeburg standing up to the emperor in the sixteenth century suggests the importance of the church's visible confession and faithful life, but Paulson resists this conclusion even while supporting ecclesial resistance against rulers who impose laws upon the church. Paulson, *Lutheran Theology*, 255–64.

49. Elsewhere, Paulson makes a similar error with regard to natural law. Paulson says that the shape of love is known on the basis of natural law, which is understood by reason. Paulson uses natural law as part of his argument that procreation is naturally connected to marriage. In so doing, Paulson fails to acknowledge how social structures and tacit narratives affect interpretation. In other words, many conclusions of natural law thinking are hardly universally accessible facts but interpretations of moral reasoning from within Christendom. That does not make such conclusions wrong; it makes them traditioned. Steven D. Paulson, "No Church of Christ without Christ," in *Seeking New Directions for Lutheranism: Biblical, Theological, and Churchly Perspectives*, ed. Carl E. Braaten (Delphi, NY: ALPB Books, 2010), 191–92.

50. On the story of politics as a particular danger of the church today, see my "Theology in a Post-Christian Context: Two Stories, Two Tasks," *Concordia Theological Journal* 4, no. 2 (Spring 2017): 43–57.

51. Stanley Hauerwas and William H. Willimon, "Why Resident Aliens Struck a Chord," in *Good Company: The Church as Polis* (Notre Dame: Notre Dame University Press, 1995), 62. Hauerwas' more recent assertions are not as stark, but he remains critical of reformation thinking. For example, Stanley Hauerwas, *The Work of Theology* (Grand Rapids, MI: Eerdmans, 2015), 59: "In short, the Lutheran emphasis on justification became the breeding grounds for the development of Protestant liberalism and the subsequent moralization of Christian theology." I agree with Hauerwas' larger point that justification divorced from a substantial Christology emphasizes how individuals come to faith. I would also argue, however, that Christology without justification turns Christology into legalism, mysticism, or philosophy.

52. Hauerwas and Willimon, "Why Resident Aliens," 62.

53. Hauerwas and Willimon, "Why Resident Aliens," 62.

54. Stanley Hauerwas, *Sanctify Them in the Truth: Holiness Exemplified* (Nashville, TN: Abingdon, 1998), 74.

55. In Reformed ecclesiology, Horton, *People and Place*, largely avoids this by locating the proclamation of the Word within the story of God's covenant with his people, opening space for considering the church in terms of God's story as a gathered people. Peterson, however, thinks Horton falls into the same trap: *Who Is the Church*, 53. Among Lutherans, Kolb may avoid this by tying horizontal righteousness so closely to vertical righteousness. See Kolb, *Christian Faith*, 261–68.

56. Nicholas M. Healy, *Hauerwas: A (Very) Critical Introduction* (Grand Rapids, MI: Eerdmans, 2014), 39. John Webster states the critique more starkly: "The Church is the center of gravity in Hauerwas' work." John Webster, "Ecclesiocentrism," review of Nicholas M. Healy, *Hauerwas: A (Very) Critical Introduction*, *First Things* 246 (Oct. 2014): 55.

57. See Hauerwas's response to Healy in *Work of Theology*, 266–78. Robert Dean also considers his book a response to Healy: Robert John Dean, *For the Life of the World: Jesus Christ and the Church in the Theologies of Dietrich Bonhoeffer and Stanley Hauerwas* (Eugene, OR: Pickwick, 2016), 5n.17.

58. Hauerwas would undoubtedly agree, but his logic invites a reversal of the proper directionality.

59. Compare David H. Kelsey, *Eccentric Existence: A Theological Anthropology*, vol. 1 (Louisville, KY: Westminster John Knox, 2009), 113–19, who sees an instrumentalizing of God in anthropology when a logic of coming to faith is prioritized over a logic of belief.

60. God's work of salvation must indeed retain its centrality. When the focus is on individual salvation, however, it devolves into how one "gets saved" rather than *God's* work of salvation. For a salutary critique of mission before message that cuts against an emphasis on visibility, see Horton, *People and Place*, 248–56. John Webster also offers important caveats against the tendency to identify the moral work of the church with God's work: *Word and Church*, 211–30. Although I agree with Webster and Horton that the church must prioritize its message of who God is and what God does, the question is not whether Christians will live publicly, but by which story will they live publicly in the world. Without describing the visible life of the

church, Christians easily slip into a life lived according to a story that is not the story of Israel's God who reveals himself in Christ through the Spirit.

61. See, for instance, Melanchthon's Apology VII–VIII: Kolb and Wengert, eds., *Book of Concord*, 174–83.

62. To be clear, I agree that the church is rightly described as hidden. First, even the audible Word and visible sacraments that make the church are only recognized as God's Word by eyes and ears of faith. Second, the Spirit's presence in the church and Christians is not a matter of empirical recognition. Third, Protestant dogmatics emphasized the hiddenness (or invisibility) of the church against a Roman Catholic understanding of the church as institution where visible fellowship mattered most. This final reason was important during Christendom, but in my view is less important today. The first reason for the church's hiddenness, however, reminds the church to eschew human success and power because God works in the ways of the cross. Such hiddenness is thus necessary, but cannot be a hedge against the church's visible obedience in the world. For Bonhoeffer's view that the church is both invisible and visible at the same time, hidden in the marks of the church yet visible in a concrete community and its life, see Kirsten Busch Nielsen, "Community Turned Inside Out: Dietrich Bonhoeffer's Concept of the Church and of Humanity Reconsidered," in *Being Human, Becoming Human: Dietrich Bonhoeffer and Social Thought*, ed. Jens Zimmermann and Brian Gregor (Eugene, OR: Pickwick, 2010), 93–94. For a broader dogmatic discussion of visibility and invisibility, see Webster, *Word and Church*, 96–113.

63. See my "Narrating the Church at the Dusk of Christendom: How the Loss of Predominance Affects Congregations," *Concordia Journal* 43, no. 4 (2017): 29–41; and "Theology in a Post-Christian Context," 43–57.

64. Mark Sayers, *Disappearing Church: From Cultural Relevance to Gospel Resilience* (Chicago: Moody Publishers, 2016), 18: "These beliefs have not so much been argued as assumed. They are not enforced; rather, they are imbibed."

65. On the privatization of the Christian faith and the church, see Robert Wuthnow, *America and the Challenges of Religious Diversity* (Princeton, NJ: Princeton University Press, 2005). On church captivity to politics, see James Davison Hunter, *To Change the World: The Irony, Tragedy, and Possibility of Christianity in the Late Modern World* (Oxford: Oxford University Press, 2010).

66. For example, Edmund Schlink, Ökumenische Dogmatik: Grundzüge (Göttingen: Vandenhoeck & Ruprecht, 1983), 537–724; Peter Brunner, "Von der Sichtbarkeit der Kirche," in *Pro Ecclesia: Gesammelte Aufsätze zur dogmatischen Theologie*, vol. 1, 2nd ed. (Berlin: Lutherisches Verlagshaus, 1962), 205–12; Anders Nygren, *Christ and His Church*, trans. Alan Carlsten (Philadelphia: Westminster, 1956); and K. E. Skydsgaard, *One in Christ*, trans. Axel C. Kildegaard (Philadelphia: Muhlenberg Press, 1957), 77–112, esp. 94–112.

67. For example, David S. Yeago, "'A Christian Holy People': Martin Luther on Salvation and the Church," *Modern Theology* 13, no. 1 (1997): 101–20; Holze, ed., *Church as Communion*; Jenson, *Systematic Theology*, vol. 2; Braaten, *Mother Church*; and Tjørhom, *Visible Church—Visible Unity*.

68. Hütter, *Suffering Divine Things*; Cheryl M. Peterson, "The Church," *Lutheran Quarterly* 30, no. 1 (2016): 43–59; Peterson, "Lutheran Principles for Ecclesiology," in *Critical Issues in Ecclesiology: Essays in Honor of Carl E. Braaten*, ed. Alberto L. García and Susan K. Wood (Grand Rapids, MI: Eerdmans, 2011), 148–71; Peterson, *Who Is the Church*; and, less strictly pneumatological, Leopoldo A. Sánchez M., "More Promise Than Ambiguity: Pneumatological Christology as a Model for Ecumenical Engagement," in *Critical Issues in Ecclesiology: Essays in Honor of Carl. E Braaten*, ed. Alberto L. Garcia and Susan K. Wood (Grand Rapids, MI: Eerdmans, 2011), 189–214.

69. These options reflect Stephen Pickard's "natural heresies" of the church. When the Spirit is concretized in the church, the risk is what Pickard calls "sacred inflation," which is an over-identification of the church with God. When the Spirit is concretized in the story of the world, the church is, in Pickard's terms, "de-sacralized," which is when church becomes another human project in the world, and the world's projects are sacralized as God's own. Stephen Pickard, *Seeking the Church: An Introduction to Ecclesiology* (London: SCM Press, 2012), 61–73.

70. The idea that practices are essential for creating Christian identity and enacting the church's mission has become ubiquitous in contemporary ecclesiology. Part of this is the on-going influence of Lindbeck, Hauerwas, and the "Yale school" mentioned in the introduction. For a description of this "new ecclesiology" and a critique of it, see Nicholas M. Healy "Practices and the New Ecclesiology: Misplaced Concreteness?" *International Journal of Systematic Theology* 5 (2003): 287–308.

71. *Suffering Divine Things*. A shorter version of Hütter's argument to which I will also refer regularly is: "The Church as Public: Doctrine, Practice, and the Holy Spirit," in *Bound to Be Free: Evangelical Catholic Engagements in Ecclesiology, Ethics, and Ecumenism* (Grand Rapids, MI: Eerdmans, 2004), 19–42.

72. Hütter, *Suffering Divine Things*, 158.

73. Hütter, *Suffering Divine Things*, 22.

74. Hütter, "Church as Public," 19.

75. Hütter, *Suffering Divine Things*, 3. Compare Yeago, "'A Christian, Holy People,'" 101–4.

76. For example, when evangelicals read the Bible as a scientific textbook, they play the fact/value game, arguing that the Bible is about facts. Also noteworthy is the apparent eagerness of evangelical Christians to employ the standard tools of American capitalism—marketing, advertisements, and media—ostensibly in service of Christ. Compare Hütter, "Church as Public," 32: "The ironic result is that a 'political theology' that attempts to 'politicize' the church can only and unavoidably deepen the church's irrelevance and undermine the church's public (political) nature by submitting and reconditioning the church according to the *saeculum's* understanding of itself as the ultimate and normative public."

77. Hütter, *Suffering Divine Things*, 3.

78. Hütter, *Suffering Divine Things*, 161. Based upon Hannah Arendt's work on the polis, Hütter develops a "structural concept of the public" that makes public and political synonymous (161–62). He states, "a 'public' . . . is characterized by four constitutive features: (1) a specific telos; (2) mutually binding principles expressed in

distinct practices, laws, and doctrines; (3) a 'moveable' locale; and (4) the phenomenon of 'freedom.'"

79. Hütter, *Suffering Divine Things*, 27.
80. Hütter, *Suffering Divine Things*, 69–93.
81. Hütter, *Suffering Divine Things*, 112–13.
82. Hütter, "Church as Public," 28.
83. Hütter, *Suffering Divine Things*, 107.
84. Hütter, *Suffering Divine Things*, 109.
85. Hütter, "Church as Public," 37.
86. Hütter, "Church as Public," 38: "Doctrine and core practices—as they enable the church to be that public in which the announcement of God's *oikonomia*, discipleship, and the formation of other practices and habits take place—are the Spirit's work although they do not exhaust, by far, the Spirit's work."
87. Hütter, *Suffering Divine Things*, 158. Emphasis original.
88. Hütter, *Suffering Divine Things*, 158.
89. Hütter, *Suffering Divine Things*, 158.
90. Hütter asserts that the church has its authoritative status in its pathos, suffering God's work and Word, not on its own (*Suffering Divine Things*, 158). Hütter's assertion accurately reflects a reformational understanding of justification, but Hütter's church is so idealized that it seems impossible for the church to be disordered and sinful. See Michael Mawson, "The Spirit and the Community: Pneumatology and Ecclesiology in Jenson, Hütter, and Bonhoeffer," *International Journal of Systematic Theology* 15, no. 4 (2013): 459–62.
91. Hütter, *Suffering Diving Things*, 144–45. To show the full context:

This constitutes neither a reification of the Spirit nor an incorporation of the church into the deity as the fourth *hypostasis*. The church remains strictly separate from the Holy Spirit insofar as it perpetually receives what the Spirit creates in it and is thus pathically determined by the Spirit's poiesis.

92. Hütter recognizes that the Holy Spirit works more broadly than the church, but he does not explore what this means. Hütter, "The Church as Public: Dogma, Practice, and the Holy Spirit," *Pro Ecclesia* 3 (1994): 358–59; and Hütter, *Suffering Divine Things*, 250n.135.
93. Hütter, *Suffering Divine Things*, 133.
94. Hütter, *Suffering Divine Things*, 133.
95. Healy, "Practices and the New Ecclesiology," 296–99; and Mawson, "Spirit and the Community," 461–62. In Mawson's words, "The problem, then, is that Hütter's account of the church as receiving the Spirit through its core practices, at least by itself, does not seem sufficiently to acknowledge how the Holy Spirit might be at work even in spite of the church and its practices" (p. 461).
96. Compare Hütter, *Suffering Divine Things*, 132–34.
97. For example, Joel Biermann, "Sanctuary: The Congregation as Haven in a Hostile World," in *Inviting Community*, ed. Robert Kolb and Theodore J. Hopkins (St. Louis: Concordia Seminary Press, 2013), 195–207.

98. For example, the narrative of *ressentiment*: Hunter, *To Change the World*, 107–9.

99. Compare Paulson, "Do Lutherans Need a New Ecclesiology," 231: For Hütter, "creation is outside this communion [of God and the church in the Eucharist], although it is being drawn in, and the church will always be *set against* the created world as a 'mystery.'" Emphasis added.

100. Miroslav Volf and Maurice Lee, "The Spirit and the Church," in *Advents of the Spirit: An Introduction to the Current Study of Pneumatology*, ed. Bradford E. Hinze and D. Lyle Dabney (Milwaukee: Marquette University Press, 2001), 383.

101. Pickard, *Seeking the Church*, 61–73.

102. Among those who have used the Trinity for such a purpose, see, for example, Catherine Mowry LaCugna, *God for Us: The Trinity and Christian Life* (San Francisco: Harper, 1991); and Miroslav Volf, *After Our Likeness: The Church as the Image of the Trinity* (Grand Rapids, MI: Eerdmans, 1998).

103. For a critique of communion ecclesiology along a similar trajectory for lacking the concrete connections between Christ and his cross and the life of the church, see Joseph L. Mangina, "The Cross-Shaped Church: A Pauline Amendment to the Ecclesiology of *Koinōnia*," in *Critical Issues in Ecclesiology: Essays in Honor of Carl E. Braaten*, ed. Alberto L. García and Susan K. Wood (Grand Rapids, MI: Eerdmans, 2011), 68–87.

104. Kathryn Tanner, *Christ the Key* (Cambridge: Cambridge University Press, 2010), 223.

105. Tanner, *Christ the Key*, 223, quoting Karen Kilby, "Perichoresis and Projection," *Blackfriars* 81 (2000): 442. Daniel Wade McClain notices a similar problem: "What (Not) to do with the Trinity: Doctrine, Discipline, and Doxology in Contemporary Trinitarian Discourse," *Anglican Theological Review* 100, no. 3 (2018): 606–12.

106. Tanner, *Christ the Key*, 208–9.

107. Among pneumatological ecclesiologies in the Lutheran tradition, Cheryl Peterson grounds church in God's economy, which is why she uses the *missio Dei* as her starting point instead of communion ecclesiology. Peterson, *Who is the Church*, 94. Despite the *missio dei* starting place, however, it seems to me that Peterson's account emphasizes the story of the church rather than the story of God in Christ. See, for instance, Peterson, "The Church," 50–51, and Peterson, *Who is the Church*, 105–14.

108. As I describe above, Hütter situates the church in God's economy but without the requisite Christology.

109. Volf and Lee, "The Spirit and the Church," 383. Peterson (*Who is the Church*, 122) misreads Volf and Lee on this point as retreating from the Christological focus of Western theology when they are trying to add pneumatology, not take away Christology.

110. Volf and Lee, "The Spirit and the Church," 384. Compare Yves Congar's comment: "The health of pneumatology is in Christology." Cited in Kilian McDonnell, "A Response to D. Lyle Dabney," in *Advents of the Spirit: An Introduction to the Current Study of Pneumatology*, ed. Bradford E. Hinze and D. Lyle Dabney (Milwaukee: Marquette University Press, 2001), 263.

111. Compare Tanner, *Christ the Key*, 240–41: "Jesus' relations with the Father and Spirit make his whole life one of worshipful, praise-filled, faithful service to the Father's mission of bringing in the kingdom; that is to be the character of our lives too, both in and out of the church, as we come to share Jesus' life." This applies even better to the church as a whole before applying to individuals as members of Christ's body.

112. Robert W. Jenson, "The Strange New World of the Bible (2008)," in *Theology as Revisionary Metaphysics: Essays on God and Creation*, ed. Stephen John Wright (Eugene, OR: Cascade Books, 2014), 152.

113. Dietrich Bonhoeffer echoes this point in his notion of the Bible as "the book of the church." DBWE 3, 22. Jens Zimmermann asserts, for Bonhoeffer, "Christ is the inner logic of the scriptures that unifies the Old and New Testaments." Jens Zimmermann, "Reading the Book of the Church: Bonhoeffer's Christological Hermeneutics," *Modern Theology* 28, no. 4 (2012): 773.

114. Tanner, *Christ the Key*, viii.

115. David Scaer's dictum "all theology is Christology" recognizes that only in Christ and his humiliation unto death on a cross do we know God truly. David P. Scaer, "All Theology Is Christology: An Axiom in Search of Acceptance," *Concordia Theological Quarterly* 80, no. 1–2 (2016): 49–62. Luther's Theology of the Cross confesses much the same thing. The classic secondary text is Walther von Loewenich, *Luther's Theology of the Cross*, trans. Herbert J.A. Bouman (Minneapolis: Augsburg, 1976).

116. Leopoldo Sánchez offers a pneumatological Christology in the Lutheran tradition that relates Christ and the Spirit through the narrative of Christ's mission while affirming the orthodoxy of the ecumenical councils and creeds of the early church. In God's economy, Jesus receives the Spirit, bears the Spirit, and gives the Spirit to the church. Jesus is thus constituted by his relation to the Spirit (and the Father), and the Spirit is constituted by his relation to Jesus (and the Father). These relations are known in the scriptural narrative. Leopoldo A. Sánchez M., *Receiver, Bearer, and Giver of God's Spirit: Jesus' Life in the Spirit as a Lens for Theology and Life* (Eugene, OR: Pickwick, 2015). For other helpful accounts of Spirit Christology, see Raniero Cantalamessa, *The Holy Spirit in the Life of Jesus: The Mystery of Christ's Baptism*, trans. Alan Neame (Collegeville, MN: The Liturgical Press, 1994); and Ralph Del Colle, *Christ and the Spirit: Spirit Christology in Trinitarian Perspective* (New York: Oxford University Press, 1994).

Chapter 2

Dietrich Bonhoeffer's Christology in Ecclesiological Perspective

Dietrich Bonhoeffer's theological analysis of *Act and Being* exposes two concerns with twentieth-century theology—categorized as being theology and act theology—that share similarities with the problems of introspection and individualism in the Lutheran ecclesiology of the previous chapter. As Bonhoeffer describes it, being theology suffers primarily from the problem of transcendence, making God available within the anthropological realm. Being theology thus turns human beings inward to themselves or to their churches rather than outward to God in Christ, which is a similar problem to the introspection of Hütter's pneumatological ecclesiology. Act theology, according to Bonhoeffer, suffers from the problem of historical existence wherein Christian faith and identity are located in heaven rather than on earth.[1] Individual faith is created by God through the Word, but one's historical life in the world is incidental theologically, similar to how the Lutheran ecclesiology of the Word focuses on the individual encounter by the Word and deemphasizes the visible life of the community.

The first section of this chapter investigates the similarities of *Act and Being*'s repair of twentieth-century theology with contemporary Lutheran ecclesiology, suggesting Bonhoeffer's Christology as a fruitful direction for my own project. The remainder of the chapter examines Bonhoeffer's 1933 Christology lectures to display his logic that binds church and world in relation to the transcendent Christ who gives himself to his creatures in the humiliation *pro-me*. In Bonhoeffer's Christology, Christ is outside of the church, yet fully present in it through the external Word. Through this account, Bonhoeffer's lectures prioritize the Christ-church and the Christ-world relations over the church-world relation, independently establishing the church and the world in Christ while linking their identities in the one story of the divine economy. Bonhoeffer's Christology brings together

Christ, church, and world in the narrative of Christ's humiliation in the flesh, establishing the church and the world in relationship to the Lord Jesus, and calling the church to the mission of the Lord in the world, empowered by the Spirit.

ACT AND BEING AND LUTHERAN ECCLESIOLOGY

As Bonhoeffer surveys the theological (and philosophical) landscape of the early twentieth century in his Habilitationsschrift, *Act and Being*, the Berlin theologian categorizes contemporary thought according to two types: being theology and act theology. On the one hand, Bonhoeffer describes being theology. The label "being theology" does not designate a single theology, but a variety of theologies that share the characteristic of making knowledge of God possible anthropologically.[2] For example, when theology is understood as a system of objective, cognitive propositions, God becomes "understandable and subject to classification" within the human sphere.[3] Additionally, when revelation is understood as religious experience, and these experiences are elevated to "objective status," God is known within one's experience.[4] Bonhoeffer also sees being theology in a third way in Roman Catholicism's emphasis on the institution of the church—"whoever is in this institution is in God"—and in conservative Protestantism's notion of verbal inspiration— which turns the Bible into an object of study containing true facts about God.[5]

The most important form of being theology with which Bonhoeffer interacts is the theology of Karl Holl, the eminent Luther scholar, church historian, and Bonhoeffer's teacher.[6] Holl argues, on the basis of early Luther, that Christianity is "a religion of conscience."[7] The pinnacle of religion for Holl is *Anfechtungen*, the terrors of conscience, which placed Luther "directly and alone" before God, and even "Christ himself seemed to vanish."[8] Ultimate knowledge, Holl asserted, originates from a direct encounter of God and the individual in the conscience. For Bonhoeffer, however, Holl's understanding of Luther is nothing more than a sophisticated version of theology as a religious experience, turning one inward to the conscience rather than outward to Christ and the Scriptures.[9] Bonhoeffer sums up Holl's theology: "Because the human being is able to hear and have God within his conscience, he is able to understand himself from within his conscience as his most authentic possibility of being human."[10] Holl's theology, like being theology generally, makes sense of one's historical existence—establishing theologically the value of one's visible, historical life—but it excludes God's transcendence. As a result, being theology turns people inward to find God within themselves. In this understanding of God's encounter with humanity, people are directed to their own cognitive abilities, their own experiences, or their own church. But such introspection is the essence of sin—*cor curvum in se*.[11] "Christ is not present," Bonhoeffer asserts, "as long as I still reflect on myself."[12]

On the other hand, *Act and Being* describes act theology as the diametric opposite of being theology, which attempts to secure God's transcendence but becomes unhinged from history (and fails to secure transcendence).[13] The most important representative of act theology is Karl Barth, Bonhoeffer's friend and mentor, and a key figure in Bonhoeffer's own theological development.[14] Against all being theologies that make knowledge of God possible for humanity, Karl Barth emphasizes God as wholly other, unknowable except by God's initiative and grace.[15] Corresponding to this understanding of God's transcendence, Barth argues for a contingent concept of revelation, which means that revelation is not generally available to humanity but is contingent upon God's freedom. Revelation, hence, can never be conceived as temporal or historical: "God's act in revelation has no material or temporal extension, no history as such, no place in the world as its concrete expression. God is free, never subject to the control of human interests."[16]

Although Bonhoeffer affirms the Swiss theologian's contingent concept of revelation, the Berlin theologian sees a problem arise from Barth's solution. To save God's transcendence, Barth's act theology places revelation and faith outside of history, in the eschatological frame. For Barth, revelation is never graspable in space and time.[17] God's promises have no historical location to which one can point and say, "Here is God," allowing a person to grasp God's Word as received in human history.[18] Barth's act theology, therefore, creates a problem of historical existence.[19] "According to Barth, no historical moment is *capax infiniti*, so that empirical human activity—be it faith, obedience—is at best reference to God's activity and in its historicity can never be faith and obedience itself."[20]

These two problems of transcendence and historical existence roughly correspond to the two problems of Lutheran ecclesiology. On the one hand, Reinhard Hütter's ecclesiology of the Spirit exhibits a similar problem to being theology: introspection. When the Spirit is not clearly identified in the public story of God's salvation in his Son Jesus, the church loses its outward reference to the transcendent God and turns inward to itself (or to the world in other versions). On the other hand, the Lutheran ecclesiology of the Word shares similarities to Barth's act theology, which focuses outward on God's external Word but loses the historical, public existence of the church. When God's work of justification is understood only in terms of the logic of performative speech, the church as a visible community on earth within human history falls apart.

Since Bonhoeffer developed his "person-concept of revelation" as an alternative to these two problems,[21] Bonhoeffer's theology offers promise to correct twenty-first-century Lutheran ecclesiology in the midst of similar problems. At the heart of Bonhoeffer's person-concept of revelation is not a general anthropology but a specific Christology: the person of Jesus Christ.[22] Bonhoeffer's Christology, best exemplified in his "Christology Lectures" of 1933, thus secures both Lutheran ecclesiology of the Word's outward orientation to God in Christ and the public visibility of the church, emphasized by Hütter's pneumatological ecclesiology.

CHRIST, CHURCH, AND WORLD IN BONHOEFFER'S CHRISTOLOGY LECTURES

Bonhoeffer's 1933 Christology lectures were delivered during the final term of his formal appointment at the University of Berlin before nearly two-hundred students.[23] Although neither a published version nor more than two pages of Bonhoeffer's own lecture notes exist, extensive student notes offer something more than a detailed outline of the lectures.[24] In them, Bonhoeffer establishes Christ, church, and world as three prongs of his Christological framework. Bonhoeffer first prioritizes the identity of Jesus' person, the "who" question, acknowledging Christ as the transcendent Son of God who revealed himself in his human history and continues to be present in the church as the risen one.[25] Second, Bonhoeffer understands Christ's relationship to the church in terms of the *pro-me* structure of Christ, the risen Christ present in the church to condemn, forgive, and call to discipleship.[26] Third, Bonhoeffer confesses Christ as the center of history and the world, establishing the world also in relationship to Jesus and distinct from Christ's relationship to his church.[27] Bonhoeffer uses Lutheran Christological categories—not without criticism—to bring together Christ, church, and world while recognizing history as the arena of this encounter between the transcendent God and his creatures.

Transcendence and the Priority of Christ's Identity

Bonhoeffer begins the 1933 Christology lectures with a seemingly odd discussion of epistemology and its relationship to Christology. Although he makes no direct reference to Karl Barth, Bonhoeffer places his Christology within the framework of the problem of transcendence that was essential to Barth's thought. Barth's early theology developed in direct response to this problem as represented by Ludwig Feuerbach.[28] In *The Essence of Christianity*, Feuerbach turns theology into anthropology and anthropology into theology: the essence of Christianity is the conflation of humanity and God in the incarnation.[29] Against Feuerbach, Barth establishes God as subject and never as object.[30] Barth argues that a "real wall" exists between God and the world that cannot be broken from the human side.[31] The wall between God and the world "holds even during and after revelation" since revelation is always an *act* and never an existing thing that can be grasped and manipulated as an object.[32] The nature of revelation, then, is indirect and contingent, never simply available to humanity. Barth builds the same indirect and contingent nature of revelation into his understanding of the person of Jesus, constructing an "eschatological reservation" into his Christology.[33] Even after Barth grounds his theology in Christology instead of eschatology, the critical distance between God and the world that Barth had found in eschatology was not diminished. For Barth, the Logos is the subject of the life of Jesus so that the Trinitarian person is revealed and hidden dialectically in Jesus of Nazareth.[34] Even in Jesus, the wall between God and the world stands.

In the Christology lectures, Bonhoeffer follows Barth in recognizing the significance of God's transcendence, but Bonhoeffer establishes it Christologically rather than formally. According to Bonhoeffer, Jesus is transcendent precisely as a man, as a person. Bonhoeffer claims, "This human person [Jesus] is *the transcendent*."[35] Barth had established God's transcendence with a subject-concept of God that refused to allow God to become an object,[36] but Bonhoeffer establishes Christ's transcendence in his historical reality as a person.[37] Jesus is transcendent because he is a person who is free to give himself and encounter reality from the outside.[38] For Bonhoeffer, human beings know the ultimate reality only because God became a human creature, entered into time and space, and made himself known.[39]

Bonhoeffer specifies the transcendence of Christ by considering classification systems in *Wissenschaft*, academic scholarship. "All scholarly questions can be reduced to two fundamental questions," Bonhoeffer says. "First, what is the cause of X? Second, what is the meaning of X?"[40] In both the natural sciences—the first question—and the arts and humanities—the second question—the object is known by classifying it in relationship to existing categories.[41] The human logos asks the "how" question—how does this object fit into my classification system?—in order to understand what is unknown by what is already known. If the object defies classification, the human logos makes a better system to incorporate the new object. No matter what, the human logos refuses to be *confronted* by the object. The human logos always demands control.[42] In this way, Bonhoeffer describes the problem of transcendence that Barth also found: human beings in sin treat reality, including revelation, as an object under their control so that they are not confronted or transformed.

Against the notion that the right question for Christology is the "how" question that tries to classify Jesus, Bonhoeffer contends that Christology properly asks the "who" question: "Who are you?"[43] This is the question, prompted by the divine Logos, that human beings need to ask in order to know Jesus. To ask this question, however, human reason needs to die first to its demands for control at the hand of the Word. Christ does just this, putting human beings to death in their sin, by confronting them as the Truth, the Logos of God. In fact, Christ negates the "how" question completely. Since Jesus is unable to be categorized as an object under human power, human reason is "dethroned," and the only question left to ask is "the question of faith: Who are you? Are you God's very self?"[44] This is the quintessential question of Christology, for Bonhoeffer, which is also "the question about transcendence," precisely because it asks about the identity of Christ's person, recognizing him as the Son of God who encounters from the outside.[45] The "how" question, on the other hand, is the "question about immanence," which asks *how* Christ exists, *how* Jesus can be God, or *how* Jesus is present in the world.[46] The "how" questions seek to learn about Jesus in order to classify him within human systematic thinking, but the "who" question is the response of one who is confronted by Christ. The "who" question is the question of faith.

Bonhoeffer moves to direct theological reasoning by connecting the prior epistemological claims to the doctrine of sin. According to Bonhoeffer, even when humans ask the "who" question, "we are speaking the language of obedient Adam, but we are *thinking* the 'how' of the fallen Adam."[47] This is a corollary of original sin, which Bonhoeffer defines using Luther's phrase the *cor curvum in se*, the heart turned in on itself. Like the heart, the thinking of fallen human creatures is curved in on itself.[48] Such sinful thinking manifests when human beings assert authority over Christ by making him a part of their system rather than hearing his Word which kills the sinner, leads to the question of faith, "Who are you?", and results in the confession of the church. Although the "who" question is the proper Christological question, sinners cannot ask the question in themselves. Instead, "one can legitimately ask *who* only after the self-revelation of the other to whom one puts the question has already taken place."[49] In other words, the question that is at the heart of proper Christology—Who are you, Jesus?—can only be posed after Jesus has already given himself to a person in faith and the answer is known. Christ controls his own revelation and can only be identified after he gives himself from the outside.

The "who" question becomes more pointed as Bonhoeffer describes Christ's identity no longer in formal terms but in the narrative of Jesus' life and his encounter with humanity. In his life and ministry, Jesus questioned and challenged human beings, their knowledge of God and themselves, but they rejected him and killed him so that the human logos would not be condemned and killed by the Counter Logos (of God). But in the resurrection, Christ stands over humanity as the risen one over whom no one has any power, and Christ confronts his murderers with the same question, Who are *you*?[50] In this confrontation with Jesus, there are only two possibilities, "the human being must either die or kill Jesus."[51] As the risen Lord, Christ confronts humanity in order to condemn human persons in their sinfulness, justify them, and lead them to confess him as the transcendent Son of God. Only then is the "who" question properly answered.

Bonhoeffer retains the priority of Christ's identity in his interpretation of the fifth-century council of Chalcedon as Bonhoeffer turns to understanding the historical Christ in the second half of the Christology lectures. In the section "Critical Christology," the Berlin theologian explicates formulations of ecumenical councils and the Lutheran tradition over and against other positions, historical and contemporary.[52] As one would expect, Bonhoeffer describes the positions addressed at Chalcedon in terms of the heretical Monophysite and Nestorian positions, which Chalcedon rejected.[53] Bonhoeffer also interprets Chalcedon as making it illegitimate to speak about the two natures separately from the one person: "it is no longer permissible to talk about the human and divine natures of Jesus Christ as about things or facts."[54] Instead, "we can only enter in faith."[55] In other words, Bonhoeffer sees the four negative formulations of Chalcedon—Jesus Christ is one person with two natures *without confusion, change, distinction*, or *separation*—as emphasizing the oneness of Jesus' person who is fully divine and fully human. "There is only *one* Christ. But he has two natures."[56] As such, Bonhoeffer thinks Chalcedon "cancels itself out" by using the language of the two natures even as it "demonstrates that these concepts are inappropriate and heretical forms."[57] For Bonhoeffer, Chalcedon formulated a doctrine of Christ using the traditional language of the two natures, but the whole point was to overcome the language of the two natures and focus instead on the one person who is God and man. Although the Berlin theologian recognizes the importance of keeping divinity and humanity separate in the abstract,[58] he follows Luther and the Lutheran tradition in moving away from talking about Christ's natures to confess the one concrete human person Jesus, who is God.[59]

Consequently, Bonhoeffer follows the development of the *unio hypostatica*, the personal union, and the *communicatio idiomatum*, the communication of attributes between the natures and the person of Jesus, as doctrines that convey the unity of Christ's person in the Lutheran tradition. Bonhoeffer calls the *genus majestaticum*—the kind of sharing in which the attributes of the divine nature are shared freely with the human nature in the person of Jesus—"the core of Lutheran theology,"[60] but he is largely critical of the whole enterprise of specifying the relationship between Christ's divine and human natures. From Bonhoeffer's perspective, the Protestant tradition dwells upon the relationship between abstract humanity and abstract divinity rather than driving toward a confession of the identity of Jesus. Although I would suggest that

Bonhoeffer misses the critical side of the *genus majestaticum*—which asserts the unity and transcendence of the person of Jesus in the state of exaltation so that wherever Jesus wishes to be, he is there as God *and* man, particularly in keeping his promise in the Eucharist[61]—Bonhoeffer rightly points out the common temptation to analyze *how* Jesus is present instead of focusing on the *identity* of the person of Jesus who is present.[62] The driving question of the Protestant tradition of Christology, according to Bonhoeffer's interpretation, is: "How shall we think about the difference of the two natures and the unity of the person?"[63] Chalcedon, however, rules out this question in favor of the question of identity: "Who is this human being who is said to be God?"[64]

For all of this emphasis on identity, the "who" question, the structure of Bonhoeffer's lectures actually depicts Jesus first as the present Christ before he describes him as the historical Christ. Robert John Dean suggests, thus, that it is a "legitimate question" whether Bonhoeffer has sufficiently placed Christ outside of the church to stand against it.[65] According to the structure of the lectures, Bonhoeffer seems to prioritize Christ's work and presence over his historical identity as Jesus of Nazareth, thereby threatening to reduce Jesus to his relationship to his creatures.[66]

At the beginning of his lectures on the present Christ, however, Bonhoeffer relates the person and work of Christ in an important way. Many Bonhoeffer commentators emphasize the way that the Berlin theologian connects and relates Christ's person with Christ's work,[67] but in the context of the Lutheran tradition, the way that Bonhoeffer distinguishes Christ's person and work is even more important. Bonhoeffer recalls Melanchthon's famous dictum: "Hoc est Christum cognoscere, beneficia eius cognoscere," to know Christ is to know his benefits.[68] According to Bonhoeffer, this settled the question of the relationship between Christ's person and works for much of the Lutheran tradition by knowing Christ solely on the basis of his works. Bonhoeffer thus sees the Christologies of Schleiermacher and Ritschl as natural developments from Melanchthon's dictum in which Christology is settled on the basis of soteriology.[69] Bonhoeffer argues that this reverses the proper order of Christology and soteriology: "Luther's thinking is that it is the person through whom the works are to be interpreted."[70] Conceptually, then, Bonhoeffer establishes the identity of Christ as the foundation for understanding his work. As such, what Norman Nagel says about Luther's Christology is also true about Bonhoeffer's: Christ's "person is the unshakeable ground of the salvation he achieved—*qualis persona, talia opera*."[71]

Even though Bonhoeffer describes Christ first as the present Christ, Bonhoeffer argues that the person proceeds the work. Robert John Dean is correct that the lecture's structure pushes toward collapsing Jesus' historical identity into his presence,[72] but the bigger problem in Bonhoeffer's lectures is the paucity of the Bible in the lectures.[73] Bonhoeffer guards formally against collapsing Christ's person into his work, but Bonhoeffer's Christology needs a fuller biblical account to establish Christ's historical identity as the transcendent one in reality. For Bonhoeffer, Christ must be known on the basis of revelation in order for one to be encountered by Jesus, be remade to trust in him, and be brought to confess him in truth. Bonhoeffer acknowledges that Christ's person and Christ's work are not separate—they are interrelated in complex ways—but Christology asks first about his person, the Son of God who became man in time and history, and only then about his work.[74] The identity of the transcendent man Jesus must be prioritized theologically over his salvific presence.[75]

Christ *Pro-Me* in the Church

At the same time that the lectures give precedence to Christ's person and identity, Bonhoeffer's Christology lectures also emphasize the present Christ who is "*pro-me*" in the church and the world. Through the *pro-me* structure of Christ, Bonhoeffer roots the doctrine of justification in the person of Jesus Christ as he is present *hic et nunc*, here and now, "in the church as person."[76] Jesus is not present in the church as an object to be manipulated but as a person to encounter his creatures. Hence, Bonhoeffer rejects the Christology of his teacher Wilhelm Hermann as well as that of Albrecht Ritschl because they make Christ into a power instead of a person.[77]

The risen Christ who is present in the church is the human Jesus. He is present in the church now as a human being, and he is eternally present because he is God.[78] Bonhoeffer refuses to veer off into speculation about how a human being could be present everywhere, or how God could enter time and space. Instead, Bonhoeffer centers his reflection upon the God-man Jesus Christ himself.[79] In this way, Bonhoeffer shifts the Christological focus from the relationship of divinity to humanity (the incarnation) to the relationship of Jesus to the world (the humiliation). In his own words, "the problem has shifted: it is not the relation of God and human in Jesus Christ, but rather than relation of the God-human, as already given, to the ὁμοίωμα σαρκὸς," the likeness of (sinful) flesh, quoting Romans 8:3.[80] In changing his focus to the relationship between Christ and the world, Bonhoeffer does not abandon Christology for soteriology, but describes the concrete history of Christ's person as the humiliated One who came in the likeness of sinful flesh, which both identifies Christ and describes his mission. Although Christ's identity is prior to Christ's work, person and work cannot be separated: "I cannot think of Jesus Christ in his being-in-himself, but only in his relatedness to me."[81] *Pro-me* is not a mere descriptor of his work; this is at *the core of his person*. "His being-Christ is his being-for-me."[82] Christ's promeity is not a supra-historical concept, but a description of the historical

Christ's identity and work: "The *pro-me* structure refers first of all to the historical Jesus."[83] In dogmatic terms, justification is intrinsic to the person and identity of Jesus. Jesus' story that identifies him as the Lord is at the same time the story of the justification of sinners, who are brought into the church, the new humanity.

Bonhoeffer describes Jesus' *pro-me* structure in the threefold form of Word, Sacrament, and church-community (*Gemeinde*).[84] As Word, Christ is the truth, not an idea of the truth but truth as concrete Word spoken to his creatures. Christ is not an idea to be manipulated and judged by human reason, nor is he a mere prophet who speaks another's word.[85] Christ is the spoken Word directly addressed to people, creating community through the truth.[86] As the direct address of God, Christ has the content of law and gospel, "commandment and forgiveness."[87] Now exalted, Christ is still present as the Word, giving himself to his people in preaching. In Bonhoeffer's conception, God's Word and human words are not mutually exclusive. Instead, just as the Son of God became a human being, these human words are truly the Word of God because of Christ's presence in the church as Word in proclamation.[88]

Christ is also present in the church as Sacrament *pro-me*. For Bonhoeffer, Christ's presence in the Sacrament speaks to God's re-creation of the sinful world. "Sacrament exists only where God, in the midst of the world of creatures, names an element, speaks to it, and hallows it with the particular word God has for it by giving it its name."[89] Within the sinful, creaturely world, Christ is present in the Sacrament in bodily form. The scandal in the Sacrament is *not* how Jesus could be present in material things, which would amount to asking the "how" question, "How do divinity and humanity relate in Christ's person to permit his sacramental presence?" Instead, the humiliation of the Son of God who hides in bread and wine is the true scandal of the Eucharist. Through this focus on the humiliation, Bonhoeffer directs the issue of sacramental presence back to the "who" question: "Who is the Christ who is present in the Sacrament?"[90] Bonhoeffer answers, "The God-human, the Exalted One! . . . His being sacrament is his being humiliated in the present. It is not an incidental aspect of his God-human substance, but rather his existence is a humiliated existence."[91] In centering Christ's sacramental presence in the humiliation, Bonhoeffer points to Jesus' willingness to become the "stumbling block," to enter the world "in the likeness of sinful flesh" and "in the form of a servant."[92] Under these hidden, weak forms, Christ makes himself present in the Sacrament as a creature for creatures, recreating bread and wine to be elements of the new creation through which he gives his own body and blood through physical matter for physical creatures.[93] At the same time that Jesus willingly gives himself in created things, Jesus is the Creator who makes sinners into new creatures.[94] In the sacraments, the Creator humbles himself to be present in created elements for creatures, and in so doing makes them participants in his own life and mission.

Finally, Bonhoeffer describes Jesus as present *pro-me* as church-community. Bonhoeffer's point is not that Jesus takes form as individual Christians who become "Christ" for their neighbors, but that Jesus is present corporately as a church-community which is called to live as and is the new humanity.[95] Here, too, Bonhoeffer emphasizes the bodily form that Christ takes in the church. The church-community is the body of Christ in reality and not merely as a metaphor or image.[96] Bonhoeffer asserts, "The concept of the body as applied to the church-community is not a functional concept referring to the members but is instead a concept of the way in which the Christ exists who is present, exalted, and humiliated."[97] The God-man Jesus Christ takes form in the church-community in humility to reveal himself, judge, forgive, and continue his mission in the world.

In this threefold form of the *pro-me* structure of Christ in the church, Bonhoeffer describes Jesus as the Son of God who is yet the humiliated One, the incognito stumbling block, present in hidden ways in the church in time and space. Jesus, a true, historical man, who is true God, gives himself in the Word, the sacraments, and the congregation in visible and historical forms. These forms are hidden, only seen by faith, but Christ truly takes concrete, historical form in these three ways in the present.

CHRIST *PRO-ME* IN THE WORLD

According to the lecture notes, Bonhoeffer spent about twice as long on the form of Christ's *pro-me* structure in the church than the place of Christ *pro-me* in the world. Though briefer, Bonhoeffer's comments on Christ's place in the world must not be overlooked because Bonhoeffer refuses to understand Jesus only in relation to the church. Christ is Lord of all and must be recognized as Lord and center of all things.[98] In placing the Lord Jesus at the center of reality, Bonhoeffer refuses to allow the secular to become an autonomous realm free from the Word of God. Instead, Bonhoeffer orients the whole world to Christ and Christ to the whole world. In three sub-sections—Christ as the center of human existence, the center of history, and the center of nature—Bonhoeffer confesses Jesus to be both the limit and the center of all. The Christ-centeredness of reality is not a matter of empirical proof, accessible by all people through natural reason, but a matter of *preaching* in which the story and person of Christ is proclaimed as both limit and goal of each person's story, history's story, and nature's story.[99]

First, Bonhoeffer acknowledges Christ as the center of human existence, since Jesus is both "the judgment and the justification."[100] Bonhoeffer sees the story of humanity in forensic terms, in a public arena of judgment, where humanity is both judged and justified in Jesus Christ. Christ fulfilled the law, revealing humanity's sin, corruption, and brokenness, and he justifies humanity by standing in humanity's place. Even for the fallen world that does not know or believe in Jesus, Bonhoeffer affirms that Christ's ministry, death, resurrection, and coming again in judgment are at the heart of humanity's story.[101]

Second, Bonhoeffer recognizes Christ as the center of history since history is "essentially messianic history."[102] Bonhoeffer describes the story of the world as the story of promise and fulfillment of the Messiah. Hence, Israel is the "place where God fulfills this promise."[103] Bonhoeffer sees the world in sin striving to achieve *its own* messianic history, each government attempting to fulfill history and be the hope of the people—this lecture was delivered in the midst of the National Socialist government striving to be Germany's hope—but in Jesus all of these ambitions are crushed and destroyed. The center of history is not visible power or glory, but the humiliation of the Son of God.[104] Only Jesus is the Messiah, not any state or world leader, especially one striving to become the savior through power.[105] Only the story of Jesus constitutes the world's true story in which the state is given its limited goals of law and order and subject to the preaching of the church.[106]

Third, Bonhoeffer acknowledges Christ as the center of nature, the limit of all other creatures because Christ is the new who reveals the old as old. At the same time, Christ brings liberation to nature which is in bondage to sin, freeing it from its sinfulness as mute, dumb, and cursed. Christ is the bearer of the new age, the new creation, which is present in a hidden way in the sacraments as Christ frees nature to speak God's own words of freedom and forgiveness even as the old age persists.[107] As in human existence and history, Christ is the center of nature by being the mediator, who stands in the place of creatures, *pro-me*, and reveals its center not as power and glory but as the humiliation of God's Son.

SUMMARY OF BONHOEFFER'S CHRISTOLOGY

Charles Marsh distinguishes between Bonhoeffer's theology and Karl Barth's theology by noting Barth's emphasis on the *aseity* of God—God's being or identity in himself—and Bonhoeffer's stress on the *promeity* of God—God's being or identity for me.[108] Although Bonhoeffer refuses to think of Christ apart from the incarnate one at work in history for the good of his creation, Bonhoeffer follows Barth in emphasizing identity over presence, primary objectivity over secondary objectivity, using Marsh's categories.[109] Bonhoeffer refuses to allow Christ to become an object under human control. Instead, Christ is transcendent in his person, and he encounters his creatures as the Lord and the Son of God. At the same time, Bonhoeffer radically connects identity with presence in a Lutheran fashion so that the distinction between primary and secondary objectivity is overcome in favor of the person of Christ. Promeity—justification—is intrinsic to Christ's person and identity.[110] Jesus is not simply the Lord *per se* in some abstract divine freedom;[111] Jesus is the humiliated Lord *pro nobis* and *precisely as such* Jesus is the revelation of God and the center of the church and the world.

Even with his "Barthian twist," Bonhoeffer's Christology remains "deeply Lutheran,"[112] although he does not articulate the unity of Christ's person in the same manner as classical Lutheranism. Lutheran dogmatics traditionally employs the *communicatio idiomatum*, the communication of attributes between the natures and person of Christ, to express the unity of Christ's person,[113] but, as we saw above, Bonhoeffer shies away from its formulations.[114] Nonetheless, the Berlin theologian stands in deep continuity with the Lutheran tradition by emphasizing the unity of the person of Jesus, especially in the affirmation that "Jesus the human being is God."[115] By focusing on the incarnate Christ whose identity is made known in Holy Scripture, Bonhoeffer's Christology combats both the Reformed tradition that abstracts the Son of God from the person of Jesus and some recent thinkers who employ the *communicatio* soteriologically but apart from the concrete identity of Jesus.

On the one hand, Bonhoeffer's Christology stands apart from Barth, who considers the Logos to be the proper Christological "person" of Jesus of Nazareth,[116] and even constructs an "eschatological reservation" into his Christology to retain the difference between God and man.[117] According to this understanding of Reformed Christology, the Logos is not entirely circumscribed by the historical Jesus on earth, but remains in heaven in relationship to the Father and the Spirit.[118] Against this so-called *extra calvinisticum*,[119] Bonhoeffer contends that no hidden subject, the Logos, exists behind the actions of the historical Jesus.[120] Instead, the historical Jesus is the Son of God without caveat or remainder. For Bonhoeffer, with the Lutheran tradition, the humanity of Jesus is in such close communion with the divinity that Jesus even makes himself present in the Eucharist in his person as God and man, as he promised.[121] God is present historically and visibly on earth in Jesus Christ not merely in acts that appear and disappear in time, but in a person who was present as depicted in the Gospels, is present in the church by the Spirit, and will be present eternally when he comes again. Bonhoeffer's Christology thus diverges from Barth and the Reformed tradition in asserting unequivocally that Jesus of Nazareth is God in the flesh.

On the other hand, Bonhoeffer's understanding of the person of Jesus must be contrasted also with those who have used the Lutheran doctrine of the *communicatio idiomatum* soteriologically without a proper account of

Christ's identity.[122] For instance, Johann Anselm Steiger claims that Hegel took up Luther's understanding of the *communicatio* philosophically:

> In a later time, it would be Hegel who, being serious philosophically about this heritage from the Reformation, defined changeableness, history and the self-emptying of the Spirit, thus that which appears accidental at face value, as substance and as the essential.[123]

In doing so, Hegel turned the historical reality of the Son of God into a philosophical reality.[124] In Hegel, the identity of Jesus as God and man became an essential philosophical truth, grasped in the anthropological sphere, and leading quite naturally to Feuerbach, as Barth asserted.[125]

More recently, Daniel Peterson contends for a "radical Lutheran" view of Christ that rejects the *extra calvinisticum* in a fully kenotic Christology.[126] Peterson seems to be in agreement with Bonhoeffer's emphasis on the humiliation as he uses Luther's notion of the *communicatio idiomatum* to assert that Christ has taken "into his divine nature what is ours—damnation and death."[127] For Peterson, however, *kenosis* and *communicatio* are not primarily descriptors of Christ's person and work, a matter of the divine history to which the Holy Scripture authoritatively testifies, but are symbols for the Christian community to learn to recognize "Godding" and "Pentecosting" moments in the world.[128] In Peterson, Christ's historical identity is overcome by a theory, and salvation becomes possible in the anthropological sphere by recognizing "Christ" in the "other."[129]

Bonhoeffer's Christology does not turn the communication of attributes into a philosophical idea because Bonhoeffer prioritizes the identity of Christ and understands Jesus materially according to his concrete history in the Bible.[130] Although Bonhoeffer's Christology lectures do not cite Scripture very often,[131] Bonhoeffer's account begins and ends with the biblical story of Christ. Near the beginning of the lectures, Bonhoeffer justifies his notion of Jesus the counter logos by an abbreviated account of Christ's story,[132] and his positive construction of Christology is a narrative of the humiliation of Christ.[133] Additionally, as Robert John Dean observes, Bonhoeffer employs the German term *Menschgewordene* instead of *Inkarnation* or *Fleischgewordene*. Bonhoeffer does so "to emphasize God's complete identification with humanity," and Dean argues, "the particular human life lived by the God-man Jesus Christ."[134] In line with this, Bonhoeffer asserts, "The Christ who is present today is the historical Christ. He is the Jesus of history."[135] In identifying the Lord of the world who makes himself present in the church with Jesus of Nazareth, known in the Bible, Bonhoeffer's Christology requires a storied account of the Christ. The narrative of the Bible must be told to confess this man as true God who bore the sin of the world in his humiliation, was raised from the dead through the Holy Spirit, and continues to be present in humility in the church and the world.[136]

CONCLUSION: THE RELEVANCE OF BONHOEFFER'S CHRISTOLOGY FOR ECCLESIOLOGY

Following the importance of the problem of transcendence in Karl Barth, Dietrich Bonhoeffer's Christology prioritizes the transcendence of the Christ as the one who is the Son of God in person. At the same time, Bonhoeffer establishes history as the arena for the Word and work of God through an account of Christ the historical man who lived, died, rose again, and continues to be present on earth as the risen Lord. In this way, Bonhoeffer's Christology offers a solution to the contemporary impasse of Lutheran ecclesiology. While Lutheran ecclesiology tends toward individualization or ecclesial introspection, as we saw in the last chapter, Bonhoeffer's Christology establishes the church in relationship to both Christ and the world within the narrative of the triune God. The church is directed outside of itself to its Lord, while also established as the body of Christ in the world that also belongs to the Lord. The risen Christ, who is the Jesus of history and the center of the world, is present in the church by the Word, sacraments, and church-community.

Bonhoeffer distinguishes between the Christ-church and Christ-world relations, which are both prior to the church-world relation. Bonhoeffer first binds ecclesiology and Christology together without dissolving one into the other. In Bonhoeffer's own words, "The community of faith is God's final revelation as 'Christ existing as community [Gemeinde],' ordained for the end time of the world until the return of Christ."[137] In describing the church as "Christ existing as church-community [Gemeinde],"[138] Bonhoeffer expresses Christ's identity as the risen One, who makes himself present in the church. Stated differently, because of Christ's identity and promise, the church is the body of Christ. Bonhoeffer explicitly demonstrates the Christological priority of his ecclesiological definition in a 1940 newsletter to Finkenwalde alumni:

> In [the ascension] the heavenly Christ is in fact utterly present to the earth; he fills his church-community, and with it and through it he fills all in all (Eph. 1:23); for through the church-community he gradually permeates the entire world, which belongs to him, and fills it with his active presence.[139]

Jesus *is* the risen Lord, not confined to the past, and as the living Lord he gives himself in the church, encountering humanity through the sacraments, preaching, and service of the church. Thus, Bonhoeffer's "definition" of church—"Christ existing as church-community"—is not a definition of church *per se*. It is first a statement about Jesus.[140] Christ makes himself present through the church.[141] Because of who Christ is, the church is what it is as the body of Christ, the people of God called to Christ's mission.

For this reason, Bonhoeffer's definition of the church—"Christ existing as church-community"—does not give license for the church to act like "an extension of the incarnation," the institution with divine power and privilege.[142] If "Christ existing as church-community" were first about the church rather than the Christ, the church would be directed toward itself, and its own life would establish the identity and work of Christ in the world. Otherwise stated, if the church determines the presence and activity of Christ—as a guaranteed extension of the Son of God into the present—Bonhoeffer's definition would grant church-communities nearly unchecked divine authority. As Michael Horton recognizes, when the church is understood as an extension of the incarnation, then "in the place of [Jesus'] historical life stands the church in all of its (or rather, his) glory."[143] As a Christological definition, however, the church is not defined as having divine authority, but by the story of the humiliated Son of God. The church that knows itself in Christ is not an extension of the incarnation, as a repository of divine power, but it *is* the body of Christ.[144] The church knows itself from Christ's story; is continually reformed by his identity, work, and teaching through the Spirit; and is made a participant in his mission of witness and service to God by grace. The church, therefore, is defined by Christ, according to Bonhoeffer's Christology, not as some philosophical idea, but as the Lord who humbled himself for us and our salvation, according to the Scriptures.

Bonhoeffer describes Christologically not only the church but also the world. The world is not to be determined chiefly by its relation to the church, but in its relationship to the Lord Jesus. This too prevents the church from asserting a triumphalistic arrogance in its mission to the world. The world is not absent or removed from the story of Christ, but a participant, even if an unknowing one, in the Messianic history of God. By grounding the world in Christ distinctly from the church, Bonhoeffer's Christology allows the church and the world to be distinct yet deeply united, as will be further explored in the next chapter.

NOTES

1. Michael P. DeJonge, *Bonhoeffer's Theological Formation: Berlin, Barth, and Protestant Theology* (Oxford: Oxford University Press, 2012), 5: "To the question, 'Where do we stand?', Bonhoeffer answers that we stand at a theological impasse, oriented either to the [historical] world or to the [transcendent] Word."

2. DeJonge, *Bonhoeffer's Theological Formation*, 16.

3. DBWE 2, 103.
4. DBWE 2, 104.
5. DBWE 2, 104. Bonhoeffer rightly warns against a view of verbal inspiration in which the Bible is a true object of study rather than the voice of the living God. Instead of locating God's Word in doctrinal content understood by a reader as external information, verbal inspiration should emphasize that Bible is truly the Word of the living God in which God encounters humanity through the Bible's words to repent and believe. The material understanding of inspiration I have suggested takes form in the Lutheran tradition in terms of the doctrine of perspicuity, stated as the dictum *sacra scriptura sui ipsius interpres*—sacred Scripture is its own interpreter. Bonhoeffer himself speaks in much the same way about the living Word of God even while criticizing verbal inspiration in "Contemporizing New Testament Texts," in DBWE 14, 413–33. See also Wolf Krötke, "Dietrich Bonhoeffer and Martin Luther," in *Bonhoeffer's Intellectual Formation: Theology and Philosophy in His Thought*, ed. Peter Frick (Tübingen: Mohr Siebeck, 2008), 58–59.
6. DBWE 2, 141–44. DeJonge, *Bonhoeffer's Theological Formation*, 118: "Bonhoeffer's rejection of being-theology is directed primarily at . . . a particularly insidious form of the [second] type of being theology, the Lutheran theology of conscience," namely, Holl's theology. For an overview of Holl that places him within his historical context, see James M. Stayer, *Martin Luther, German Saviour: German Evangelical Theological Factions and the Interpretation of Luther, 1917–1933* (Montreal: McGill-Queen's University Press, 2000), 18–47. For an excellent analysis of Bonhoeffer's relationship to Holl, see Michael P. DeJonge, *Bonhoeffer's Reception of Luther* (Oxford: Oxford University Press, 2017), 16–41.
7. Karl Holl, *What Did Luther Understand by Religion?*, ed. James Luther Adams and Walter F. Bense (Philadelphia: Fortress, 1977), 48
8. Holl, *What Did Luther Understand by Religion*, 77–79. For more on Holl's disparaging of Christology, see Stayer, *Martin Luther, German Saviour*, 43–44.
9. See Holl, *What did Luther Understand by Religion*, 51–53n.28, for evidence of Holl's internalizing tendency.
10. DBWE 10, 401.
11. DBWE 2, 137, on the *cor curvum*:

> God has become a religious object, and human beings themselves have become their own creator and lord, belonging to themselves. It is only to be expected that they should now begin and end with themselves in their knowing, for they are only and utterly 'with themselves' in the falsehood of naked self-glory.

12. DBWE 2, 142.
13. DeJonge, *Bonhoeffer's Theological Formation*, 56–68. Bonhoeffer explains that early Barth ironically fails to secure transcendence because he establishes it formally in thought rather than materially in the content of who God is. In other words, transcendence in Barth is an idea affirmed conceptually, but not established in reality. There is an interesting parallel here with Lutheran ecclesiology. The logic of performative speech turns the preached Word inward into the human experience of the Word even though the externality of the Word is affirmed conceptually.

14. For Barth's relationship to Bonhoeffer, see DeJonge, *Bonhoeffer's Theological Formation*, esp. 36–55. See also Andreas Pangritz, *Karl Barth in the Theology of Dietrich Bonhoeffer*, trans. Barbara and Martin Rumscheidt (Grand Rapids, MI: Eerdmans, 2000), and Andreas Pangritz, "Dietrich Bonhoeffer: 'Within, Not Outside,' the Barthian Movement,'" in *Bonhoeffer's Intellectual Formation*, ed. Peter Frick (Tübingen: Mohr Siebeck, 2008), 245–82. For Bonhoeffer's understanding of Barth in this period, see Eberhard Bethge, *Dietrich Bonhoeffer: A Biography*, rev. ed., ed. Victoria J. Barnett (Minneapolis: Fortress, 2000), 73–81.

15. This emphasis on God's transcendence and the corresponding critique of religion was muted but never abandoned in later Barth. See Barth's late programmatic essay, "The Humanity of God," in *The Humanity of God* (Atlanta: John Knox, 1960), 37–65.

16. Charles Marsh, *Reclaiming Dietrich Bonhoeffer: The Promise of His Theology* (New York: Oxford University Press, 1994), 10.

17. DBWE 2, 124: for Barth, "God *is* in the divinely wrought, existential act of faith" only. Emphasis original.

18. I'm alluding to one of Bonhoeffer's favorite *freely* quoted dictums from Luther about Jesus: "This is the human being to whom you should point and say, this is God." Bonhoeffer, "Lectures on Christology," in DBWE 12, 318. See 318n.44 for the derivation of the quote.

19. DeJonge, *Bonhoeffer's Theological Formation*, 20–21.

20. DBWE 2, 84. Notice the confessional reference to the Lutheran and Reformed arguments concerning the finite and the infinite and the ability of the infinite to be known or believed in finite things. See James H. Burtness, "As Though God Were Not Given: Barth, Bonhoeffer, and the *Finitum Capax Infiniti*," *Dialog* 19, no. 4 (1980): 249–55; and DeJonge, *Bonhoeffer's Reception of Luther*, 42–76.

21. DeJonge, *Bonhoeffer's Theological Formation*, 56–82.

22. DBWE 2, 110–13. DeJonge, *Bonhoeffer's Theological Formation*, 77.

23. For a short historical introduction to these lectures, see Bethge, *Bonhoeffer*, 219–20.

24. DBWE 12, 299n.1. The critical edition of Bonhoeffer's works, *Dietrich Bonhoeffer Werke*, follows the transcription of just one student, Gerhard Riemer. An earlier publication of Bonhoeffer's lectures, called *Christ the Center*, reconstructed the lectures based upon seven different students' notes. I use the more recent critical edition.

25. Bonhoeffer's "Introduction" accomplishes this (DBWE 12, 300–10), supported by his understanding of historical/critical Christology from the second half of the lectures.

26. DBWE 12, 310–23.

27. DBWE 12, 324–27.

28. DeJonge, *Bonhoeffer's Theological Formation*, 39–40. On the development of Karl Barth's theology, see Bruce L. McCormack, *Karl Barth's Critically Realistic Dialectical Theology: Its Genesis and Development 1909–1936* (Oxford: Clarendon, 1995).

29. Ludwig Feuerbach, *The Essence of Christianity*, 2nd ed., trans. Marian Evans (London: Kegan Paul, Trench, Trübner, & Co., 1890), accessed via Project Gutenberg (http://www.gutenberg.org/files/47025/47025-h/47025-h.htm), x:

It is not I, but religion that worships man, although religion, or rather theology, denies this; it is not I, an insignificant individual, but religion itself that says: God is man, man is God; it is not I, but religion that denies the God who is *not* man, but only an *ens rationis*,—since it makes God become man, and then constitutes this God, not distinguished from man, having a human form, human feelings, and human thoughts, the object of its worship and veneration.

30. DeJonge, *Bonhoeffer's Theological Formation*, 39–40.
31. Karl Barth, *The Word of God and the Word of Man*, trans. Douglas Horton (New York: Harper & Row, 1957), 257.
32. DeJonge, *Bonhoeffer's Theological Formation*, 40. Compare Barth, *Word of God and Word of Man*, 257: there is a "real wall between God and the world which God both razes *and reestablishes* in Christ." Emphasis added.
33. McCormack, *Barth's Critically Realistic Dialectical Theology*, 328: "The shift from an eschatological to a Christological grounding of theology could take place with no weakening of the eschatological reservation."
34. DeJonge, *Bonhoeffer's Theological Formation*, 74–75. Compare McCormack, *Barth's Critically Realistic Dialectical Theology*, 327: "The Subject of this human life—we may liken this to Kant's conception of an unintuitable, noumenal self—was at every point the Second Person of the Trinity."
35. DBWE 12, 301. Emphasis added.
36. DBWE 2, 85: In Barth, "God remains always the Lord, always subject, so that whoever claims to have God as an object no longer has *God*."
37. DeJonge, *Bonhoeffer's Theological Formation*, 68–77.
38. DBWE 2, 128: "The person 'is' free from the one to whom it gives itself."
39. DBWE 12, 301.
40. DBWE 12, 301.
41. DBWE 12, 301.
42. DBWE 12, 302.
43. DBWE 12, 302.
44. DBWE 12, 302.
45. DBWE 12, 302.
46. DBWE 12, 302.
47. DBWE 12, 303. Emphasis original.
48. DBWE 12, 303.
49. DBWE 12, 303. Christology is an ecclesial discipline that does not question the *that* of revelation in Christ (p. 304). Thus, Bonhoeffer's Christology requires the church in the same way as his understanding of Scripture as "the book of the church." DBWE 3, 22. See also Martin Kuske, *The Old Testament as the Book of Christ: An Appraisal of Bonhoeffer's Interpretation*, trans. S. T. Kimbrough, Jr. (Philadelphia: Westminster Press, 1976), 28–31.
50. DBWE 12, 305.
51. DBWE 12, 307.
52. DBWE 12, 331–53. Recently, Stephen Plant has argued that Bonhoeffer's Christology lectures "privilege modernity" in a way that does not do justice to the

theology of the early church, especially the councils. Plant, "'We believe in one Lord, Jesus Christ': A Pro-Nicene Revision of Bonhoeffer's 1933 Christology Lectures," in *Christ, Church, and World: New Studies in Bonhoeffer's Theology and Ethics*, ed. Michael Mawson and Philip G. Ziegler (London: T&T Clark, 2016), 45–60. Plant is right to observe Bonhoeffer's thin engagement with the councils—I suspect that Bonhoeffer allows the questions of Harnack to dominate his approach—and he is also correct that Lewis Ayres' understanding of Nicaea provides a better way forward than Bonhoeffer's modern approach. As Plant says, the modern approach tends to devalue the ancient councils as Greek-influenced negative theology and makes positive Christology a matter of individual theologians. Bonhoeffer is guilty of both to a degree, but Plant neglects three things that present Bonhoeffer's lectures in a more positive light. First, Bonhoeffer was using the best historical work of his day, that of Adolf von Harnack. Following Bonhoeffer's lead is not following Harnack but the best contemporary historians, like Ayres. Second, Plant's criticism of Bonhoeffer uses Nicaea to show the constructive side of ancient Christology whereas Bonhoeffer focuses on Chalcedon, which *is* primarily negative. Bonhoeffer's characterization of the councils as negative theology should not be applied to all Christology of the ancient church but his understanding of Chalcedon as the central Christological council. Third, Bonhoeffer *does* interpret Chalcedon positively despite his broad characterization of it as negative theology. For Bonhoeffer, Chalcedon demands recognition of the unity of Jesus' person which pushes toward a narrative approach from below that confesses the man Jesus as true God. Bonhoeffer's constructive Christology is built on this understanding of Chalcedon. See DBWE 12, 352–53.

53. For a historical and theological overview of Chalcedon, see Jaroslav Pelikan, *The Emergence of the Catholic Tradition*, vol. 1 of *The Christian Tradition: A History of the Development of Doctrine* (Chicago: University of Chicago Press, 1971), 226–77.

54. DBWE 12, 342.

55. DBWE 12, 342.

56. DBWE 12, 342. Emphasis original.

57. DBWE 12, 343.

58. So also the Lutheran tradition: see Paul R. Hinlicky, *Luther and the Beloved Community: A Path for Christian Theology after Christendom* (Grand Rapids, MI: Eerdmans, 2010), 63–65.

59. On Luther's Christology, see Hinlicky, *Luther and the Beloved Community*, 31–65; Paul R. Hinlicky, "Luther's Anti-Docetism in the Disputatio de divinitate et humanitate Christi (1540)," in *Creator est Creatura: Luthers Christologie als Lehre von der Idiomenkommunikation*, ed. Oswald Bayer and Benjamin Gleede (Berlin: de Gruyter, 2007), 139–85; and Norman E. Nagel, "*Martinus*: 'Heresy, Doctor Luther, Heresy!' The Person and Work of Christ," in *The Seven-Headed Luther: Essays in Commemoration of a Quincentenary, 1483–1983*, ed. Peter Newman Brooks (Oxford: Clarendon, 1983), 25–49.

60. DBWE 12, 345.

61. Compare DeJonge, *Bonhoeffer's Reception of Luther*, 74: "There is also a way of reading the majestic genus not as a reversion to illegitimate 'how' thinking but as a form of legitimate 'how' thinking within 'who' thinking. Such 'how' thinking could perhaps be characterized as a descriptive ontology of the present person of

Christ, precisely what Bonhoeffer names as the task of Christology." DeJonge further observes that this stems from the "est"—"This man is God"; "This is my body"—which Bonhoeffer finds central.

62. With the categories of presence and identity, I am following Hans W. Frei, *The Identity of Jesus Christ: The Hermeneutical Bases of Dogmatic Theology* (Philadelphia: Fortress, 1975).

63. DBWE 12, 350.

64. DBWE 12, 350.

65. Robert John Dean, *For the Life of the World: Jesus Christ and the Church in the Theologies of Dietrich Bonhoeffer and Stanley Hauerwas* (Eugene, OR: Pickwick, 2016), 33:

> Although there are hints within the lectures that it is possible for Christ to stand over and against the church, as evidenced in the Counter Logos narrative at the beginning of the lectures and the concluding comments of the lectures which speak of Christ being an offense or stumbling block to the church, on the basis of the lectures as a whole this is a legitimate question.

66. Compare Nagel, "*Martinus:* 'Heresy, Doctor Luther, Heresy!'" 43: "Bonhoeffer asserts that the person of Jesus Christ is his work."

67. For example, Karsten Lehmkühler, "Christologie," in *Bonhoeffer und Luther: Zentrale Themen ihrer Theologie*, ed. Klaus Grünwaldt, Christiane Tietz, and Udo Han (Velkd, 2007), 55–78. Sometimes, though, the interconnection can collapse Christ's person into his work, threatening to lose the unique identity of Jesus. When, for instance, Bonhoeffer's definition, "Christ existing as church-community," is primarily an ecclesiological claim rather than a Christological one, the identity of Jesus can be elided into his presence in the church. I'm afraid that Jennifer McBride's use of Bonhoeffer begins to move this direction even as she does much well with regard to the church's public witness. Jennifer M. McBride, "Christ Existing as Concrete Community Today," *Theology Today* 71, no. 1 (2014): 92–105.

68. DBWE 12, 308.

69. DBWE 12, 308. To be clear, this is hardly a fair reading of Melanchthon's 1521 *Loci*. At least in the first edition, Melanchthon's intention is to say that Christ cannot be merely known by facts, but must be trusted as the Son of God who encounters sinners as their Savior. Philip Melanchthon, *Commonplaces: Loci Communes 1521*, trans. Christian Preus (Saint Louis: Concordia, 2014), 24–25.

70. DBWE 12, 308. The two kinds of righteousness are also apparent here in Bonhoeffer. See Robert Kolb, "Luther on the Two Kinds of Righteousness: Reflections on his Two-Dimensional Definition of Humanity at the Heart of his Theology," *Lutheran Quarterly* 13 (1999): 449–66. Compare Luther, *Sermon on the Mount*, LW 21, 267: "So all the works of a Christian are of a good kind because the tree is sound."

71. Nagel, "*Martinus:* 'Heresy, Doctor Luther, Heresy!'" 43. I say this contra Nagel's understanding of Bonhoeffer from the same.

72. Dean, *Life of the World*, 33.

73. Compare Jaroslav Pelikan, "Bonhoeffer's *Christologie* of 1933," in *The Place of Bonhoeffer: Problems and Possibilities in his Thought*, ed. Martin E. Marty (New York: Association Press, 1962), 162–63.

74. DBWE 12, 310:

In this way, the Christological question is shown to have theological priority over the soteriological question. I must first know who it is who does something before I can know what it is that the person has done. Nevertheless, it would be wrong to conclude that person and works should be considered separately.

75. In agreement with Frei, *Identity of Jesus*, 6: "The right order for thinking about the unity of Christ's identity and presence is to begin with his identity."
76. DBWE 12, 310.
77. DBWE 12, 311.
78. DBWE 12, 312.
79. DBWE 12, 312–13.
80. DBWE 12, 313.
81. DBWE 12, 314.
82. DBWE 12, 314.
83. DBWE 12, 315.
84. The German *Gemeinde* (traditionally "congregation" in theological contexts) is translated in the DBWE as "church-community" most of the time. This translation reminds the reader that Bonhoeffer uses *Gemeinde* in a broader sense than a single congregation, but he does have a concrete entity in mind, which is often congregations.
85. DBWE 12, 316–17.
86. DBWE 12, 316.
87. DBWE 12, 317. Christ as Word of law and gospel takes concrete form in *Discipleship*. See my "Luther and Bonhoeffer on the Sermon on the Mount: Similar Tasks, Different Tools," *Concordia Theological Journal* 7, no. 1 (Winter 2020): 33–58.
88. DBWE 12, 318.
89. DBWE 12, 319.
90. DBWE 12, 322.
91. DBWE 12, 322.
92. 1 Cor. 1:23, Rom. 8:3, and Phil. 2:7, respectively.
93. DBWE 12, 322. Bonhoeffer's understanding of the exalted Christ as humiliated may seem odd, but Luther speaks the same way. Johann Anselm Steiger, "The *Communicatio Idiomatum* as the Axle and Motor of Luther's Theology," *Lutheran Quarterly* 14, no. 2 (2000): 136.
94. DBWE 12, 323.
95. DBWE 12, 323.
96. Compare Robert W. Jenson, Robert Jenson, *Systematic Theology*, vol. 1 (Oxford: Oxford University Press, 1997), 204–6. Bonhoeffer avoids the language of Christ's body as "object" that Jenson uses. Bonhoeffer's notion is closer to "promise." See also DBWE 15, 422.
97. DBWE 12, 323.
98. DBWE 12, 324.
99. Twice in this short section Bonhoeffer says that Christ's centrality cannot be proven, only proclaimed. DBWE 12, 325 and 327.

100. DBWE 12, 324.

101. Bonhoeffer's understanding of justification in terms of the world's story compared to the church has much in common with a minor Lutheran dogmatic distinction between objective and subjective justification. Justification as the center of the world's story is similar to objective justification while justification in the church, preaching, and sacrament has more in common with subjective justification. To my mind, Bonhoeffer's distinction between Christ *pro-me* in the church and the world is more accurate biblically and more helpful dogmatically by thinking in terms of church and world and the presence of Christ rather than the misleading labels "objective" and "subjective."

102. DBWE 12, 325.

103. DBWE 12, 325.

104. DBWE 12, 325.

105. Considering the summer 1933 date of these lectures, the critique of Hitler as Führer is clear, if indirect.

106. Bonhoeffer says, "The church judges and justifies the state," on the basis of its true and proper goals of "law and order." DBWE 12, 326.

107. DBWE 12, 327.

108. Marsh, *Reclaiming Dietrich Bonhoeffer*, vii–ix.

109. Compare Marsh, *Reclaiming Dietrich Bonhoeffer*, 14–15: Barth's account of revelation "admirably accents certain doxological themes—God's sovereignty over all things, his provenience in grace—yet in Bonhoeffer's estimation this view does not sufficiently characterize genuine Christian theological reflection."

110. On promeity in Bonhoeffer, see Philip Ziegler, "Christ for Us Today—Promeity in the Christologies of Bonhoeffer and Kierkegaard," *International Journal of Systematic Theology* 15, no. 1 (2013): 25–41.

111. Compare Derek W. Taylor, *Reading Scripture as the Church: Dietrich Bonhoeffer's Hermeneutic of Discipleship* (Downers Grove, IL: IVP, 2020), 86: "The ongoing historical presence of the God-man allows Bonhoeffer to overcome the limits of classical metaphysical geometry and thereby uphold God's divine freedom without sacrificing Christ's promeity."

112. Jens Zimmermann, "Suffering with the World: The Continuing Relevance of Dietrich Bonhoeffer's Theology," in *Dietrich Bonhoeffer Jahrbuch 3: 2007/2008*, ed. Clifford J. Green, et al. (Gütersloh: Gütersloher Verlagshaus, 2008), 314.

113. Robert Kolb and Timothy J. Wengert, eds., *The Book of Concord: The Confessions of the Evangelical Lutheran Church* (Minneapolis: Fortress, 2000), 616–34; Martin Chemnitz, *The Two Natures in Christ*, trans. J.A.O. Preus (Saint Louis: Concordia, 1971); and Steiger, "*Communicatio Idiomatum* as the Axle and Motor," 125–58.

114. Although critical of the *genera* broadly, Bonhoeffer does say that the *genus majestaticum* is "the core of Lutheran theology," recognizing its importance in Lutheran theology. DBWE 12, 345.

115. DBWE 12, 354. On the continuity with Luther, compare Robert W. Jenson, "Luther's Contemporary Theological Significance," in *The Cambridge Companion to Martin Luther*, ed. Donald K. McKim (Cambridge: Cambridge University Press,

2003), 277: In Luther's Christology, person is "the central concept, and is used very much in the modern sense, for the protagonist of a history."

116. DeJonge, *Bonhoeffer's Theological Formation*, 74.

117. McCormack, *Barth's Critically Realistic Dialectical Theology*, 328.

118. For Barth's understanding of the *extra calvinisticum* and how he developed on this point, see Darren O. Sumner, "The Twofold Life of the Word: Karl Barth's Critical Reception of the Extra Calvinisticum," *International Journal of Systematic Theology* 15, no. 1 (2013): 42–57.

119. This Reformed doctrine that Lutherans have called the *extra calvinisticum* most clearly depicts the difference from Lutheran Christology. According to Anglican theologian Christopher Holmes—using John Webster—this doctrine intends to refer the person of Jesus back to his eternal relationship with the Father and the Spirit. Holmes has argued that Bonhoeffer's Christology lacks a full Trinitarian reference and needs the *extra calvinisticum* to point back to the eternal Trinity. For Bonhoeffer, however, the whole point of highlighting the person of Jesus as the God-man is that one of the Trinity has entered into time and space, and Jesus of Nazareth is the Son of God without remainder. There is no need to point beyond Jesus to the Trinitarian relationships through a separate doctrine since the Son is on earth. To be clear, Jesus is the Son *of God* and bearer *of the Spirit*, but such Trinitarian reference is the identity of the man Jesus. Therefore, the *extra calvinisticum* can only serve to point beyond the man Jesus rather than confessing him and his history as the fullness and identity of God. Since this "backward reference" is properly seen in Christ's humiliated history on earth, the *extra calvinisticum* only bypasses God's self-revelation in Christ. Christopher R.J. Holmes, "Bonhoeffer and Reformed Christology: Towards a Trinitarian Supplement," *Theology Today* 71, no. 1 (2014): 28–42.

120. DeJonge, *Bonhoeffer's Theological Formation*, 51.

121. On the Eucharist, compare Hermann Sasse, *This Is My Body: Luther's Contention for the Real Presence in the Sacrament of the Altar* (Minneapolis: Augsburg, 1959), 342:

> Christ is present [in the Supper], the entire Christ, God and man, our Mediator and High Priest through whom we have forgiveness of sins, our King whose glory is still hidden to human eyes, our Brother as true man, He in us and we in Him when we receive the Sacrament for the assurance and confirmation of His presence with all its blessings: forgiveness, life, and salvation.

122. I say this in agreement with Michael Horton that the Lutheran understanding of the *communicatio* can diminish the humanity of Jesus—*but only* when abstracted from the concrete history of Jesus in the Bible. The *communicatio* should demand a substantial account of the humiliation (and incarnation) of the Son of God, and his relation to the Spirit in his fully human life. Michael S. Horton, *Lord and Servant: A Covenant Christology* (Louisville, KY: Westminster John Knox, 2005), 170–1. See also pp. 160–77 for Horton's broader discussion.

123. Steiger, "*Communicatio Idiomatum* as the Axle and Motor," 148.

124. Bernd Wannenwetsch, *Political Worship: Ethics for Christian Citizens*, trans. Margaret Kohl (Oxford: Oxford University Press, 2004), 41–43.

125. Even David Robinson, who is sympathetic to Hegel, admits that Hegel "may well be subject to Luther's criticism of theologians who speak of the 'bare God,' or 'God merely as such'" in that Hegel does not emphasize the external Word. David S. Robinson, *Christ and Revelatory Community in Bonhoeffer's Reception of Hegel* (Tübingen: Mohr Siebeck, 2018), 127–28.

126. Daniel J. Peterson, "Beyond Deep Incarnation: Rethinking Theology in Radical Lutheran Terms," *Dialog: A Journal of Theology* 53, no. 3 (2014): 246.

127. Peterson, "Beyond Deep Incarnation," 243.

128. Peterson, "Beyond Deep Incarnation," 248. Some, including Peterson, read Bonhoeffer's prison letters to say something similar, interpreting Bonhoeffer's more radical statements about Christ—the man for others, for instance—as a transcendental experience of Christ in the other. Wolf Krötke harshly but accurately comments, "Many of the adventurous (mis)construals of Bonhoeffer's thought about Jesus as the essential 'experience of transcendence' and his 'being there for others' could have been avoided had his interpreters been even half as knowledgeable of Luther's Christology as he was." Krötke, "Bonhoeffer and Luther," 62.

129. Gerhard Forde rightly polemicizes against attempts to "put roses on the cross," which explain away the death of Jesus through a theory. "The Work of Christ," in vol. 2 of *Christian Dogmatics*, ed. Carl E. Braaten and Robert W. Jenson (Philadelphia: Fortress, 1984), 5–99. By way of theory, salvation becomes certain because of a system instead of the historical work and promises of God in Christ. Something like this happens in Diane Virginia Bowers, "Martin Luther and the Joyful Exchange Between Christ and his Christian: Implications for the Doctrine of Justification and the Christian Life," PhD diss. (Graduate Theological Union, Berkley, CA, 2008), 234–41. Bowers tries to find a model for justification that appeals to post-modern people, but ends up losing the concrete, historical Jesus. Even with worthwhile goals, Bowers does not avoid the danger of overcoming the unique identity of Jesus with her model.

130. DBWE 12, 310: "Only through Christ's own revelation do I have opened to me his person and his works."

131. Pelikan, "Bonhoeffer's *Christologie* of 1933," 162–63.

132. DBWE 12, 305–7. This story is focused on the cross and is more critical in character, but opens the door to the humiliation of Christ as the positive account.

133. DBWE 12, 353–60.

134. Dean, *For the Life of the World*, 39.

135. DBWE 12, 328.

136. A fuller account of the narrative of Christ is one way to fill the pneumatological lacuna in Bonhoeffer. For this critique of Bonhoeffer, see Alexander S. Jensen, "Schleiermacher and Bonhoeffer as Negative Theologians: A Western Response to Some Eastern Challenges," *St. Mark's Review* 215, no. 1 (2011): 15–17. For a sort of defense of Bonhoeffer (or at least a description of Bonhoeffer's understanding of the Spirit in "inscribing the church through its encounter with the Word into the unfolding drama of salvation"), see Robert J. Dean, "A Matter of Mission: Bonhoeffer, the Bible, and Ecclesial Formation," *Didaskalia* 28 (2018): 49–74. Compare also Dean, *For the Life of the World*, 95; and Taylor, *Reading Scripture as the Church*, 86–88.

137. DBWE 2, 112.

138. DBWE 1, 189–90. On Bonhoeffer's understanding and use of the phrase, see Michael Mawson, *Christ Existing as Community: Bonhoeffer's Ecclesiology* (Oxford: Oxford University Press, 2018), 138–43. For a study sensitive to the Hegelian roots, see Robinson, *Christ and Revelatory Community*, 25–62.

139. DBWE 16, 480.

140. Recognized in part by Christiane Tietz, "Bonhoeffer on the Ontological Structure of the Church," in *Ontology and Ethics: Bonhoeffer and Contemporary Scholarship*, ed. Adam C. Clark and Michael Mawson (Eugene, OR: Pickwick, 2013), 41: "To be clear, 'Christ existing as community' is not a metaphysical claim about the church. Rather, it describes what takes place concretely when one church member becomes Christ to the other. It is when we become Christ to the other in the church-community that then Christ is present. This occurs in the structure of being with-each-other and in the action of being for-each-other." Tietz is right to see "Christ existing as community" as a claim about Christ and his presence, but Tietz's description threatens to reduce Christ's presence in the church to interpersonal interactions. Instead, Christians *are* Christ to each other by virtue of their baptism and unity with Christ in his body by the Spirit; it is not a matter of becoming so. Tietz's recognition of the "*structure*" of "with-each-other" suggests the same thing, but her focus is on certain actions rather than participation and presence according to Christ's promise.

141. Compare Richard B. Hays, "The Story of God's Son: The Identity of Jesus in the Letters of Paul," in *Seeking the Identity of Jesus: A Pilgrimmage*, ed. Beverly Roberts Gaventa and Richard B. Hays (Grand Rapids, MI: Eerdmans, 2008), 195: "After the resurrection, Jesus' identity is not confined to a localized physical body; he embraces and receives into himself all those whom he calls. Consequently, he manifests his identity to the world through this complex corporate reality." Hays continues to summarize Paul's view: "The church really *is* the body of Christ, because Christ lives in us."

142. For a review and critique of this idea, see Mark Saucy, "Evangelicals, Catholics, and Orthodox Together: Is the Church an Extension of the Incarnation?" *JETS* 43, no. 2 (2000): 193–212.

143. Michael S. Horton, *People and Place: A Covenant Ecclesiology* (Louisville, KY: Westminster John Knox, 2008), 12. See also pp. 155–89 on Horton's understanding of the *totus Christus*.

144. DBWE 15, 422:

> Church is not a community of souls, as is claimed today, nor is church merely the proclamation of the gospel; that is to say, church is not only the pulpit, but church is the real body of Christ on earth. Church is an ordered and differentiated commonwealth constituted on this earth by, and grounded in, God. Just as Jesus Christ was not a truth or an idea but flesh, that is to say, a human being in the body, likewise the church is the earthly body of the heavenly head.

Chapter 3

Christ-Church-World

The Christological Center of the Church-World Relation

Dietrich Bonhoeffer's Christology binds church and world to Christ while acknowledging Jesus as the Lord *extra se* who encounters through the Word. By recognizing the church in its relationship to Lord Jesus, both desiderata of Lutheran ecclesiology are established: justification's outward reference to God, retaining God's transcendence, and the nature of the church as a visible community participating in the economy of God, retaining the church's historicity. By grounding the church on the Lord Jesus who humbled himself to death on the cross, the church is turned away from itself to the Word of God to receive its identity and mission in Christ by the Spirit. In addition, Christ's concrete presence in the church generates a real community in the world, formed by the Spirit through the Scriptures and called to follow Christ in his mission to the world. Bonhoeffer's Christology accomplishes both desiderata through the dialectical character of the Christ-church relation, which is explored in this chapter. In addition, Bonhoeffer's Christology opens the way to a hermeneutical ecclesiology that not only identifies the church but shapes the church-world relationship. By grounding the church-world relationship on both the Christ-church and Christ-world relations, the Word of Jesus not only creates the church but forms it for faithful witness in the world.

This chapter unfolds the Christ-church-world complex of relations, developing the dialectics of the Christ-church and church-world relations. These dialectics, in turn, enable reading and preaching the Scriptures to identify the church as Christ's body and form congregations into Christ's cruciform mission. This chapter first delineates the relationship between Christ and the church as a dialectic of lordship and presence, following from Christ's simultaneous transcendence and gracious condescension as articulated in Bonhoeffer's Christology. Bonhoeffer himself employs this dialectic in his scriptural hermeneutics, as we will see, establishing Christ's relationship to the church via the Word. Then, I examine the church-world relation in light of Christ, investigating some apparent inconsistencies in how Bonhoeffer articulates the church-world relation across his corpus. I situate this apparent inconsistency within Bonhoeffer's broader Christological logic, arguing that the church is *both* distinct from the world *and* fully part of the world at the same time, thereby accounting for both the continuity and discontinuity across Bonhoeffer's thought. The story of Jesus will come to the fore as the storied identity of the church, creating this people to be a distinct community called to Christ's mission in the world of which it is one.

CHRIST FOR AND AGAINST HIS CHURCH: A CHRIST-CHURCH DIALECTIC

As Bonhoeffer describes the Christ-church relation, Jesus *is* both the gracious Servant who is present in the church in Word, Sacrament, and community and the transcendent Lord who encounters his church from the outside. The Christ-church relation thus requires a dialectic, recognizing Christ as present in the church, graspable in the means of grace, and at the same time the Lord who calls the church to repentance and obedience. In Bonhoeffer's words, "The unity between Christ and his body, the church, demands that we at the same time recognize Christ's lordship over his body."[1] To use the language of Ephesians 5, the church is the body of Christ, but it is also his bride, gladly submissive to the bridegroom who gives himself to make his bride holy.[2] Hence, the dialectic of Christ's presence and lordship is a "real historical dialectic," not merely formal or conceptual,[3] following from what the Scriptures say of Christ's relationship to the church. In other words, the Christ-church relation must be described dialectically not because it is convenient or clever, but because Christ *is* both present in the church and transcendent over it.[4] This "dynamic tension" between Christ and the church must not be smoothed over or elided, but the tension is itself the way forward for proclaiming the church's identity and mission.[5]

The first part of the dialectic affirms that the crucified and risen Christ abides in his church, giving of himself in the Word and the sacraments, present when his people gather for preaching, prayer, confession, witness, service, and justice. The church is none other than the mouthpiece of God,[6] the community wherein God speaks and gives of himself for forgiveness of sins and new life in Christ by the Spirit. In fact, the presence of Christ in the church is less of a conclusion from Bonhoeffer's Christology and more of a presupposition.[7] In Bonhoeffer's logic, one can only ask about Christ and reflect upon him theologically "because Christ is the Christ who is present" in the church.[8] Otherwise stated, that the crucified Jesus is risen from the dead, exalted to the right hand of the Father, and is present now according to his promises is a *first principle* for Christian theology. And where Christ is, there he creates and forms his church by the Spirit. Christ gives of himself in his church by the external Word and Sacrament, assuring his people of their identity as children of God, and bringing new sheep into his sheepfold.[9] Christ is present in his church *for* his church through the Spirit.[10]

Although Christ's presence in his church is an essential presupposition for ecclesiology, the Christ-church relationship cannot be dictated solely by the presence of Christ in the church for two closely related reasons. First, sounding only the melody of Christ's presence in the church fails to explain ecclesial sinfulness, and second, it leaves no room for the *semper ecclesia reformanda est*, Christ's call for the church to repent continually and follow him faithfully.[11] Both of these arose in connection with the ecclesiology of Reinhard Hütter in chapter 1. In Hütter's thought, the church is the actualization of the mission of the Spirit so that the sinfulness of the ecclesial community is nearly ruled out.[12] In this way, the church is turned inward to itself and lacks the outward reference to the story of God in Christ that forms Christian community for faithfulness and obedience to the mission of God rather than contemporary politics. When the church knows itself only by its unity with God and God's mission—for instance, by the presence of Christ in it—the church is overidentified with God, believing itself to be the instantiation of the work of God and becomes deaf to the Word that points out its sinfulness and calls it to obedience to God's mission.

At the same time that Bonhoeffer confesses the presence of Christ in the church—"Christ existing as church-community"[13]—Bonhoeffer's Christology also establishes the second part of the dialectic: the outward orientation of the church to Christ, placing the church under Christ the Lord to attend to his alien Word of law and gospel. Bonhoeffer resists idealism that separates the visible and the invisible church through the church's relationship to Christ, enabling theological description of the community as both truly Christ's body and truly sinful at the same time.[14] Bonhoeffer asserts, the "church is a ministry from God," even the presence of the living Christ,[15] and at the same time it is "part of the world, a lost, godless, cursed vain, evil world," even the "evil world in its most potent form."[16] Thus, the church as Christ's body is not disconnected from the concrete community that continues to sin, needs the forgiveness of Christ, and lives in Christ's promise in the world. The recognition of the church as the body of Christ in the real world of time and space does not merely signify that the church has two aspects: a hidden righteousness in Christ and a visible, historical identity.[17] Instead, the congregation *is* a historical community that exists in this sinful age, and *is* the body of Christ in a particular place.[18] For this reason, the church itself, not just individual Christians but the community as a whole, is *simul congregatio sanctorum et peccatorum*.[19] The church is both a holy community and a sinful community at the same time because Christ is both present in the church-community and the Lord standing outside of it and *against* it. Jesus calls the church to repentance and gives himself to it by his Spirit in the Word to be shaped into his cruciform mission.

Through a dialectical account of the Christ-church relation, two cardinal errors of separating Christ from his church and overidentifying Christ and his church are avoided. On the one hand, the church can be so removed from the presence of the risen Christ that imitating Jesus is the only way to follow his mission. In an *imitatio Christi* model, the church is called to follow Christ in discipleship and mission not by being formed into his story through the Word and the Spirit but by imitating his actions. Whether in the liberal version of being taught and inspired by a religious virtuoso[20] or in the conservative version of applying Jesus' teachings and following his behavior,[21] both separate the church from the risen Christ. The church rather than the living Christ through the Spirit is the primary actor of God's mission.[22]

For Bonhoeffer, by contrast, moral formation is not a matter of Christians determining how to emulate Jesus; instead, formation is passive as Christ fashions his people. Christ is present in and transcendent over the church to shape it into his own form, not as Christian people act but as Christ acts upon them. Bonhoeffer writes,

> Formation occurs only by being drawn into the form of Jesus Christ, by *being conformed to the unique form of the one who became human, was crucified, and is risen*. This does not happen as we strive "to become like Jesus," as we customarily say, but as the form of Jesus Christ himself so works on us that it molds us, conforming our form to Christ's own (Gal. 4:19). Christ remains the only one who forms. Christian people do not form the world with their ideas. Rather, Christ forms human beings to a form the same as Christ's own.[23]

For Bonhoeffer, the church does strive to follow Jesus, but it can never form itself into him. By an "asymmetrical agency," Christ is the one who forms the church into his mission even as the church is called to obey the Word of Jesus.[24] The *imitatio Christi* model reverses the direction of formation, making the church the primary agent of formation rather than Christ himself. In the *imitatio Christi* model, the church makes Jesus part of its story by trying to do his works, but Bonhoeffer places the priority on Christ who sends his Spirit by the Word, thus forming the church into his story and mission as the church suffers his Word and work.[25] Christ is not merely a teacher or an example, but the Lord who makes himself present in the church to bring people into his kingdom and call his church to conform to his mission.

On the other hand, the Christ-church dialect also prevents the church from falling into triumphalism by overidentifying itself with Christ. At its worst, an overidentification of Christ and the church enables the institution to act as if it were Christ himself regardless of its actual conformation to the Word of Jesus.[26] Roman Catholic theology, for instance, has occasionally conflated the church and Christ such that being a member of Christ's church is identical to being in communion with the Roman Curia.[27] When the institution is conflated with Christ, the church's status quo is confused with God's will, and any criticism of the institution is an attack on God himself.[28] Among Lutherans, Robert Jenson has been accused of "erasing the distinction between Christ and the church" because the church *is* the body of Christ ontologically, not analogically.[29] Although Michael Horton's accusations are overstated,[30] Jenson's idealistic descriptions of the church and his overarching concern for ecumenism can lose sight of the messiness of the church in the world.[31] When the church is understood to be Christ's body *without* a clear orientation of the church to the living Jesus of Nazareth, the church demarcates itself from the world, considers itself better than the world, and fails to live Christ's mission in it.[32]

Bonhoeffer can confess the presence of the risen Christ in the church unequivocally while orienting the church to Christ *extra se* because the risen Christ is none other than the historical Jesus. The church cannot assume that presence of Christ, which is "cheap grace";[33] instead, it believes that the same Jesus was not only killed upon a cross, but raised from the dead, ascended into heaven, and truly present by the Spirit in the world as he promises. This Jesus is transcendent over his church—as the Creator who humbly made himself nothing for us and our salvation—and he graciously makes the church part of his mission through his presence within it.

Bonhoeffer establishes both poles of the Christ-church dialectic by shifting the church's identity from a focus upon what it has received—the invisible, hidden aspect of faith—to the One from whom the church receives its identity. Bonhoeffer's Christology makes this shift by establishing the church on the basis of Christ's presence by the Spirit. Without Christ's presence, there is no church.[34] At the same time, the Christ present in the church is the historical Jesus, the person who confronts and creates the church by the Word, and shapes it into his mission.[35] The story, therefore, that defines the church, judges it, and forms its mission does not belong to the church, but is the story of the Lord Jesus and his humiliation. The church knows itself rightly by being oriented to Christ *extra se*, hearing Christ's Word of repentance and forgiveness by the external Word, and being made a participant in his mission.

BONHOEFFER'S SCRIPTURAL HERMENEUTICS AND THE CHRIST-CHURCH DIALECTIC

Because Christ *is* both the transcendent Lord and the one who is graciously present in the church, Bonhoeffer does not merely affirm a Christ-church dialectic in the abstract. Rather, the Christ-church dialectic permeates Bonhoeffer's biblical hermeneutics, showing how Bonhoeffer reads the Scriptures in light of Christ's identity and relationship to his church, enabling preaching and teaching that orients the church to Christ and his mission.[36] Bonhoeffer's biblical hermeneutics demonstrate the Christ-church dialectic in action, illuminating how Bonhoeffer sees Christ at work through the Bible to identify the church in him and call it to repentance for its sin and obedience to his mission.

Bonhoeffer's understanding of Scripture across his corpus exhibits three key strands, which are apparent in a 1935 lecture to seminarians, titled "Contemporizing New Testament Texts."[37] First, Bonhoeffer refuses to interpret the Bible as a mere object of academic research, understanding it instead as "the book of the church."[38] In this way, the Christ-church relation takes center stage in Bonhoeffer's hermeneutics since Christ's identity is confessed in the church, and he is the key to the Scriptures. Second, Bonhoeffer interprets the Bible in light of the sinfulness of humanity and the church, reading the Bible as the Word of Christ who stands outside of the church and speaks *against* it and its attempts at gaining power and privilege. The third strand of Bonhoeffer's hermeneutics confesses that the Bible is God's living Word in which God himself speaks to evoke repentance, faith, and obedience. In this final strand, the risen Christ is present in his church by the Spirit, not to offer mere knowledge, but to speak a Word that kills his church in its sin and re-creates his people, bringing them into his story and ministry. Bonhoeffer offers his hermeneutics not merely to understand the Bible, but so that the Christian church would know itself within God's story of Holy Scripture. Within this story, Christ is the transcendent Lord, and the church acknowledges itself both as sinful, attending to Christ speaking *against* it in recognition of its need for forgiveness and obedience, and as justified, knowing Christ present in his body *for* his people.

In the notion that the Bible is "the book of the church," Bonhoeffer makes the Christ-church relation central to reading the Scriptures.[39] Bonhoeffer expounds this first strand of his hermeneutics primarily against the German Christian movement that sought to fuse together Germanness with Christianity in order to have a church that was "relevant" to the German people.[40] German Christians created a relevant Bible by forcing God into a contemporary ideology or narrative and refusing to allow God to place humanity within his story.[41] In developing a relevant German religion, German Christians offered new interpretations of the Bible that made Scripture fit with their principles.[42] For example, Ludwig Müller, the Reich Bishop, head of most of the German Protestant church and a leading German Christian, published a work in 1936 titled *Deutsche Gottesworte*, the *German Word of God*. The project was intended to be evangelistic by reaching out to Germans estranged from religion with an appealing message.[43] In the tract Müller rid the Sermon on the Mount of any sign of weakness or gentleness in Jesus because those traits were not acceptable to modern Germans.[44] Müller wrote, "'For you, my comrades in the Third Reich, I have not translated the Sermon on the Mount but Germanized it.'. . . The blessing of the meek [Müller] interpreted as: 'Happy is he who always observes good comradeship. He will get on well in the world'; and [about] the cross [Müller says]: 'Take pains to maintain a noble, calm attitude, even to one who insults or persecutes you.'"[45] In Müller's Germanizing of God's Word, Christ became a Nazi spokesman in order to make the Bible palatable to the modern German.

In contrast to German Christian interpretations of the Bible that emphasize the present moment and its story—as well as historical critics who turn the Bible into a relic of past history[46]—Bonhoeffer interprets the New Testament within the church's confession of God's story in Christ Jesus, that is, as the book of the church. The church, then, reads the Bible, understands it, and proclaims it within its acknowledgment of Christ's lordship, not as knowledge abstracted from Jesus. As such, proper biblical interpretation is dependent upon the church's confession that "Jesus is Lord," and its recognition of its place under the Lord. In "Contemporizing New Testament Texts," Bonhoeffer argues that Christ fills the entire Scripture, and both the Old and the New Testament witness to him.[47] In his own words, "Holy Scripture is . . . as a whole *the witness* of God in Christ, and in every passage the point is to make the character of this word as a witness audible."[48] Every text speaks about the identity and mission of God who makes himself known in the Son and by the Holy Spirit, and the Bible must be read as a book that is ultimately about this Triune God and God's work.[49] As such, the Bible is properly interpreted in a contemporary way not by pulling out doctrines as eternal truth or connecting the Bible to some relatable anecdote, but by underscoring the Bible's witness to Jesus the Savior.[50]

As a result of his understanding of the Bible as the book of the church, Bonhoeffer is not afraid to offer interpretations that sound more like the Christological readings of the ancient church than the exposition of a modern biblical scholar.[51] For example, in *Prayerbook of the Bible*, Bonhoeffer understands Jesus not only as the object of the psalms' words and the Lord of whom the psalms speak, but Bonhoeffer also puts every psalm into the mouth of Jesus, believing him to be the one who prayed the psalms in his life on earth and continually prays them as the high priest at the Father's right hand.[52] With this Christological center in place, Bonhoeffer does not object to allegorical interpretation of the Bible. As long as the content of the exposition is Jesus and only the text of the Bible itself is confessed to have the power to witness in this allegorical way, Bonhoeffer believes, "one must grant to allegorical ... interpretation a measure of freedom" in the church.[53] Bonhoeffer is comfortable with allegory because proclaiming the Bible is less about positing the historic meaning that original hearers would have understood—which would give less freedom to allegory—or about connecting the Bible to the contemporary world—which can make allegorical interpretations dangerous—and more about connecting the Bible to the Savior of the world, Jesus the Christ.[54] As the Bible is understood in light of God's story of creation, human rebellion, and redemption, so the text is applicable to the hearers, who are also creatures, rebels against the Creator, and redeemed by Jesus. The Holy Spirit brings people into this story, "inscribing" them into "the drama of salvation" and incorporating them into the church through the Word.[55]

This first strand of Bonhoeffer's hermeneutics—recognizing the Bible as the book of the church—ensures that the lordship of Jesus and the reality of his story are established prior to reading the text. The church does not read the Bible apart from its relationship to Jesus Christ, but in it. The church reads the text *as* the community that acknowledges "Jesus is Lord," not separate from this confession.[56] Only in faith that Jesus is Lord and Savior can the Bible be properly interpreted and proclaimed. This presupposition of Biblical hermeneutics establishes the basis of the Christ-church dialectic. Only where Christ is present and believed can the Scriptures be read and proclaimed faithfully, but such belief does not reduce Jesus to the church. Jesus is the Lord who makes the church what it is by his presence, and he orients the church to himself through the Word. Through the Bible and biblical preaching, Christ is both transcendent over and present in the church, speaking against it to bring his people to repentance and obedience, and giving himself to be grasped by faith, establishing the church's identity and mission.

In the second strand of his hermeneutics, Bonhoeffer recognizes that the Bible must be read differently in light of sin. The biggest problem in biblical interpretation, Bonhoeffer suggests, is not irrelevance, ignorance, or historicity, but sin.[57] The Berlin theologian sees that sinful human beings avoid the sharp edges of Scripture, evade Christ's Word of repentance, and twist the Bible to fit their own agendas. Even Christians tend to fashion the Bible's story into a nice, easily digestible message that requires very little of the hearers, but Bonhoeffer argues that the Bible's true message does not seem nice or good to natural humanity.[58] Rather, the Bible's central message is an alien one, one that comes from the outside and does not conform to sinful human nature. The true message of the Bible is the cross of Jesus Christ, which is exactly "where God wants us to find him. It is not at all a place that we find pleasant or that might be clear a priori, but a place alien to us in every way, a place utterly repugnant to us."[59] The message of the Bible, with the cross of Christ at its center, does not coincide with the nature of humanity. Rather, the Bible's message cuts against the grain of sinful humanity, as an alien message of sin and grace that transforms human perceptions and reality *in toto*.

If the Bible's message is alien to sinful humanity, "one cannot simply read the Bible like other books."[60] In sin, human beings interpret the Bible so that it will support their sinful projects, give them the power they desire, and tell them what they want to hear. In fact, that's how Christians too—intentionally or not—read it. In a lecture to young ecumenical church leaders, at Gland, Switzerland, in 1932, Bonhoeffer asserts, "We prefer our own thoughts to those of the Bible. We no longer read the Bible seriously. We read it no longer against ourselves but only for ourselves."[61] Bonhoeffer claims that Christians read the Scriptures to confirm their current beliefs and practices, and support themselves and their power rather than being confronted by the Spirit of God in the Word. Because of this sinful tendency to read the Bible for one's own advantage, Bonhoeffer contends that the church must learn to read it against itself, hearing God speak not what it wants to hear but his Word of law and repentance. By attending to God's external Word, the church is encountered by the Bible's alien message and opened to hear the good news of God's free grace in Christ.

According to "Contemporizing New Testament Texts," Christians fail to read the Bible against themselves when they mine the Bible for "eternal truths with which I am already familiar."[62] These truths can be intellectual truths like the doctrine of grace or an ethical principle like loving one's neighbor or a universal insight into human nature. When the Bible is understood like this, the meaning of the text is already known, and that doctrine or ideology sits comfortably with people. In Bonhoeffer's words, "the norm of contemporizing resides within us; the Bible is the material to which this norm is applied."[63] Instead of letting the Bible speak its alien Word, the Bible becomes merely a guide to point out what is already believed. Finding in the Bible a universal, intellectual, or moral truth seems like an easy way to make the Bible relevant since the message resonates with the hearers, but such a reading gets the Bible wrong. By reading it for oneself and not against, such an interpretation misses entirely the Bible's "otherness."[64] Scripture's true message, Bonhoeffer insists, is offensive and alien and must be so because God is God—the Creator, Judge, and only Savior—and humans are proud, self-centered sinners, constantly searching for power over others and over God.

Because the alien message of the Scriptures proclaims the sinfulness of the church and the good news of the transcendent Lord, Bonhoeffer argues that Christians must learn to read the Bible against themselves, not naming those sinners out there, showing how sinful *they* are. Rather, Christians need to read the Bible against their own sinful disposition, their own power-plays, and their own failures to follow the humiliation of the Lord Jesus. Only when the church listens to the Bible's interrogation of its own community and ministry—attending to the Bible's questions, challenges, and story—can the church be sure that it is on the right track in interpreting Scripture.[65] Proper interpretation of the Bible means that the church recognizes and confesses that it too is sinful, standing under the judgment of the cross and in need of its redemption.

This second strand of Bonhoeffer's hermeneutics distinguishes between the church and the Lord, recognizing that Christ stands against his church. The church can never think of itself as simply and only unified with the Lord. To be clear, the church confesses the lordship of the crucified and risen Jesus and trusts that he is present within it by his promise in preaching and the sacraments. At the same time, the church acknowledges its sinfulness and listens to Christ who is outside of the church and stands as its judge and Lord. Bonhoeffer's hermeneutics, therefore, presume and establish ecclesial sinfulness, orienting the church to Christ in repentant humility.

The third and final strand of Bonhoeffer's hermeneutics affirms that "God is speaking to us in the Bible."[66] For Bonhoeffer, the Bible is not a repository of ideas or doctrines; it is speech, God's speech to his creatures. In traditional dogmatic language, Bonhoeffer declares the Bible to be the *viva vox Dei*, the living voice of God.[67] Bonhoeffer repudiates the notion that the Scriptures primarily give information or teach true doctrine. Rather, the Scriptures are the very voice of God that brings Jesus to sinners. In "Contemporizing New Testament Texts," Bonhoeffer rejects the idea that the commandments and parenesis of the New Testament should be understood as eternal principles or natural laws. Instead, Bonhoeffer argues that the commands and parenesis of the New Testament are

> commandments of a Lord, in which the commandment is only understood correctly where the Lord is recognized. A commandment without a Lord is nothing, and the basis, the content, and the goal—that is, the fulfillment of the commandment is always the Lord, specifically as the Crucified.[68]

Bonhoeffer insists that he is not minimizing the commandments; rather, he acknowledges them as the Word of Jesus that calls to repentance, faith, and obedience.[69] For Bonhoeffer, only when the Bible is read in this way, as the Word of Jesus that evokes faith and obedience, are the Scriptures read correctly. The Bible is not a treasury of ideas, but the living voice of a person, the Lord Jesus Christ, that brings one to repentance, creates trust in the heart, and commands that one to follow him.[70] According to this third strand, the

Scriptures are rightly interpreted when they are recognized as this active, living speech of Jesus, as a dynamic encounter of God with his creatures.[71] Jesus first brings sinners to himself through the Word by the Spirit, and then sinners learn to read the Bible in such faith, confessing their on-going sinfulness on the way of obedience.

In acknowledging the Bible as God's living voice, Bonhoeffer affirms the presence and activity of the crucified and risen Jesus through the text and in the church. As the Word, Jesus makes the words of the Bible and biblical preaching his own, and the Spirit makes Jesus present in the church for his people. This strand completes the Christ-church dialectic. The church's sinfulness and the necessity of Jesus standing against his church are only one side of the coin. This other side is that Jesus makes himself present in the church through the living voice of God's Word so that he and his promises might be grasped. Jesus is the transcendent Lord, but he does not exercise that authority far from the church but within it,[72] fully present in his body by the Word even as the church must be oriented to the Lord *extra se* in repentance, faith, and obedience. Bonhoeffer's hermeneutics enact and enable the proclamation of the Christ-church dialectic for shaping the church's identity and mission.

CHURCH AND WORLD CHRISTOLOGICALLY CONSIDERED

Bonhoeffer's Christology informs a Christ-church dialectic in which Christ is both present in the church, incorporating the church into him and his work, and he is the transcendent Lord outside the church, calling it to repentance, faith, and obedience. The Christ-church dialectic is fundamental to my project, but it is only one leg of the Christ-church-world triad that constitutes the church's identity and mission. This section focuses on the Christ-world and church-world legs of the triad, showing how Bonhoeffer's Christology not only identifies the church in Christ while retaining Christ's transcendence, but it also shapes the church's mission in the world Christologically. This section establishes a church-world dialectic on the basis of the prior Christ-church and Christ-world relationships wherein the church is distinct from the world but also in solidarity with it.

Recent ecclesiology has concentrated on the relationship between the church and the world, but the dynamic remains unsettled.[73] Most theologians acknowledge that the church must not disappear into the world nor should the world be sacralized as such.[74] Most also agree that a sectarian church that refuses interaction with the world is equally problematic.[75] Despite this broad agreement, the church-world relationship remains the center of much debate. Dietrich Bonhoeffer's Christology sculpts the church-world relation through the prior Christ-church and Christ-world relations.[76] Both a strong distinction of church from world and the unity of church and world in Christ are present in Bonhoeffer's theology, stemming from the same Christological center.[77] Reading these seemingly contradictory tendencies together in Bonhoeffer's Christology results in a church-world dialectic of distinction and solidarity, flowing from the Christ-church and Christ-world relationships. This dialectic opens the way for preaching and teaching the church's mission in and with the world Christologically in a non-triumphalistic manner.

The Church-World Relation in Bonhoeffer's Theology

During the German church struggle and the ecclesiastical turmoil of the 1930s, Bonhoeffer stressed the church's unique identity in Christ as a community distinct from the world.[78] Bonhoeffer begins *Life Together* by commenting on the church's existence in the midst of enemies, "scattered, held together in Jesus Christ *alone*, having become one because they remember *him* in the distant lands, spread out among the unbelievers."[79] *Life Together* thus establishes the church in Christ as a community distinct from the world, distinct both in its love[80] and in its practices.[81] *Discipleship* develops the contrast between church and world yet more starkly. Beginning with the antithesis between cheap grace and costly grace, Bonhoeffer refuses to think of the Christian life and the church apart from Christ.[82] Bonhoeffer argues that one's faith is only pleasing to God, and hence truly faith, when the Christian is obedient to Christ.[83] One's vocation too—even though the doctrine of vocation in Lutheran theology is often understood in the context of creation—is only pleasing to God when the Christian is following Christ.[84]

The Berlin theologian expands the logic of Christian discipleship to include the church: a community is only truly a church-community when it refuses the ways of the world and follows Jesus in its *visible* life.[85] Accordingly, Bonhoeffer sees the distinction of church and world as essential to the church's identity in Christ: "separation [of Christians and non-Christians] *necessarily* takes place in the call by the Word."[86] Baptism institutes this separation of God's people from the sinful world, inaugurating a wholly new life in Christ.[87] Baptism divides, but it also unifies, bringing Christians into the church-community, through which they "take a step out of the world, their work, and family," and "they visibly stand in the community with Jesus Christ."[88] In this visible community, the way of Jesus is to be followed both through personal practices[89] and through the church's unique polity, established by Jesus.[90] Bonhoeffer definitively grounds the distinction of the church from the world.

To understand the logic of Bonhoeffer's construal of the church-world distinction, the Christological foundation needs to be explored.[91] In *Discipleship*, the church-world distinction stems from the Christ-church relation. Most importantly, Bonhoeffer ties the church to Christ as deeply as possible: "The church is the present Christ himself."[92] What Bonhoeffer means is that Christ is the new Adam, the new human being, who is renewed in God's own image and is part of the new age, God's coming Kingdom that is already present proleptically.[93] By baptism into Christ, the church too is the new human being and is Christ's body, not in some metaphorical way but in actuality: "Christ is the church."[94] The Berlin theologians retain Christ's transcendence and lordship over the church,[95] but his emphasis lies on the identity of the church in Christ and thus the dissimilarity of the church from the world that lives at variance with the ways of the Lord.[96] The distinction between church and world becomes starkest in *Discipleship* as Bonhoeffer describes the church's identity and life as a visible community in the world and not an invisible matter of faith. The centrality of the church's visibility in the world follows the logic of the incarnation: "The body of Christ takes up physical space here on earth."[97] Hence, Bonhoeffer describes the church as "the body of the exalted Lord,"[98] enfleshed in preaching,[99] sacraments,[100] and church order.[101] The church of Christ knows itself, its identity, its mission, and its ways from the person of Jesus and his ministry, not from the ways of the world.[102] Bonhoeffer's radical Christological understanding of the church leads to the church-world distinction as a commitment to the presence of the risen Son of God in the church.

In addition to grounding the distinction between the church and the world, Bonhoeffer's Christology also brings church and world deeply together. Scholars often find such thinking in his later works—*Ethics* and *Letters and Papers from Prison*—sometimes attributing the change to a different period in his life, usually his participation in the coup against Hitler.[103] Bonhoeffer's *Ethics*, for instance, closes the gap between church and world as it refuses two-sphere thinking, affirming "the one realm of the Christ-reality, in which the reality of God and the reality of the world are united."[104] In the prison letters, the Berlin theologian binds church and world christologically as he writes about "the claim of Jesus Christ on the world that has come of age."[105] Bonhoeffer's theological letters criticize how Christian theology normally "aim[s] to save some room for religion in the world or over against the world."[106] Instead of an antagonistic approach, Bonhoeffer asserts the necessity of a "nonreligious interpretation of theological concepts,"[107] which does not try to turn the world into something it is not—weak or vulnerable—but proclaims God's Word that reigns where the world is strongest.[108] According to Bonhoeffer, "Christ wishes to liberate humans for genuine worldliness" rather than making them into religious people.[109] Even more, Bonhoeffer believes that Christ is present in the midst of world's worldliness, as the one who is "weak and powerless in the world and in precisely this way, and only so is at our side and helps us."[110] Bonhoeffer's later works thus emphasize the affirmation of the world as Christ's own world rather than the distinction between church and world that marks *Discipleship* and the works of the Finkenwalde period.

The later works do describe the world more positively than during the Finkenwalde period, but the Christological center remains the same as in Bonhoeffer's earlier theology.[111] In *Ethics*, Bonhoeffer does not abscond from the Christological identity of the church, but unites the world to Christ and Christ to the world. The first chapter of the reconstructed *Ethics*, "Christ, Reality, and Good: Christ, Church, and World," focuses on Christian ethics, how the church and Christians live in the world. Rather than concentrating on the identity of the church in Christ to help Christians navigate life in the world, as *Discipleship* does, Bonhoeffer identifies the true reality of the world as the reality of God in Christ. In the person of Jesus Christ and his work of reconciliation, the world finds its true ontology: "The whole reality of the world has already been drawn into and is held together in Christ. History moves only from this center and toward this center."[112] As Bonhoeffer's Christology lectures had earlier understood the story of the world as the story of Jesus Christ,[113] so *Ethics* underscores this point, confessing the world's reality in Christ.

Ethics does not deny the necessity of polemics against idolatry, injustice, and evil in the world, but it refuses to separate church and world because Christ is the center of both. In fact, the church speaks polemically against the world *for the sake of* "a better worldliness."[114] The church should not demand that the world become a religious world but affirm it as created and redeemed by God in Christ. In a striking similarity to *Discipleship*,[115] Bonhoeffer argues that the church is properly distinct from the world, and the church must determine its own structure in Christ, even as it recognizes the world as created and redeemed. The church's distinction, however, is not for its own sake: "The space of the church is not there in order to fight with the world for a piece of its territory, but precisely to testify to the world that it is still the world, namely, the world that is loved and reconciled by God."[116] If *Discipleship* demands that the Christ-church relationship proceeds the church-world relationship, *Ethics* mandates that the Christ-world relationship also proceeds the church-world relationship.[117]

What is different about *Ethics*, and even *Letters and Papers from Prison*,[118] therefore, is not that Bonhoeffer vitiates the Christ-church relationship so prominent in *Discipleship*, but that he expands upon the Christ-world relationship and begins to think the church-world relationship on the basis of both the Christ-world and the Christ-church relations.[119] To be clear, the Berlin theologian never abolishes nor denies the necessity of thinking church-world from Christ-church.[120] Bonhoeffer's polemic against religion, for example, is not a polemic against Christ, the church, or God's Word—as the death of God theologians and a few evangelicals have believed[121]—but a polemic against an apologetics of religiosity that tries to prove the necessity of an omnipotent God while actually relying on an idea of God as a crutch.[122] In addition, *Letters and Papers* does not demand establishing the world on its own terms—a truly independent foundation of the world apart from the church[123]—but mandates a thoroughly Christological understanding of all reality, God and the world.[124] As Bonhoeffer himself comments,

> What matters is not the beyond but this world, how it is created and preserved, is given laws, reconciled, and renewed. What is beyond this world is meant, in the gospel, to be there *for* this world . . . in the biblical sense of the creation and the incarnation, crucifixion, and resurrection of Jesus Christ.[125]

By seeing the world in and through Christ, Bonhoeffer develops a church-world dynamic through the Christ-world relation without abolishing the necessity of the Christ-church relation prominent in *Discipleship*.[126]

Distinction and Solidarity in the Church-World Relation

Bonhoeffer's Christology grounds the two seemingly opposite assertions between which contemporary theology has often floundered: the church must be distinct from the world, grounded in Christ alone, and the church and world are truly united in one reality in Jesus. In Christ, both assertions can stand together. The church is distinct from the world as the community in which Jesus is present by his promises, and in which he makes himself known by his Spirit. At the same time, the world is an essential participant in God's creation, Christ's reconciliation, and the coming consummation by the Spirit. In this light, the church is in solidarity with the world: created, sinful, reconciled to the Father, and waiting in hope for the final restoration of all things.[127]

Bonhoeffer's understanding of the church-world relation, therefore, takes a storied framework that grounds this church-world dialectic.[128] All things exist as created, broken in sin, and redeemed by Christ Jesus, for Bonhoeffer,[129] because the true story of the world is "the holy history of God on earth" that Scripture narrates.[130] Bonhoeffer's typology of the world does not express everything there is to say about any aspect of the world, but it does recognize the world in its complexity as theological. In fact, the church *must* see the world theologically.[131] The world is created by God and under the lordship of Jesus Christ; the world is fallen under sin and in need of judgment and reconciliation; the redemption of the world has already come in Christ who will finish his work when he comes again and makes all things new through the Spirit. To see the world in any other way is not to see with biblical eyes.

Although the world only knows itself to be creation, fallen, and redeemed in light of God's Word—"the church precedes the world epistemologically"[132]—*all* of reality exists in this three-fold typology that signifies the story of God. The church cannot be dichotomized and separated from the world as if the church was not constituted by the same story. To be sure, the distinction between church and world is necessary, but that distinction must not become a dichotomy. Hence, in Bonhoeffer's view, "The church belongs to the world-reality, just as world-reality belongs to the church."[133] In view of creation, sinfulness, redemption, and the coming judgment, church and world are bound together in the one story of God in Christ.

In the narrative of the triune God, the dialectic of the church-world relation emerges, showing the church's distinction from the world and the church's solidarity with the world.[134] The church must be distinguished from the world because the church knows itself aright in Christ alone. In view of its identity in Jesus, the church cannot understand itself first in and through the world, but in and through the Lord in whom church and world are bound. After all, the world does not understand itself within the story of creation, sin, and redemption. As such, part of the church's calling is to remind the world that it is world, as Stanley Hauerwas frequently asserts.[135] Because the world does not know itself within the story of God, "the primary social task of the church is to be itself—that is, a people who have been formed by a story that provides them with the skills for negotiating the danger of this existence, trusting in God's promise of redemption."[136] For this reason, the church fails in its task when it capitulates to the world and serves only or primarily on the world's terms.[137] The story of Jesus Christ must be the center of the mission of the church, and ecclesiology cannot be content with an understanding of mission that does not proclaim Jesus Christ as Lord and Savior of the world. The mission of the church is Christ's; it does not belong to human beings to do what society or the government wants the church to do. As the community identified in Christ and oriented to him, the church witnesses to the world that it does not belong to itself but to its Creator.

Under each main rubric of the story of God—creation, sin, and redemption—the church both stands in solidarity with the world and is distinct from the world. As created, the church is in solidarity with the world as dependent upon the Creator. The church did not create itself, nor is it in control of its own story or destiny. In the same way, the world was formed by God's voice and lives from the breath of his mouth. The world is the material that God called "good" in the beginning, which God made for community with himself and all creation. God eternally affirmed the goodness of creation when the Word assumed human nature and took residence in the womb of Mary. The incarnation is God's "Yes" to his creation, affirming it as his creative handiwork. As Bonhoeffer confesses clearly, the church does not ascend above the materiality of the world, nor become more than creatures. Christians *are* simply human creatures, who depend upon the Creator for food, clothing, breath, and life itself, "Being a Christian does not mean being religious in a certain way . . . . Instead, it means being human, not a certain type of human being, but the human being Christ creates in us."[138] As such, the church is not different from the world in its fundamental ontology, and it should not seek to be so. Church and world are creatures of the Creator, receiving all good things from his hand and continually reliant upon him.

The church's difference from the world is not that the church is better or greater than the world, but that it realizes and confesses its dependence upon God.[139] The church knows itself as created, and is called to witness to the world that it too is created. In this solidarity, the church can learn to see goodness, truth, and justice in the world not as accidental, but as part of God's story, reflections or parables of God's reign in Christ.[140] Such a perspective is not a solidarity from above—in which a savior comes to be in solidarity with a vulnerable population to help—it is a real solidarity in the story of God. The church and the world are in the same place vis-à-vis God's action and work. Hence, the church is *with* the world, not merely called to mission for it.[141]

As fallen, the church is also in solidarity with the world, but it differs from the world in that the church recognizes and repents of its sin. Both church and world stand under the rule and judgment of Christ the Lord, as sinners in themselves, and having no righteousness of their own. The church, however, admits this sinfulness before God in confession and repentance, and this repentance shapes the church's relation to the world.[142] In confession, the church stands in solidarity with the world at the same time that it witnesses to the world, confessing its brokenness and witnessing to the Lord Jesus who comes in the promise of forgiveness. In this way, the church is both prophet to the world—admitting the idolatry and sin of many political, economic, and social games played in North America—and sister of the world, praying for the world, and working in discipleship to make God's justice come here and now in faithfulness to Jesus Christ. The church is bound with the world as truly sinful, yet also distinct from it, confessing sin, witnessing to the world, and praying for all. Without this difference, the church fails in its faithfulness to Jesus Christ.

When the world is construed in terms of the redemption of Christ, the same tension emerges. On the one hand, the world is the object of God's love and redemption. As such, the church does not have ontological primacy vis-à-vis salvation. In other words, salvation and redemption do not belong to the church; salvation belongs to God who graciously gives it to the world. The church is the community in the world that hears this Word, believes it, and is called by God into mission. As such, there is no room in the church for triumphalism, whether intellectual or moralistic. God's salvation is eschatological, part of the coming of Jesus Christ; it is his *adventus*, delivered only in his coming, not the *futurum* that the church or society is able to construct on its own.[143] Church and world are both redeemed by the death and resurrection of Jesus, and await his coming again to make all things new. On the other hand, the church knows Jesus as the Lord, and witnesses to his redemption by word and deed. The church testifies to Christ's reign as it gathers together people from all walks of life, all socioeconomic and racial backgrounds, to drink from one cup and eat of one bread. The church witnesses to the redemption of Christ as it enters into the lives of the homeless and the poor, not only to give but to receive from them as those loved by Christ.[144] The church confesses the lordship of Jesus as it seeks to end racial disparity and bring justice to whole communities.[145] The church bears witness to the reign of Christ as it forgives the sins of heinous criminals, even murderers and pedophiles who repent. The church attests to the coming of Jesus as it proclaims the message of good news only in this one, the crucified and risen Savior of the world. The church confesses Jesus and his present, but still coming, reign; the church does not control the Lord or his reign, even as Christ rules now in the church by his promise. Since redemption belongs to Christ, the church remains in solidarity with the world under Jesus even at the same time that it is distinct from the world in pointing to Christ alone as Savior and Lord.

In this way, the church-world dialectic, like the Christ-church dialectic, is not merely grammatical or logical but real.[146] The church-world relationship is properly addressed dialectically because the Scriptures reveal both entities to be created, sinful, and redeemed at the same time. In fact, because the church and the world are dynamic communities, ecclesiology cannot specify the church's proper disposition toward the world in the abstract. Whether the church must first affirm the world or first speak prophetically against the world or first listen to Christ to know itself in him depends upon the context.[147] Hence, the dialectics of Bonhoeffer's Christology do not specify the church-world relationship in the abstract, but enable preaching and teaching that shapes the church's identity in Christ and calls it to faithfulness to concrete mission in Christ's world.

The church is neither elevated over the world nor is it merged into it. Instead, the church is both distinguished from the world but also deeply connected to it in Christ. Within the framework of creation, sin, and redemption, the church stands as sister to the world as those who have received life from the hand of the Creator, are curved in upon themselves in sin, and can do nothing to save themselves. At the same time, the church is distinct from the world as the community that acknowledges this story and believes in the salvation of God in Christ's cross, resurrection, and continued work through the Spirit. The church is distinct from the world and deeply interconnected with the world as participants in the mission of the Lord of the church and the world, Jesus Christ.

CONCLUSION: TOWARD A STORY-SHAPED ECCLESIOLOGY FOR THE LOCAL CHURCH

The church is not defined in itself but in its fundamental relationships, the Christ-church-world triad. Following Bonhoeffer's Christology, the church is first identified through the simultaneous presence and transcendence of the Lord. The church is Christ's body in which he gives himself graciously in Word and sacrament and through which he continues his ministry. Concurrently, the church is under Christ, oriented to the Lord Jesus who stands outside of it. In addition, the church is identified in relation to the world, but the church-world relation does not have an independent status. Instead, the church-world relation is determined by the prior Christ-church and Christ-world relations.[148] On the one hand, the church is distinct from the world as it knows itself in Christ and its relationship to the world only in the crucified Lord and his mission.[149] On the other, the world is created by God, broken in sin, and redeemed by Christ, and this story of God in Christ encompasses both church and world within the one Christ-reality. "Belonging completely to Christ, one stands at the same time completely in the world."[150] The church has no ontological priority over the world but stands in solidarity with it vis-à-vis the reality of God in Christ. Yet, the church is simultaneously distinct from the world as it brings Christ to the world by the Word, witnessing to the world of its true reality as created, sinful, and reconciled to God in Jesus.

The dialectics of the Christ-church-world triad stem from and are enacted by the story of Christ proclaimed through the Word. The church receives its identity through the Word and is formed into his story by the Spirit. Hence, narrative is the proper form for ecclesiology, not because narrative is in vogue,[151] but because the story of Christ establishes reality, identifying the church, the world, and their proper relationship. Christ's humiliated history with his creatures renders the church and the world in the narrative of his incarnation, ministry, death, resurrection, ascension, continued presence in the Spirit, and his coming again in judgment.[152] In the gospel, received via preaching and the sacraments, the church comes to know Jesus by faith as Lord, and it comes to know itself as called into his cruciform mission.

Although the narrative of Jesus calls the church to follow him in his ministry, the story of Jesus does not belong to the church as a narrative of its own to be manipulated. In fact, a narrative ecclesiology primarily concerned with "the story of the church" can lead to an unhelpful introspection as if the church were the center of its own story.[153] Instead, the church is *given* its story, receiving it as a gift from God.[154] As a gift, the church's story cannot be constructed from the side of the church, even though it is always received and interpreted from this side.[155] Rather, in Bonhoeffer's words, "only in Holy Scripture do we get to know our own story."[156] The Scriptures themselves incorporate sinful creatures into God's story, shaping them for Christ's mission. Through the proclamation of the Scriptures,

> we are uprooted from our own existence and are taken back to the holy history of God on earth. There God has dealt with us, and there God still deals with us today, with our needs and our sins, by means of the divine wrath and grace. What is important is not that God is a spectator and participant in our life today, but that we are attentive listeners and participants in God's action in the sacred story, the story of Christ on earth.[157]

According to Bonhoeffer, the proclamation of the Word causes the church to attend to its true history, the story of Jesus Christ. Through preaching and the sacraments, Jesus speaks to the church *extra se* so that it recognizes the reality of God's judgment and mercy and becomes a participant in Christ's own story by faith. Such preaching also opens the eyes of the church to know the world in light of Christ and follow Jesus in obedience to his mission in the same.

In addition to taking a storied form, an ecclesiology grounded in Bonhoeffer's Christology emphasizes local congregations and ministries. To be clear, the church that is identified by Christ's story and called into his mission is not a particular congregation or denomination but the whole communion of saints, the *una sancta*. Nevertheless, Bonhoeffer's Christology does not merely name the church in the abstract, but describes specific congregations theologically. Both the presence of Christ in the concrete, embodied practices of the Word—preaching, confession and absolution, and the sacraments—and the logic of Christ's story specify local congregations and ministries as places where Christ is to be grasped and his ministry proclaimed in word and deed. According to the former, God hallows out a part of creation—audible words, bread, wine, and water—giving forgiveness and life through tangible means to restore sinners to true creatureliness.[158] These gifts of Christ's presence are necessarily local, given to local congregations, and the gifts shape each congregation as Christ's body called to proclaim and embody Jesus in a particular place.[159] According to the latter, the logic of Christ's story, the church is called to ministry in particular places and cultures just as Jesus himself inhabited Galilee, Judea, and Jerusalem, serving particular people: prostitutes, lepers, Pharisees, and zealots.[160] The catholicity of the church does not come from an ideal or abstract church that can be presumed to be universal, but from the ministry and call of Jesus to preach, administer the sacraments, and embody his kingdom to the whole world. Such work is and must be local even as Christ's Word is universal.

While the locality of the church might seem obvious, ecclesiology often does not address concrete congregations, but is focused on a pure, abstract church instead of actual communities in need of resources to repent and be faithful to Christ.[161] Attending to Christ's story should mean that congregations are attentive to local matters of justice, peace, and mercy, listening closely to God's Word to hear how and where Christ is calling a local congregation to repentance, forgiveness, and mission.[162] The local community's needs, both congregational and broader community, should shape the church's service and witness because the local community is recognized as part of Christ's one story with the church.[163] James K. A. Smith's words equally apply to my project: "The Christian *ekklēsia* must be not only liturgical but also local; it must transform not only hearts but also neighborhoods; its worship must foster not only discipleship but also justice—indeed, disciples who are passionate about justice."[164] An ecclesiology rooted in Bonhoeffer's Christology takes seriously the local concrete nature of ministry and its visible work not only in preaching the gospel but in public service to the community.[165]

Ecclesiology thus expressed refuses to think of the church apart from Christ. The church's identity is a sinful community of sinners that is yet his own body, part of his story and ministry. This is not an identity the church possesses separately from Christ, but it receives this identity through his Word and by his Spirit delivered in preaching and the sacraments. In the same way, the church does not control its mission but receives it from Jesus through its identity in him. As such, the church's mission to the world and the shape of that mission requires continual attention to the story of God in Christ. Through the proclamation and teaching of Christ, each local congregation is called to repentance and obedience to Jesus and his mission. Ecclesiology should not get hung up on ideal models or practicalities, but should enable proclamation of God's Word interpreted Christologically that brings true repentance and a renewed sense of calling to Christ's mission in the world.

NOTES

1. DBWE 4, 220.
2. Ephesians 5:23–32. Compare Robert W. Jenson, "The Bride of Christ," in *Critical Issues in Ecclesiology: Essays in Honor of Carl E. Braaten*, ed. Alberto L. García and Susan K. Wood (Grand Rapids, MI: Eerdmans, 2011), 1–5.
3. DBWE 1, 62. Michael Mawson, "Christ Existing as Community: The Ethics of Bonhoeffer's Ecclesiology," PhD diss. (University of Notre Dame, South Bend, IN, 2012), 72–73:

> Through the church the "real dialectic" that governs and underlies all reality is disclosed and made apparent. Through the church it is revealed that all human reality is radically qualified in terms of God's judgment and grace. This qualification is then expressed through the Christian doctrines of the primal state, sin and reconciliation.

4. This dialectic also fits with Augustine's understanding of the Christ-church relation in the *totus Christus*, as explained by J. David Moser, "*Totus Christus*: A Proposal for Protestant Christology and Ecclesiology," *Pro Ecclesia* 29, no. 1 (2020): 5–9 and 12–17. For instance, Moser summarizes one part of Augustine's view:

> *Totus Christus* denotes a kind of metaphysical identity between Christ and the Church, such that the "whole thing" (*totum*) is Christ. But this spiritual entity is not composed of two distinct entities that become numerically identical, or one and the same thing. Christ and the Church are distinct in one way and united in another: distinct in their being, we might say, since God and creatures are distinct, but united by the Holy Spirit. (9)

5. Fleming Rutledge, *The Crucifixion: Understanding the Death of Jesus Christ* (Grand Rapids, MI: Eerdmans, 2015), 33. Calling such tensions "dynamic tensions," Rutledge contends, "There is no midpoint compromise between paradoxical affirmations; the way ahead is found *in the tension itself*."
6. Compare Martin Luther's notion of the church as "God's mouth house": Robert Kolb, "The Sheep and the Voice of the Shepherd: The Ecclesiology of the Lutheran Confessional Writings," *Concordia Journal* 36 (2010): 328–30.
7. DBWE 12, 304.
8. DBWE 12, 310.
9. For the importance of the external Word in Bonhoeffer, see Paul R. Hinlicky, "*Verbum Externum*: Dietrich Bonhoeffer's Bethel Confession," in *God Speaks to Us: Dietrich Bonhoeffer's Biblical Hermeneutics*, ed. Ralf K. Wüstenberg and Jens Zimmermann (Frankfurt am Main: Peter Lang, 2013), 189–215.
10. Christiane Tietz recognizes the presence of Christ in the church in Bonhoeffer's "dialectic of faith and church," following Ernst Feil's interpretation of *Act and Being*. In my view, such a dialectic exists in Bonhoeffer but follows from the prior dialectic of Christ and his church. See Christiane Tietz, "Bonhoeffer on the Ontological Structure of the Church," in *Ontology and Ethics: Bonhoeffer and Contemporary Scholarship*, ed. Adam C. Clark and Michael Mawson (Eugene, OR: Pickwick, 2013), 44–45.

11. On the importance of this kind of repentance in the church, see Darrell L. Guder, *The Continuing Conversion of the Church* (Grand Rapids, MI: Eerdmans, 2000).

12. See chapter one.

13. DBWE 1, 189–90.

14. Compare Kirsten Busch Nielsen, "Community Turned Inside Out: Dietrich Bonhoeffer's Concept of the Church and of Humanity Reconsidered," in *Being Human, Becoming Human: Dietrich Bonhoeffer and Social Thought*, ed. Jens Zimmermann and Brian Gregor (Eugene, OR: Pickwick, 2010), 93: for Bonhoeffer, "the 'invisible' church is at the same time the 'visible' church." For Bonhoeffer's notion of the church's invisibility, see also Karina Juhl Kande, "Biblical Metaphors in Dietrich Bonhoeffer's Understanding of The Church," in *God Speaks to Us: Dietrich Bonhoeffer's Biblical Hermeneutics*, ed. Ralf K. Wüstenberg and Jens Zimmermann (Frankfurt am Main: Peter Lang, 2013), 133–36.

15. DBWE 12, 263.

16. DBWE 12, 262.

17. This is the implication of David Daniel's understanding of Luther on the church. See David P. Daniel, "Luther on the Church," in *The Oxford Handbook of Martin Luther's Theology*, ed. Robert Kolb, Irene Dingle, and L'ubomír Batka (Oxford: Oxford University Press, 2014), 333–52.

18. Compare DBWE 12, 264: "It is one and the same church, its visible form and its hidden divinity."

19. Eva Harasta, "One Body: Dietrich Bonhoeffer on the Church's Existence as Sinner and Saint at Once," *Union Seminary Quarterly Review* 62, no. 3–4 (2010): 17–34.

20. On the liberal version, see Bernd Wannenwetsch, "The Whole Christ and the Whole Human Being: Dietrich Bonhoeffer's Inspiration for the 'Christology and Ethics' Discourse," in *Christology and Ethics*, ed. F. LeRon Shults and Brent Waters (Grand Rapids, MI: Eerdmans, 2010), 87.

21. Compare Sherwood G. Lingenfelter and Marvin K. Mayers, *Ministering Cross-Culturally: An Incarnational Model for Personal Relationships*, 2nd ed. (Grand Rapids, MI: Baker Academic, 2003), 22–23:

> The *practice* of incarnation (i.e. a willingness to learn as if we were helpless infants) is the first essential step toward breaking this pattern of excluding others. Missionaries, by the nature of their task, must become personally immersed with people who are different. To follow the example of Christ, that of incarnation, means undergoing drastic personal reorientation . . . . Moreover, they must do this in the spirit of Christ, that is, without sin. While most of us may not face situations requiring total reorientation, the *incarnation principle* can also be applied effectively in family and church life.

Emphases added. For a more recent example, see Greg Finke, *Joining Jesus on his Mission: How to be an Everyday Missionary* (Elgin, IL: Tenth Power, 2014).

22. Compare Walter Rauschenbusch's social gospel movement that called churches to follow *the spirit of Christ* and get involved in social mission. The problem with Rauschenbusch is not that the gospel of Christ shapes the church and its life, but

that Christ's mission is reduced to something churches are able to do by their own power and Christ's unique identity as Lord and God is overcome by an instrumental Christology. See Walter Rauschenbusch, *Christianity and the Social Crisis* (1907; reprint, New York: Macmillan, 1916), esp. the final chapter, 343–422.

23. DBWE 6, 93. Emphasis original.

24. Joseph McGarry, "Formed While Following: Dietrich Bonhoeffer's Asymmetrical View of Agency in Christian Formation," *Theology Today* 71, no. 1 (2014): 108: "Christian formation is determined by an asymmentrical agency, in which formation in Christ is a byproduct of the church's discipleship to Christ, even as such formation is not—indeed cannot—be its original objective."

25. Compare Wannenwetsch, "Whole Christ," 87: "The problem with the idea of Jesus as moral exemplar whose works are to be emulated is that it assumes these works can be taken on their own, in abstraction from the person of Christ."

26. Stephen Pickard, *Seeking the Church: An Introduction to Ecclesiology* (London: SCM Press, 2012), 64: "When the divine Christ is transposed into the Church, the Church becomes the singular and determinative authoritative voice of the Divine" (64).

27. For a summary and criticism of the tendency in Roman Catholicism to conflate Christ and the church, see Horton, *People and Place*, 155–64. See also Avery Dulles, *Models of the Church*, expanded ed. (New York: Image Books, 2002), 35–38, for an internal Roman Catholic critique.

28. Compare Pickard, *Seeking the Church,* 61–62.

29. Horton, *People and Place*, 167.

30. Horton's paragraph that states what Jenson "seems to be saying" is not connected nearly enough to what Jenson does say (*People and Place*, 167). Jenson does not *erase* the distinction of Christ and the church nor does he *abolish* the real character of the church as a human community, as Horton insinuates. For example, Jenson, *Systematic Theology*, 2:213: "We may not so identify the risen Christ with the church as to be unable to refer distinctly to the one and then to the other"; and 2:174: "The church is not an invisible entity; she is the, if anything, all too visible gathering of sinners around the loaf and cup."

31. Compare Michael Mawson, "The Spirit and the Community: Pneumatology and Ecclesiology in Jenson, Hütter, and Bonhoeffer," *International Journal of Systematic Theology* 15, no. 4 (2013): 457–59.

32. On the connection of Christ-church conflation and the church-world relation, see Pickard, *Seeking the Church*, 65–66.

33. DBWE 4, 43–56.

34. Compare DBWE 2, 131: "Because theology turns revelation into something that exists, it may be practiced only where the living person of Christ is itself present and can destroy this existing thing or acknowledge it."

35. See chapter 2 on the Christology lectures. The logic that the church is defined not in itself but in reference to Christ is not an enigma of those lectures but a thorough-going orientation in Bonhoeffer's thought. As a sampling, I see the same logic at work in *Discipleship* as Christ separates individuals from their self-determined relationships before giving them brand new community in him, which he determines (DBWE 4, 98–99). The logic is apparent in "Ethics as Formation": Christians are

formed by Christ and take on his form but never do the forming by their own ideas of power (DBWE 6, 93). This is also the logic of *Life Together* as Bonhoeffer describes the story of Holy Scripture as our story (DBWE 5, 62) and Christian righteousness as alien, *extra nos* (DBWE 5, 31). Finally, it is the logic of *Act and Being*: "Human beings, when they understand themselves in faith, are entirely wrenched away from themselves and are directed towards God" (DBWE 2, 135).

36. The intimate connection of scriptural hermeneutics and ecclesiology in Bonhoeffer has been highlighted most recently by Derek W. Taylor, *Reading Scripture as the Church: Dietrich Bonhoeffer's Hermeneutic of Discipleship* (Downers Grove, IL: IVP Academic, 2020). For Bonhoeffer's commitment to God's Word, see Philip Ziegler, "Dietrich Bonhoeffer: A Theologian of the Word of God," in *Bonhoeffer, Christ, and Culture*, ed. Keith L. Johnson and Timothy Larsen (Downers Grove, IL: IVP Academic, 2013), 17–37.

37. DBWE 14, 413–33.

38. DBWE 3, 22.

39. DBWE 3, 22. For more details on Bonhoeffer's view of the Bible as a book of the church, see Martin Kuske, *The Old Testament as the Book of Christ: An Appraisal of Bonhoeffer's Interpretation*, trans. S. T. Kimbrough, Jr. (Philadelphia: Westminster Press, 1976), 28–31. Karl Barth is an important figure in reading the Bible in the church. For the relationship of Barth and Bonhoeffer on the Bible, see John Webster, *Word and Church: Essays in Christian Dogmatics*, Cornerstones (London: Bloomsbury T&T Clark, 2016), 87–110.

40. DBWE 14, 413–23. Compare Ziegler, "Bonhoeffer: Theologian of the Word of God," 18.

41. DBWE 4, 414–16.

42. On the German Christians, see Doris L. Bergen, *Twisted Cross: The German Christian Movement in the Third Reich* (Chapel Hill, NC: University of North Carolina Press, 1996).

43. Eberhard Bethge, *Dietrich Bonhoeffer: A Biography*, rev. ed., ed. Victoria J. Barnett (Minneapolis: Fortress, 2000), 542, calls it an "evangelistic" work. Oliver Heil, *Die Auslegung der Bergpredigt im Dritten Reich* (Norderstedt, Ger.: GRIN Verlag, 2011), 5, emphasizes that it was addressed to Germans alienated from the church.

44. Heil, *Auslegung der Bergpredigt*, 5. The whole chapter on Müller (pp. 5–12) is instructive.

45. Quoted in and summarized by Bethge, *Dietrich Bonhoeffer*, 542.

46. Timo Laato, "Romans as the Completion of Bonhoeffer's Hermeneutics," *JETS* 58, no. 4 (2015): 709–17, recognizes this context as central to Bonhoeffer's hermeneutics.

47. DBWE 14, 424.

48. DBWE 14, 421.

49. Hence, many interpreters recognize Bonhoeffer hermeneutics as "Christological." Bonhoeffer's biblical hermeneutics are and must be Christological because Bonhoeffer is committed to understanding the Bible as a book of the church, reading it in the context of fundamental ecclesial practices like confession, worship,

proclamation, and teaching. Among those who recognize the centrality of Christology to Bonhoeffer's hermeneutics, see Jens Zimmermann, "Reading the Book of the Church: Bonhoeffer's Christological Hermeneutics," *Modern Theology* 28, no. 4 (2012): 763–80.

50. DBWE 14, 425.

51. Walter Harrelson has criticized Bonhoeffer's Christological readings of *Creation and Fall* as "gratuitous" and does not find Bonhoeffer's biblical contributions to be important to his legacy in part because of Bonhoeffer's tendency to be more homiletical and Christological than historical and literary. Walter Harrelson, "Bonhoeffer and the Bible," in *The Place of Bonhoeffer*, ed. Martin E. Marty (New York: Association Press, 1962), 115–39. Similarly, Jay Rochelle calls Bonhoeffer's work on King David "embarrassing" because the Christological center leaves no space for Jewish people to interpret the Scripture as their own (though Rochelle largely sees Bonhoeffer's exegesis positively). Jay C. Rochelle, "Bonhoeffer and Biblical Interpretation: Reading Scripture in the Spirit," *Currents in Theology and Mission* 22, no. 2 (1995): 89. Recently, some scholars have found great value in Bonhoeffer's homiletical approach to theology. For example, see Michael Pasquarello III, *Dietrich: Bonhoeffer and the Theology of a Preaching Life* (Waco, TX: Baylor University Press, 2017).

52. DBWE 5, 158–60. See also the editors' afterword in DBWE 5, 181, and Brad Pribbenow, *Prayerbook of Christ: Dietrich Bonhoeffer's Christological Interpretation of the Psalms* (Lanham, MA: Lexington Books/Fortress Academic, 2018), 53–100.

53. DBWE 14, 429.

54. Compare DWBE 14, 424:

> *The common character of the New Testament witness* is that it is Christ who performs this miracle, speaks the parable, issues the commandment, and that through such a miracle, parable, commandment, or teaching Christ is always aiming at one and the same thing, *namely, to bind human beings to himself* as the absolutely unique, historic one.

Emphases are original. The underline of "himself" is based on Bonhoeffer's own double underline in the original (DBWE 14, 424n.[59.]).

55. Robert J. Dean, "A Matter of Mission: Bonhoeffer, the Bible, and Ecclesial Formation," *Didaskalia* 28 (2018): 49–74, quoting p. 53.

56. Timo Laato ("Romans as the Completion of Bonhoeffer's Hermeneutics") properly recognizes that Bonhoeffer has attached revelation to the presence of Christ in a congregation (718), but he believes that Bonhoeffer does not sufficiently name what exactly revelation is in *Act and Being* (717–19). Latto is right that Bonhoeffer does not give a fully material account of Christ's person in *Act and Being*, which is necessary to concretize his understanding of the relationship of revelation and the Bible—in its Christological materiality and not a spiritual formality. Bonhoeffer, however, did not fail to root revelation in Christ's person, and the Christological foundation established in *Act and Being* is central to Bonhoeffer's thought thereafter. See Michael P. DeJonge, *Bonhoeffer's Theological Formation: Berlin, Barth, and Protestant Theology* (Oxford: Oxford University Press, 2012).

57. Compare John Webster's recognition that the problem faced in reading Scripture is not a matter of intelligence but sin, including "our wicked repudiation of the divine address" and "our desire to speak the final word to ourselves." Webster, *Word and Church: Essays in Christian Dogmatics*, Cornerstones (London: Bloomsbury T&T Clark, 2016), 109.

58. Compare DBWE 14, 168:

> If it is I who says where God is to be found, then I will always find a God there who in some manner corresponds to me, is pleasing to me, who is commensurate with my own nature. But if it is God who says where he is to be found, then it will probably be a place that is not at all commensurate with my own nature and that does not please me at all.

59. DBWE 14, 168.

60. DBWE 14, 167.

61. DBWE 11, 377–78.

62. DBWE 14, 420.

63. DBWE 14, 421.

64. Stephen Plant, "'In the Bible it is God who speaks': Peake and Bonhoeffer on Reading Scripture," in *Taking Stock of Bonhoeffer* (Burlington, VT: Ashgate, 2014), 52.

65. Stephen E. Fowl and Gregory Jones, *Reading in Communion: Scripture and Ethics in Christian Life* (Grand Rapids: Eerdmans, 1991), 42, and Ian Stackhouse, "The Text Has More Than Enough Thoughts: Bonhoeffer's Lectures on Preaching," in *Text Message: The Centrality of Scripture in Preaching*, ed. Ian Stackhouse and Oliver D. Crisp (Eugene, OR: Pickwick, 2014), 26. Karen Case-Green calls for defamiliarization in preaching which has some echoes of Bonhoeffer's understanding of reading the Bible against ourselves. See Karen Case-Green, "Defamiliarization: Purging our Preaching of Platitudes," in *Text Message: The Centrality of Scripture in Preaching*, ed. Ian Stackhouse and Oliver D. Crisp (Eugene, OR: Pickwick, 2014), 145–65.

66. DBWE 14, 167.

67. John Webster focuses on this point in Bonhoeffer's hermeneutics in Webster, *Word and Church*, 101–7.

68. DBWE 14, 427. Bonhoeffer likely has in mind the German Christian ideology of race and struggle as part of the natural law. Bonhoeffer refuses to allow natural law to abolish or overcome the Word of Jesus.

69. Florian Schmitz argues that "simple obedience" brings together faith and obedience, justification and sanctification, grace and discipleship in the call of Jesus and is the "leading principle behind Bonhoeffer's Biblical Hermeneutics" in *Discipleship* (and *Ethics* too). While Schmitz is right, it is only so because of Bonhoeffer's unwavering commitment to the *verbum externum* as the efficacious Word of Jesus. Florian Schmitz, "'Only the believers obey, and only the obedient believe.' Notes on Dietrich Bonhoeffer's Biblical Hermeneutics with Reference to *Discipleship*," in *God Speaks to Us: Dietrich Bonhoeffer's Biblical Hermeneutics*, ed. Ralf K. Wüstenberg and Jens Zimmermann (Frankfurt am Main: Peter Lang, 2013), 182–86.

70. Compare Jay Rochelle: "It is our relationship to the text, one might say our discipleship under the text, which is of primary importance," for Bonhoeffer. Rochelle, "Bonhoeffer and Biblical Interpretation," 87.

71. Bonhoeffer's repudiation of verbal inspiration must be understood in this light (e.g., DBWE 2, 92; DBWE 12, 331). Bonhoeffer sees verbal inspiration as an attempt to ensconce truth within the text as a static object. Because Bonhoeffer thinks that verbal inspiration establishes an inerrant repository of truth, he objects to the doctrine as a poor replacement for the presence of Jesus in the living and active Word of God that calls to repentance and forgives sins. Hence, Bonhoeffer's "liberal" rejection of verbal inspiration stands on firm Lutheran ground, and does not militate against the Scriptures as the Word of God. So also Ziegler, "Bonhoeffer: Theologian of the Word of God," 32.

72. Compare DBWE 8, 367: "God is the beyond in the midst of our lives." Although some have interpreted this in a pantheistic fashion, Bonhoeffer immediately transitions to the church and the life of the church, which is suggestive of my interpretation. Bonhoeffer's next sentence states, "The church stands not at the point where human powers fail, at the boundaries, but in the center of the village."

73. Compare Gerard Mannion, "Postmodern Ecclesiologies," in *The Routledge Companion to the Christian Church*, ed. Gerard Mannion and Lewis S. Mudge (New York: Routledge, 2008), 132: the major question for a postmodern ecclesiology "is the relationship between the church and the world, and the ecclesial attitudes and practices which relate to, shape and reflect this." As a sampling of some texts and authors that emphasize the church-world relationship, see John Milbank, *Theology and Social Theory: Beyond Secular Reason*, 2nd ed. (Malden, MA: Blackwell, 2006); Stanley Hauerwas, *A Better Hope: Resources for a Church Confronting Capitalism, Democracy, and Postmodernity* (Grand Rapids, MI: Brazos, 2000); John Howard Yoder, *The Politics of Jesus: Vicit Agnus Noster*, 2nd ed. (Grand Rapids, MI: Eerdmans, 1994); Oliver O'Donovan, *The Desire of the Nations: Rediscovering the Roots of Political Theology* (Cambridge: Cambridge University Press, 1996); Peter Scott and William T. Cavanaugh, eds., *The Blackwell Companion to Political Theology* (Malden, MA: Blackwell, 2004); and William T. Cavanaugh, *Migrations of the Holy: God, State, and the Political Meaning of the Church* (Grand Rapids, MI: Eerdmans, 2011).

74. Pickard, *Seeking the Church*, 67–73. One of the strongest cases for distinguishing the church from the world has been made by John Howard Yoder. See, for instance, Yoder, *The Priestly Kingdom: Social Ethics as Gospel* (1984; reprint, Notre Dame: Notre Dame University Press, 2011), 135–47. To be clear, I disagree with the common sectarian charge brought against this position, especially against Hauerwas who uses very similar logic to Yoder. Distinguishing church and world is necessary for ecclesiology. For the sectarian charge leveled against Hauerwas, see James M. Gustafson, "The Sectarian Temptation: Reflections on Theology, the Church and the University," *Proceedings of the Catholic Theological Society of America* 40 (1985): 83–94. For another critique of Hauerwas and Yoder and their "sectarianism" which looks at some underlying philosophical commitments, see Scott Holland, "The Problems and Prospects of a 'Sectarian Ethic': A Critique of the Hauerwas Reading of the Jesus Story," *The Conrad Grebel Review* 10, no. 2 (1992): 157–68. For Hauerwas' own

rebuttal to the charge of sectarianism, see Hauerwas, "Why the "Sectarian Temptation" Is a Misrepresentation," in *The Hauerwas Reader*, ed. John Berkman and Michael Cartwright (Durham: Duke University Press, 2001), 90–110. For an argument sympathetic to Hauerwas, see Nigel Biggar, "Is Stanley Hauerwas Sectarian?" in *Faithfulness and Fortitude: In Conversation with the Theological Ethics of Stanley Hauerwas*, ed. Mark Thiessen Nation and Samuel Wells (Edinburgh: T&T Clark, 2000), 141–60.

75. Pickard, *Seeking the Church*, 61–66 and 73–74.

76. Pickard recognizes that Christological and pneumatological heresies conjoin with these ecclesial heresies: *Seeking the Church*, 56–79. Hence, the church-world relationship requires an orthodox doctrine of God.

77. Compare Zimmermann, "Reading the Book of the Church," 771: "Incarnational Christology is the centre not only of scriptural interpretation but of understanding reality in general." Compare also Philip Ziegler's understanding of Bonhoeffer's ethics as "metaethical" which is more concerned with describing God and his grace, thus reality as moral, than prescribing human actions. Philip Ziegler, "'Completely Within God's Doing': Soteriology as Meta-Ethics in the Theology of Dietrich Bonhoeffer," in *Christ, Church, and World: New Studies in Bonhoeffer's Theology and Ethics*, ed. Michael Mawson and Philip G. Ziegler (London: T&T Clark, 2016), 101–17.

78. The church-world distinction has been emphasized in Bonhoeffer scholarship by those who interpret him in an Anabaptist light: for example, Mark Thiessen Nation, "Discipleship in a World Full of Nazis: Dietrich Bonhoeffer's Polyphonic Pacifism as Social Ethics," in *The Wisdom of the Cross: Essays in Honor of John Howard Yoder*, ed. Stanley Hauerwas, et al. (Eugene, OR: Wipf and Stock, 1999), 249–77, and Stanley Hauerwas, *Performing the Faith: Bonhoeffer and the Practice of Nonviolence* (Grand Rapids, MI: Brazos, 2004), 33–72. For a critique of the Anabaptist interpretation, especially with regard to pacifism, see Michael P. DeJonge, *Bonhoeffer's Reception of Luther* (Oxford: Oxford University Press, 2017), 142–82.

79. DBWE 5, 28. First emphasis added. Second emphasis is Bonhoeffer's.

80. DBWE 5, 38–44.

81. DBWE 5, 48–118.

82. For the antithesis between cheap grace and costly grace, see DBWE 4, 43–56.

83. DBWE 4, 67.

84. DBWE 4, 49: "A Christian's secular vocation receives new recognition from the gospel only to the extent that it is carried on while following Jesus."

85. DBWE 4, 110–14.

86. DBWE 4, 175. Emphasis added.

87. DBWE 4, 208: "The break with the world is absolute."

88. DBWE 4, 210.

89. This seems to me to be a major concern of *Life Together*. DBWE 5.

90. DBWE 4, 225–52. See David S. Yeago, "The Church as Polity? The Lutheran Context of Robert Jenson's Ecclesiology," in *Trinity, Time, and Church: A Response to the Theology of Robert W. Jenson*, ed. Colin E. Gunton (Grand Rapids, MI: Eerdmans, 2000), 201–37. Compare Bonhoeffer, "Lecture on the Path of Young Illegal Theologians of the Confessing Church, October 26, 1938," in DBWE 15, 422:

Church is not a community of souls, as is claimed today, nor is church merely the proclamation of the gospel; that is to say, church is not only the pulpit, but church is the real body of Christ on earth. Church is an ordered and differentiated commonwealth constituted on this earth by, and grounded in, God. Just as Jesus Christ was not a truth or an idea but flesh, that is to say, a human being in the body, likewise the church is the earthly body of the heavenly head.

91. For a broader study of Bonhoeffer's understanding of the world, see Ernst Feil, *The Theology of Dietrich Bonhoeffer*, trans. Martin Rumscheidt (Philadelphia: Fortress, 1985), 99–205. More recently, see Joel Lawrence, *Bonhoeffer: A Guide for the Perplexed* (London: T&T Clark, 2010), 54–76, and many essays in John W. de Gruchy, Stephen Plant, and Christiane Tietz, eds., *Dietrich Bonhoeffers Theologie heute: Ein Weg zwischen Fundamentalismus und Säkularismus?* (Gütersloh: Gütersloher Verlagshaus, 2009). Jens Zimmermann has also addressed the theme of the church-world relationship in Christ cogently: Jens Zimmermann, "Suffering with the World: The Continuing Relevance of Dietrich Bonhoeffer's Theology," in *Dietrich Bonhoeffer Jahrbuch 3: 2007/2008*, ed. Clifford J. Green, et al. (Gütersloh: Gütersloher Verlagshaus, 2008), 311–37.

92. DBWE 4, 218.
93. DBWE 4, 218–19.
94. DBWE 4, 219.
95. DBWE 4, 220.
96. Bonhoeffer's connection of the temple as the place set apart for God's gracious dwelling to Christ and the church is illuminating in this regard. DBWE 4, 223–24.
97. DBWE 4, 225.
98. DBWE 4, 226.
99. DBWE 4, 226–28.
100. DBWE 4, 228–29.
101. DBWE 4, 229–32.
102. Compare DBWE 4, 210: "Christians who are actively involved in the church-community take a step out of the world, their work, and family; they visibly stand in the community with Jesus Christ."
103. Eberhard Bethge's periodization of Bonhoeffer's life tends to emphasize these kinds of discontinuities even though Bethge sees more continuity than discontinuity across the periods. See his comments on Bonhoeffer as "man for his times" which he became in 1939: Bethge, *Dietrich Bonhoeffer,* 676–78. For an example of a scholar who sees some discontinuity between *Discipleship* and *Letters and Papers from Prison*, see Matthew D. Kirkpatrick, *Attacks on Christendom in a World Come of Age: Kierkegaard, Bonhoeffer, and the Question of "Religionless Christianity"* (Eugene, OR: Pickwick, 2011), 198–204. Kirkpatrick believes, for example, that Bonhoeffer is changing his notion of sin in *Letters and Papers*, "steering—whether consciously or not—away from Luther and Kierkegaard on this matter" (200). For the most extreme position of which I am aware, see David M. Gides, *Pacifism, Just War, and Tyrannicide: Bonhoeffer's Church-World Theology and His Changing Forms*

of Political Thinking and Involvement (Eugene, OR: Pickwick, 2011), who argues that Bonhoeffer's worldly, secular involvement in phase 4 (1939–45) has "absolutely nothing in common" with his earlier involvement in the church in phase 3, London and the Finkenwalde period (pp. 335–36).

104. DBWE 6, 58.

105. DBWE 8, 451. On Bonhoeffer's "worldly theology" and its earlier manifestations, see Clifford J. Green, "Sociality, Discipleship, and Worldly Theology in Bonhoeffer's Christian Humanism," in *Being Human, Becoming Human: Dietrich Bonhoeffer and Social Thought*, ed. Jens Zimmermann and Brian Gregor (Eugene, OR: Pickwick, 2010): 71–90.

106. DBWE 8, 429.

107. DBWE 8, 429. On this concept, see Wolf Krötke, "Dietrich Bonhoeffer's 'Nonreligious Interpretation of Biblical Concepts' and the Current Missionary Challenge of the Church," in *Karl Barth and Dietrich Bonhoeffer: Theologians for a Post-Christian World* (Grand Rapids, MI: Baker, 2019), 232–45.

108. DBWE 8, 457: "One must not find fault with people in their worldliness but rather confront them with God where they are strongest. . . . The Word of God does not ally itself with this rebellion of mistrust, this rebellion from below. Instead, it reigns." See the next chapter for more on this point.

109. Krötke, "Bonhoeffer's 'Nonreligious Interpretation,'" 236.

110. DBWE 8, 479.

111. Florian Schmitz observes this with regard to *Discipleship* and *Ethics*: "*Discipleship* and *Ethics* do not differ from each other as far as the essential Christological assumptions are concerned." Florian Schmitz, "Reading *Discipleship* and *Ethics* Together: Implications for Ethics and Public Life," in *Interpreting Bonhoeffer: Historical Perspectives, Emerging Issues*, ed. Clifford J. Green and Guy C. Carter (Minneapolis: Fortress, 2013), 151. Clifford Green also sees Bonhoeffer's "worldly theology" already in the 1933 address "Thy Kingdom Come." Green, "Sociality, Discipleship, and Worldly Theology," 71–90.

112. DBWE 6, 58. This echoes the 1933 Christology lectures in which Christ is the "center of history." DBWE 12, 325–26.

113. See chapter 2.

114. DBWE 6, 60.

115. Hence, the footnote, "See *Discipleship*." DBWE 6, 62n.1.

116. DBWE 6, 63.

117. The second chapter, "Ethics as Formation," may be an exception because it focuses on the Christ-church relationship, but even here conformation to Christ is not becoming religious but "new human beings [who] live in the world like anyone else" (DBWE 6, 95).

118. Although some see Bonhoeffer distancing himself from traditional ecclesial Christianity in the prison letters, Bonhoeffer's concern for the *disciplina arcana* shows his continuing concern for the church in its unique Christological identity. See DBWE 8, 365, 373, and 390. To understand Bonhoeffer's concept and the early church context, see John W. Matthews, "Responsible Sharing of the Mystery of the Christian Faith: *Disciplina Arcani* in the Life and Theology of Dietrich Bonhoeffer,"

in *Reflections on Bonhoeffer: Essays in Honor of F. Burton Nelson*, ed. Geffrey B. Kelly and C. John Weborg (Chicago: Covenant Publications, 1999), 114–26. The importance of the church is also revealed in Bonhoeffer's "outline for a book," chapter 3, which shows Bonhoeffer's desire for ecclesial repentance: DBWE 8, 503–4. In addition, the nonreligious *interpretation* of theological concepts is itself a way of understanding preaching and mission. As Wolf Krötke notes, Bonhoeffer recognizes the church as genuine community for others as "a necessary precondition for speaking the Word of God," but Bonhoeffer still expects it to speak God's Word. (Krötke, "Bonhoeffer's 'Nonreligious Interpretation,'" 244–45.) For another argument for the ecclesial nature of the prison letters, see Barry Harvey, "The Narrow Path: Sociality, Ecclesiology, and the Polyphony of Life in the Thought of Dietrich Bonhoeffer," in *Being Human, Becoming Human: Dietrich Bonhoeffer and Social Thought*, ed. Jens Zimmermann and Brian Gregor (Eugene, OR: Pickwick, 2010), 102–23.

119. Compare DBWE 6, 68: "This belonging together of God and world that is grounded in Christ does not allow static spatial boundaries, nor does it remove the difference between church-community and world."

120. Thus, in prison, Bonhoeffer writes, "I still stand by it [*Discipleship*]" even as he also "clearly see[s] the dangers of that book." DBWE 6, 486.

121. For a sketch of how Bonhoeffer's letters were interpreted among the death of God theologians, see Martin Marty, *Dietrich Bonhoeffer's Letters and Papers from Prison: A Biography* (Princeton, NJ: Princeton University press, 2011), 119–32. Among evangelicals, see Richard Weikart, *The Myth of Dietrich Bonhoeffer: Is His Theology Evangelical?* (San Francisco: International Scholars Publications, 1997).

122. Compare Kirkpatrick, *Attacks on Christendom*, 191: "Idealist religion has painted Christianity according to certain ideas: a belief in God as omnipotent and transcendent, of God as the answer to life, of humankind's identity forged in his weakness and guilt, of separation of the eternal from the temporal, the internal from the external. Bonhoeffer's contention is that on each point, Christianity is entirely the opposite."

123. Such an interpretation always stretched the reality of a thorough reading of Bonhoeffer's writings from prison. As Wolf Krötke has observed, Bonhoeffer's piety, including his trust in God's providence, remains quite traditional in prison, and this piety "was, without doubt, foundational for his thinking." Wolf Krötke, "'God's Hand and Guidance': Dietrich Bonhoeffer's Language for God in a Time of Resistance," in *Karl Barth and Dietrich Bonhoeffer: Theologians for a Post-Christian World* (Grand Rapids, MI: Baker, 2019), 204.

124. Wolf Krötke, "Dietrich Bonhoeffer's Understanding of God," in *Karl Barth and Dietrich Bonhoeffer: Theologians for a Post-Christian World* (Grand Rapids, MI: Baker, 2019), 166–76. See also Zimmermann, "Suffering with the World," 315–26.

125. DBWE 8, 373. Emphasis original.

126. Compare "Church and World I" in DBWE 6, 342–44, where Bonhoeffer brings together both the "exclusive claim" of Jesus—what I am naming as the Christ-church relation—and the "all-encompassing claim"—the Christ-world relation. These come together to form the church-world relation: "The more exclusively we

recognize and confess Christ as our Lord, the more will be disclosed to us the breadth of Christ's Lordship" (344).

127. Mawson, "Christ Existing as Community: The Ethics of Bonhoeffer's Ecclesiology," 70–75; and Mawson, *Christ Existing as Community*, 48–51.

128. Mawson, *Christ Existing as Community*, 50: "The decisive insight of theology, then, is that there is no such abstract standpoint or even human being; there is only ever the one who has been created, has fallen into sin, and is reconciled in Christ."

129. Bonhoeffer structures *Sanctorum Communio* according to "primal state," "sin and broken community," being in Adam, and *sanctorum communio* as being in Christ. DBWE 1, 58–134. Bonhoeffer structures *Act and Being* according to "being in Adam" and "being in Christ." As such, Bonhoeffer uses ontological categories but the basic narrative of creation, fall, and salvation functions in his categories. DBWE 2, 136–61. See also Mawson, "Christ Existing as Community: The Ethics of Bonhoeffer's Ecclesiology," 72–73.

130. DBWE 5, 62.

131. DBWE 6, 68: "To speak of the world without speaking of Christ is pure abstraction." Compare Philip Ziegler, *Militant Grace: The Apocalyptic Turn and the Future of Christian Theology* (Grand Rapids, MI: Baker Academic, 2018), 178–80: "Reconciliation in Jesus Christ is constitutive of reality," for Bonhoeffer.

132. Yoder, *Priestly Kingdom*, 11. Compare Ziegler, *Militant Grace*, 180: "Only *trust* that reality has in fact been decisively constituted by God's apocalypse in Christ underwrites 'serious' grappling with moral life in the world." Emphasis added.

133. Eva Harasta, "Bonhoeffer's Lutheran Ecclesiology and Inter-Religious Dialogue: A Dogmatic Reading of Bonhoeffer," in *Bonhoeffer and Interpretative Theory: Essays on Methods and Understanding*, ed. Peter Frick (Frankfurt am Main: Peter Lang, 2013), 247.

134. As before this is a "real historical dialectic," not a conceptual or formal one (DBWE 1, 62). Eva Harasta too recognizes this tension in Bonhoeffer who affirms "the multitude of ways in which Christ relates to reality as a whole," which "strikes a balance between the universal claim of reconciliation in Christ and the interest in the particular function of the church." Harasta, "Bonhoeffer's Lutheran Ecclesiology," 245–46.

135. For example, see Stanley Hauerwas, *Community of Character: Toward a Constructive Christian Social Ethic* (Notre Dame: Notre Dame University Press, 1981), 10: Christians are to "serve the world on their own terms; otherwise the world would have no means to know itself as the world."

136. Hauerwas, *Community of Character*, 10.

137. Hauerwas, *Community of Character*, 10.

138. DBWE 8, 480.

139. Compare Wolf Krötke, "The Church as 'Provisional Representation' of the Whole World," in *Karl Barth and Dietrich Bonhoeffer: Theologians for a Post-Christian World*, trans. John P. Burgess (Grand Rapids, MI: Baker Academic, 2019), 121: "The church is that part of the world that already realizes and represents in its life that which in Christ has been offered to all."

140. Bonhoeffer's "After Ten Years" is this kind of reading of the world. DBWE 8, 37–52. "Parables of the kingdom" is what Karl Barth calls such words of the world that speak the truth of the Word, Jesus. Karl Barth, *Church Dogmatics*, vol. 4, part 3.1, ed. G.W. Bromiley and T.F. Torrance (1961; reprint, Peabody, MA: Hendrickson, 2010), 114.

141. On the importance of "with" instead of the usual "for," see Samuel Wells, *A Nazareth Manifesto: Being with God* (Malden, MA: Wiley Blackwell, 2015).

142. Jennifer M. McBride, *The Church for the World: A Theology of Public Witness* (Oxford: Oxford University Press, 2012) stresses repentance as the mode of the church's public witness. For McBride, repentance "is the politically intelligible expression of the liturgy of confession of sin; the communal, public proclamation of the all-embracing lordship of Christ; and the church's reorientation toward this world" (147). See also Matthew D. Lundberg, "Repentance as Paradigm for Christian Mission," *Journal of Ecumenical Studies* 45, no. 2 (2010): 201–17.

143. Using the categories of Jürgen Moltmann, *The Coming of God: Christian Eschatology*, trans. Margaret Kohl (Minneapolis: Fortress, 1996), 25–26.

144. Samuel Wells' emphasis on "being with" masterfully illumines this point in light of the gospel: Wells, *Nazareth Manifesto*. See also the earlier Samuel Wells and Marcia A. Owens, *Living Without Enemies: Being Present in the Midst of Violence* (Downers Grove, IL: IVP, 2011).

145. For Bonhoeffer on race, see Reggie L. Williams, "Dietrich Bonhoeffer, the Harlem Renaissance, and the Black Christ," in *Bonhoeffer, Christ and Culture*, ed. Keith L. Johnson and Timothy Larsen (Downers Grove, IL: IVP Academic, 2013), 59–72. For my own attempt to think through race, see Theodore J. Hopkins and Mark A. Koschmann, "Faithful Witness in Wounded Cities: Congregations and Race in America," *Lutheran Mission Matters* 4, no. 2 (2016): 247–63.

146. DBWE 1, 62. See Mawson, "Christ Existing as Community: The Ethics of Bonhoeffer's Ecclesiology," 72–73.

147. Against James Davison Hunter, *To Change the World: The Irony, Tragedy, and Possibility of Christianity in the Late Modern World* (Oxford: Oxford University Press, 2010), 231, and Jane Barter Moulaison, *Thinking Christ: Christology and Contemporary Critics* (Minneapolis: Fortress, 2012), 9. Even if affirmation might be the right first move in the contemporary context, I disagree with Hunter that affirmation can be specified as the "first moment" in the church-world relationship in the abstract. The story of Christ certainly affirms the world, but in a world that refuses to see itself as creation and or act like God is King, is it right to affirm that world *first* in every circumstance? For instance, should Bonhoeffer have affirmed the Nazi world in Germany before distinguishing the church from it during the Finkenwalde period? I do not think so. Some circumstances require antithesis first and then affirmation.

148. Compare DBWE 6, 66: "The church-community's relation to the world is completely determined by God's relation to the world."

149. DBWE 6, 67–68: "The church-community is separated from the world only by this: it believes in the reality of being accepted by God—a reality that belongs to the whole world."

150. DBWE 6, 62.

151. On the importance of narrative, see Stanley Hauerwas and L. Gregory Jones, eds., *Why Narrative? Readings in Narrative Theology* (Eugene, OR: Wipf & Stock, 1997). One of the most influential thinkers on narrative for me is Alasdair MacIntyre, *After Virtue: A Study in Moral Theory* 3rd ed. (Notre Dame: Notre Dame University Press, 2007), 216: "man is in his actions and practice, as well as in his fictions, essentially a story-telling animal" (216). See also Charlotte Linde, *Working the Past: Narrative and Institutional Memory* (Oxford: Oxford University Press, 2009), 3–4: "Narrative is one very important way that institutions construct their presentations of who they are and what they have done in the past, and they use these pasts in the present as an attempt to shape their future."

152. William Cavanaugh also argues that Christ's humiliation is essential to make sense of the relationship between the church and the world. William T. Cavanaugh, "Sinfulness and Visibility of the Church," in *Migrations of the Holy: God, State, and the Political Meaning of the Church* (Grand Rapids, MI: Eerdmans, 2011), 141–69.

153. This is the critique Nathan Kerr levels against Stanley Hauerwas. Nathan R. Kerr, *Christ, History and Apocalyptic: The Politics of Christian Mission* (Eugene, OR: Cascade, 2009), 101–16. Kerr contends,

> Hauerwas conceives of Jesus' relation to the church in such a way that who Jesus is *outside* of the church can really only ever be a kind of hermeneutical function of the internal linguistic and narrative construct that is the church's habits, practices, and institutions.... Thus, when I say that Christ's identity as Lord is itself a "hermeneutical function" of the church, I am suggesting that for Hauerwas Christ is "outside" the church in a way that is reducible to the Christian community's consistent interpretation of its own "internal" story. (111, emphasis original)

154. This is also an implication of the doctrine of justification. DBWE 5, 62: "Our salvation is 'from outside ourselves' (*extra nos*). I find salvation not in my life story, but only in the story of Jesus Christ."

155. The multiple pictures of Jesus in the Scriptures, the four Gospels and the many pictures in the rest of the Scriptures, impede easy systematization, such as an all-compassing metanarrative. This is theologically significant since Christ is more than any picture of him, and his Word must judge all theological systemization.

156. DBWE 5, 62.

157. DBWE 5, 62.

158. DBWE 12, 318–19.

159. Such a local perspective does not deny the importance of ecumenism, but it would shape ecumenism to be more focused on local efforts. I would suggest that doctrinal agreement is necessary to enable faithful ecumenism at the local level. Certainly, Bonhoeffer was critical of ecumenical efforts without doctrinal substance even as he prioritized ecumenism. See Bonhoeffer, "On the Theological Foundation of the Work of the World Alliance," in DBWE 11, 356–69. For a helpful perspective on Bonhoeffer's life as a confessor of faith in ecumenical contexts, see Richard H. Bliese, "Dietrich Bonhoeffer (1906–1945)," in *Twentieth-Century Lutheran Theologians*, ed. Mark C. Mattes (Göttingen: Vandenhoeck & Ruprecht, 2013), 223–48.

160. The overall scope of my project compares favorably with James K. A. Smith, "The Logic of Incarnation: Towards a Catholic Postmodernism," in *The Logic of Incarnation: James K. A. Smith's Critique of Postmodern Religion*, ed. Neal DeRoo and Brian Lightbody (Eugene, OR: Pickwick, 2009), 3–37, who sees immanence and transcendence brought together in the "logic of incarnation." This too is my broader point simply focused around the transcendence of Christ's person that remains while he is immanent in his church. The story of Christ shows the same thing: the transcendent God dwelling in the flesh among us (John 1:14).

161. Healy, *Church, World and the Christian Life*, 9–10. Healy's chapter two is also relevant to this discussion.

162. Luke Bretherton names both listening to Scripture and listening to others as central tasks: *Christianity and Contemporary Politics: The Conditions and Possibilities of Faithful Witness* (Malden, MA: Wiley-Blackwell, 2010), 98–101. See also my "Theology in a Post-Christian Context: Two Stories, Two Tasks," *Concordia Theological Journal* 4, no. 2 (Spring 2017): 55–57.

163. Parish thinking rightly emphasizes the importance of local places and the significance of geography for mission. See Eric O. Jacobsen, *The Space Between: A Christian Engagement with the Built Environment* (Grand Rapids, MI: Baker Academic, 2012); Paul Sparks, Tim Soerens, and Dwight J. Friesen, *The New Parish: How Neighborhood Churches Are Transforming Mission, Discipleship and Community* (Downers Grove, IL: IVP Books, 2014); and Mark T. Mulder, *Congregations, Neighborhoods, Places* (Grand Rapids, MI: Calvin College Press, 2018).

164. James K. A. Smith, *Who's Afraid of Postmodernism? Taking Derrida, Lyotard, and Foucault to Church* (Grand Rapids, MI: Baker Academic, 2006), 142.

165. To be clear, the church remains hidden, just as Christ is hidden under the opposite of the cross even as he is the revelation of God in the flesh. My focus on visibility does not deny this epistemological perspective of the theology of the cross; visibility rather points toward Christ's own call to faithfulness to him. For Bonhoeffer's understanding of the entailments of the theology of the cross in discipleship and responsibility, see H. Gaylon Barker, *The Cross of Reality: Luther's Theologia Crucis and Bonhoeffer's Christology* (Minneapolis: Fortress, 2015), 421–22.

Chapter 4

Jesus Christ, Lord and Servant
A Storied Ecclesiology for Post-Christendom

The church is not properly defined in itself but in its fundamental relationships to Christ and the world. The church is the church as it knows Christ as the transcendent Lord who is graciously present within it. Hence, ecclesiology is not first about describing the church's institutional structures, but knowing Jesus and being formed into his mission in the world. To identify the church and shape its mission within the Christ-church-world triad, this chapter tells two necessary, interconnected, and mutually enriching stories of Jesus: Christ the Lord and Christ the Servant.[1] Although these two accounts could be told as one—Christ the Lord who serves or Christ the servant who rules—they are best kept distinct as two true narratives to be understood dialectically. By this method, I intend to give equal weight to the lordship and servanthood of Christ so that Christology retains the priority in shaping the church-world relation through the Christ-church and Christ-world relationships.

The Bible's narrative Christology is multifaceted, and a number of stories can be presented that identify Jesus and proclaim the good news.[2] This chapter provides the accounts of Christ the Lord and Christ the Servant both because of their prominence in Scripture and because Dietrich Bonhoeffer's work shapes the church-world relation around one or both of these narrative arcs. Bonhoeffer's Christological center remains stable, but how he employs Christology to shape the church does change. In some texts, he gives precedence to the lordship of Jesus and in others his gracious condescension and humiliation. In traditional Lutheran categories, Bonhoeffer employs Christology in order to more effectively bring the church to repentance, faith, and obedience to the triune God, to proclaim law and gospel. In my construal of these two stories, the account of Christ the Lord prioritizes the Christ-church relation and its entailments for the church-world relation.[3] The story of Christ the Servant accentuates the Christ-world relationship and its entailments for the church-world relation.⁴ By holding both narratives together in dialectical tension, the Christ-church and Christ-world relations mutually inform the church-world relation. Whereas many theologians tend to dissolve the Christ-church-world triad into one primary relationship, Bonhoeffer's Christology grounds a dialectical approach that can address both sectarianism and cultural captivity, over-identification of the church with Christ, and the dissolution of the church into the world.

This chapter offers both a critical account of Christ's story, identifying the church within the work of Christ alone and calling it to repentance and obedient discipleship, and a constructive account of Christ's mission, helping congregations imagine their mission in the world in the way of Jesus. In other words, this chapter offers ecclesiological readings of the Gospels that attend to and enact the Christ-church-world dialectics. These readings are intended to be heuristic, helping practitioners to teach and proclaim the Scriptures with concrete communities and a specific church-world relation in mind.⁵ As the Scriptures are opened to see the dynamic of Christ-church-world with Christ himself at the center, God's people are led to repentance, further faith in the Lord, and are formed by the Spirit into Christ's mission in a local community.

The chapter is organized into two major sections: Christ and the Lord and Christ the Servant. Each major section could be its own chapter, but I have chosen to place them together in one chapter to highlight the necessity of both narratives for ecclesiology. Neither story of Jesus ought to be separated from the other even as distinguishing between them is necessary for proclaiming the Scriptures with the goal of ecclesial repentance and faithfulness. The first major section begins by establishing the centrality of Jesus' lordship in the Bible before exploring the importance of this account for North America after Christendom. The biblical heart of the section comes next: the story of the Lord Jesus, which focuses on the Gospel of Luke and the Christ-church relation. Finally, I draw out the ecclesiological implications in conversation primarily with Bonhoeffer's *Discipleship*. We will see how the narrative of Jesus the Lord cements the church's identity in Christ, differentiates the church from the world by its continual orientation to Christ, and calls the church to his mission in obedient discipleship.

The narrative of the Lord Jesus cannot be divorced from the story of Christ the Servant, which follows as the second major section. The account of Jesus the Servant recognizes the suffering Servant as foundational to Paul and the Gospels, emphasizing the humiliation of the Lord and the Christ-world relation. Then, I discuss the importance of the narrative of Christ the Servant in light of the problem of politics in the North American church. The scriptural center of the section follows: the story of Christ's servanthood from incarnation to his death upon the cross reveals the shape of Christ's ministry in the world. Finally, I bring the story of Christ the servant to bear on ecclesiology in conversation with *Letters and Papers from Prison* and *Ethics*. I contend that embodying the ministry of Christ the servant entails first the church's solidarity with the world in mission from below, second giving priority to the world's welfare, and third repentance as the proper disposition of the church vis-à-vis the world.

JESUS CHRIST THE LORD: ECCLESIAL IDENTITY AND DISCIPLESHIP IN THE CHRIST-CHURCH RELATION

The predominant New Testament confession of Jesus consists of two words: *Iesus Kyrios*, Jesus is Lord. In the book of Romans, Saint Paul writes, "If you confess with your mouth that Jesus is Lord and believe in your heart that God raised him from the dead, you will be saved" (Rom. 10:9). The early church historian J.N.D. Kelly notes that "Jesus is Lord" is the "most popular" of the brief Christological confessions in the New Testament.[6] The gospel of Luke, in particular, features the title Lord prominently. New Testament scholar C. Kavin Rowe has shown how Luke's Christology unfolds the meaning of the lordship of Jesus throughout the narrative of Jesus' life.[7] In other words, as Luke renders the identity of Jesus Christ, he shows his readers who Jesus is as Lord and what his lordship means in the narrative flow of Luke's Gospel.[8]

The lordship of Jesus is thus an essential tenet of the Christian faith, and its meaning is at least twofold. On the one hand, the confession of Jesus as Lord harkens back to the Old Testament, especially the Septuagint, and the confession of Yahweh as Lord. By calling him Lord (κύριος) Jesus' identity is intricately related to the identity of the God of Abraham, Isaac, and Jacob. Rowe argues, "Luke positions κύριος within the movement of the narrative in such a way as to narrate the relation between God and Jesus as one of inseparability, to the point that they are bound together in a shared identity as κύριος."[9] For Rowe, this connection is not a *Vermischungsidentität*, a blending or mixing of identity, but a *Verbindungsidentität*, a linking of identity.[10] In fact, the God of Abraham, Isaac, and Jacob makes himself definitively known in the Lord Jesus, and the identity of Jesus is properly understood in intimate relation with his Father, God, and also in connection to the whole story of Abraham, Isaac, Israel, and their descendants.[11]

On the other hand, the proclamation of Jesus as Lord is always a counter-proclamation. That is, Jesus is proclaimed as Lord over and against other possible lords. In the New Testament period, the proclamation of Jesus' lordship naturally conflicted with the Roman confession that Caesar is lord.[12] New Testament scholar N.T. Wright points to the Johannine narrative of Jesus' trial before Pilate as a conflict between "not just two kings but two types of kingdoms."[13] Wright continues, "Pilate stands for the world, the world made by God but run by Caesar; Jesus stands for the kingdom of God, as announced by psalms and prophets, by Isaiah and Daniel."[14] In this scene where Pilate faced Jesus,

> Jesus has come, he says, to bear witness to the truth; and Pilate's famous response, "What is truth?", indicates the gulf between the two empires. Caesar's empire knows only the truth of Roman rule, the truth that comes out of the scabbard of a sword (or, as we would say, the barrel of a gun): the "truth" of taxes and whips, of nails and crosses, the truth that will swap Jesus for a brigand if that's what the crowd wants, the truth that lets Pilate wriggle of one hook while impaling Jesus on another.[15]

To confess Jesus as Lord is to renounce the coercive power and self-serving violence perpetrated by Pilate, Caesar, and all idolatrous authorities that demand the same.[16] The early Christian confession of Jesus' lordship, then, functioned polemically, pointing out idolatry and calling the church to Christ alone and to testify to his lordship over all.

In this second sense of the lordship of Jesus, especially, the confession of Jesus as Lord highlights the Christ-church relationship and the difference of the church from all other communities. The church worships *this* Lord and no other, the man Jesus of Nazareth, who was murdered on a cross but God raised his Son from the dead by the Spirit. In the Lord Jesus, the church finds life and identity, and it lives always by repentance and faith, turning to Christ, and following him.

The Necessity of the Story of the Lord in North America

Although most scholars recognize the theocentric nature of the church's identity and purpose, the American church's history reveals something quite different. Historically, the American church has acted like a chaplain to the American project.[17] Even now, the American church often acts like its purpose is therapeutic, helping individuals in their own stories of self-fulfillment.[18] The resulting individualism identifies the church according to felt needs rather than the story and mission of the triune God.[19] With church membership seemingly based upon an individual's choice and religious organizations ostensibly existing for the sake of societal or individual well-being,[20] the church in North America desperately needs to hear the story of God's work in Christ that makes the church what it is and incorporates it into the divine mission.

In the story of the Lord Jesus, the church is created not by its own choice but by God's choice and purpose. The church's origin is in the authority of the Lord's voice and call, its ongoing existence stems from his continued presence through the Spirit, and its goal is formation into Christ, which Jesus realizes in the church as it hears his Word in faith, and is shaped by the Spirit into a life of discipleship. In this way, the story of the Lord Jesus decisively distinguishes the church from any community organized by the therapeutic story of self-fulfillment.[21] The church is not a therapeutic community, intended to help an individual on her self-chosen journey. Neither is the church beholden to the nation-state to make good citizens according to the rules of the state.[22] Rather, the church lives in the ongoing story of Jesus and his mission, and its purpose comes from Christ alone. The story of Christ the Lord shows how the church takes form as a community different from the world, given its identity in Jesus, and called to witness to the world in obedience to the Lord of the world.

The Lord Jesus: A Narrative Rendering for Ecclesiology

In the story of the Lord Jesus, I am following Luke's Gospel because, as C. Kavin Rowe demonstrates, "for Luke, to narrate the life of Jesus is to write of ὁ κύριος [the Lord]."[23] The Gospel of Luke begins with the story of Zechariah and Elizabeth and the promise of their son John who is "to make ready for the Lord a people prepared" (1:17). Speaking to Mary in Luke 1, the angel Gabriel announces that God will give her son "the throne of his father David, and he will reign over the house of Jacob forever," and he will be called "the Son of God" (1:32–33). Luke thus identifies Jesus from the beginning of his story as the promised King of Israel, the Lord even in the womb of his mother (1:43) and the anointed one who has come to save his people and establish God's reign.[24]

At the time of Jesus, Israel waited in eager anticipation for the Shalom of God's reign as it suffered under Roman rule. Worse yet—though this was not as widely recognized—Israel mourned under the same tyranny of sin, death, and the devil that overshadowed the entire creation. N.T. Wright explains,

> Week after week, and year after year, Israel kept alive the memory of what YHWH had done in the past to show that he was king, both of Israel and of the whole world and so kept alive the hope that his kingdom would soon come, and his will be done, on earth as it was (they believed) in heaven. God's kingdom, to the Jew-in-the-village in the first half of the first century, meant the coming vindication of Israel, victory over the pagans, the eventual gift of peace, justice and prosperity.[25]

Following this hope, when Zechariah is filled with the Holy Spirit at John's birth in Luke 1, he prophesies that the Lord is raising up a "horn of salvation" for his people Israel as he promised of old "that we should be saved from our enemies and from the hand of all who hate us; to show the mercy promised to our fathers and to remember his holy covenant" (1:68–72). Zechariah acknowledges that Israel lies in the grasp of its enemies, in need of the salvation of the one true King.[26] Zechariah confesses the longing and hope of Israel that God is coming to fulfill his promises.[27] The King is coming to reign on earth so that his people can "serve him without fear in holiness and righteousness before him all our days," have "knowledge of salvation," and "the forgiveness of their sins" (1:74–79).

In Luke 4, the "programmatic" scene of the book, Jesus emerges from his baptism and temptation to go into Galilee anointed by the Holy Spirit.[28] The first act of his public ministry is to teach in the synagogues, proclaiming the year of the Lord's favor. In Nazareth, Jesus opens the scroll of Isaiah to read from chapter 61: "The Spirit of the Lord is upon me because he has anointed me to proclaim good news to the poor. He has sent me to proclaim liberty to the captives and recovering of sight to the blind, to set at liberty those who are oppressed, to proclaim the year of the Lord's favor" (Lk 4:18–19). With these profound words, Jesus proclaims that he is the promised Servant and Messiah. He is the one anointed by the Spirit to free God's people from their enemies, proclaim the Word of freedom to captives, heal the blind, and bring a new Jubilee, inaugurating the eschatological kingdom of God and making Israel what it is supposed to be.[29] Through Christ's presence and work, Israel will no longer be enslaved to its enemies, and the poor will no longer be in bondage; the lepers, the paralyzed, and the blind will be made whole, and the demon-possessed will be free. Jesus promises to fill the people with the Shalom of God, providing eschatological peace even in the face of opposition.[30] This proclamation of Luke 4 begins to be realized in Jesus' ministry through the rest of the story,[31] as the Lord makes visible the reign of God on the earth, primarily through preaching.[32]

The Lord's Initiative and the Repentant Response

Luke 5 establishes the community of disciples who repent of their sins, confess their faith, and proclaim the good news of the Lord and his coming kingdom. In this text, we see the proper relation of the Lord and his church.[33] The chapter begins with Jesus preaching to a crowd as the crowd presses him against the Sea of Galilee. In order to be heard by the people, Jesus enters a nearby boat, belonging to Simon Peter. The most important part of this pericope occurs when Jesus is finished teaching and he addresses Peter directly: "Put out into the deep and let down your nets for a catch" (5:4). Simon is incredulous—they had been fishing all night and caught nothing—but he obeys nonetheless. In the deep part of the lake, Peter puts down the nets, and to his consternation the nets are jammed full of fish and are ripping at the seams. Another boat is called to help, but the sheer weight of the fish begins to capsize the boats. Peter recognizes that this catch did not come from his own skill, virtue, or hard work, but from Jesus. Back on shore, Peter falls before Jesus, taking the proper posture before his Lord, and confesses, "Depart from me, for I am a sinful man, O Lord [κύριε]" (5:8).[34] Precisely because Jesus is the Lord, Simon is afraid and recognizes himself as a sinner.[35]

Luke 5 demonstrates that the lordship of Jesus requires repentance and confession, and it shows the mercy of the Lord. After all, Jesus gives Simon all of these fish, grants him a new identity in him, and calls him to follow by Christ's initiative and grace alone. In the same way, the Lord Jesus creates his church, marking sinners with the triune name in baptism and incorporating them into his body by his effort and mercy alone. Before the Lord, the church falls upon its knees, acknowledging its sinfulness and confessing its need.[36] To his church, Jesus graciously speaks, just as he did to Simon: "Do not be afraid; from now on you will be catching men" (5:10). Through the Word and work of the Lord Jesus, Simon—and by extension the church—is distinguished from the world, given identity in Christ and called to his mission.

Obedience to the Lord Jesus in Mission

At the end of the story of the miraculous catch of fish, the disciples leave everything and follow the Lord. Such obedience to Christ is a prominent feature not only of the narrative portions of Luke but also the didactic sections. In Luke 9, Jesus first acknowledges to his disciples the kind of Lord he is, the Lord of the cross. After Peter confesses him to be "the Christ of God" (9:20), Jesus tells the Twelve what it means to be the Christ: he will suffer and die at the hands of the religious leaders before being raised from the dead. For Jesus, suffering and cross are not mere coincidences of his mission; they mark his reign, and he expects them to mark the disciples' lives too. "If anyone would come after me, let him deny himself and take up his cross and follow me. For whoever would save his life will lose it, but whoever loses his life for my sake will save it" (9:23–24). To be in community with Jesus means to follow him, even to suffering and death. If Jesus is truly Lord—and anything else claiming lordship is an idol and a fraud—then the disciples must put Jesus above all, even if that means obedience unto death.[37]

What Jesus says about obedience and cross in Luke 9:23–27 is enacted in verses 57–62.[38] As Jesus sets out to Jerusalem, three people address or are addressed by Jesus to follow him. The first comes to Jesus promising to follow him wherever he goes. Jesus responds enigmatically, "Foxes have holes, and birds of the air have nests, but the Son of Man has nowhere to lay his head" (9:58). Those who try to follow Jesus without Christ's Word cannot. Christ always holds the initiative and the priority over his church, and no one follows Jesus without his prior Word.[39] To the second, Jesus calls for him to follow, but he evades the immediacy of the call, asking the "Lord" if he can first "go and bury my father" (9:59). Failing to recognize the depth of the title with which he addresses Jesus, κύριε, the man sees Christ only as a master among masters.[40] Jesus thus commands, "Leave the dead to bury their own dead. But as for you, go and proclaim the kingdom of God" (9:60). Like the first, the third approaches Jesus of his own accord, saying that he will follow the Lord but only on certain conditions. He must first say farewell to his family.[41] Jesus will not allow anything to be placed above himself, and he responds, "No one who puts his hand to the plow and looks back is fit for the kingdom of God" (9:62).

Although the whole account is instructive, Jesus' authority as Lord is accentuated in his directive to the second man. This second man appealed to bury his father, an appeal to the law of God. Jesus, however, directly opposes the law by his own authority.[42] Jesus does not even bother explaining his extraordinary demand, nor does he try to rationalize the man's options by appealing to the purpose of the mandate.[43] Instead, Jesus' authority is the point at issue, and Jesus places himself above the law. Dietrich Bonhoeffer comments, "A clear command of the law stands between the one called and Jesus. Jesus' call forcefully challenges this gap. Under no circumstances is anything permitted to come between Jesus and the one called, even that which is greatest and holiest, even the law."[44] Jesus commands obedience from his disciples, demanding that his people put aside all other things and follow him. Since Jesus is Lord, his disciples must cast off everything that prevents them from following Jesus and put him first.

The Non-Violent Way of Jesus

As Luke progresses, the verbal confrontations with the politico-religious leaders escalate and the potential for violence intensifies. In the midst of these explosive circumstances, Jesus turns expectations for his lordship upside down. Luke tells of a dispute among the disciples as to which was the greatest (22:24–30). As Jesus explains it, the Gentiles, the pagans, exercise lordship in terms of coercive power, but Jesus is different: "I am among you as the one who serves" (22:27). Although contemporary Christians too easily misunderstand Jesus to be talking about a merely heavenly or spiritual rule, Jesus' point is not that. As John Howard Yoder comments, "The alternative to how kings of the earth rule is not 'spirituality' but servanthood."[45] Jesus has come to truly rule as the Lord, but he reigns in God's way, the way of servanthood, not the way of sinful, power-hungry humanity. The Lord Jesus is not like pagan kings; he is a different kind of Lord, refusing violence and coercive power and serving in love according to the reign of God.

In the garden of Gethsemane, Jesus shows just how committed he is to the nonviolent way of God. When the mob led by Judas arrives, the disciples want to pull their swords and fight off the mob. One strikes with his sword and cuts off a ear from the high priest's servant. Jesus rebukes his disciples—"No more of this!"—and he heals the ear of his enemy (Lk 22:51). Even in the face of an armed enemy, Jesus will not deviate from his way of lordship.[46] The cross only deepens the centrality of suffering, service, and nonviolence to Jesus' lordship, disclosing the chasm between the way of the world and the way of the Lord and calling his church to live by faith and obedience to him.

Summary

The narrative of Jesus the Lord depicts the story of sinners incorporated into Christ's own body, repenting from sinful ways and finding new identity and mission in Christ alone. As I have sketched it, the story of the Lord Jesus emphasizes the Christ-church relation, though it already points to Christ's lordship over the whole world and his mission to the world in service. The narrative of the Lord emphasizes three characteristics of the Christ-church relation: Jesus' initiative in creating his disciples and sending them on his mission, the response of the church in repentance and obedience, and the distinction of the church from the ways of the world. First, the church does not stem from its own ideals, effort, or will, but from the will and work of the triune God. Jesus thus says to his disciples in John's Gospel: "You did not choose me, but I chose you and appointed you that you should go and bear fruit" (15:16). As illustrated in the story of Peter's call, Jesus creates the church by his power and will, and the church finds its origin, mission, and goal only in Jesus. Second, the story of the Lord Jesus stresses the proper response of the church in repentance and obedience. Since Jesus is Lord, the church must repent of all the ways it has acted like something else is its master and lord. Additionally, the church's mission is not self-chosen but belongs to Jesus, and congregations are called to obedience in following his mission of preaching the gospel and seeking justice in the world. The mission of Christ will receive more detail in the next section on the servanthood of Jesus, but here an emphasis on the lordship of Jesus decisively turns the church to doing Christ's mission in obedience to his way. Third, the story of the Lord Jesus stresses the church's difference from the sinful age. The church must repent of how it has incorporated worldly wisdom and worldly ways that do not correspond to the way of Christ. The church must read the

Scriptures, ready to critique itself and repent for all of the ways it has failed to know itself in Christ and follow him in obedience.

Embodying the Story of the Lord Jesus in *Discipleship*

The lordship of Jesus stands at the center of Dietrich Bonhoeffer's most famous work *Discipleship*, in which Bonhoeffer insists that the twentieth-century Protestant church in Germany must find its identity and purpose in Christ alone. Within a context that pressured Christian faith to be private and personal, Bonhoeffer proclaims the lordship of Jesus and demands obedience *in* the church and *by* the church.[47] In so doing, Bonhoeffer connects the church's identity—justification—completely in Christ (the Christ-church relation), which leads to the response of faith in obedience and mission (the church-world relation). The church's relationship with Christ is not private, nor merely spiritual, but results in a publicly formed life of faithfulness to the Lord.

Bonhoeffer's response to the ecclesial context in Germany is relevant for the North American church after Christendom. Just as Bonhoeffer's Germany attempted to render the church apolitical and private, the North American context often places the church within a therapeutic frame of individual well-being. Against these privatizing forces, an ecclesiology formed by the story of Christ the Lord focuses on the church's identity in Christ given through the Word, the church's difference from the sinful world in repentance, and its mission to God's world in proclamation and service. In the prior chapter, we saw how *Discipleship* distinguished church and world through the Christ-centered identity and purpose of the church. This section places *Discipleship* more clearly within its historical context in order to show how the story of the Lord Jesus functioned theologically and pastorally in Bonhoeffer's context and consider what the narrative of the Lord Jesus means for the church today. Otherwise stated, Bonhoeffer's portrayal and use of the Lord Jesus in *Discipleship* illumines how this story directs the church to Christ alone, distinguishes the church from the world, and calls the church back to its identity and mission found in Holy Scripture.

Discipleship began to take form in the early 1930s as Bonhoeffer became interested in the Sermon on the Mount and its relationship to the Christian life. When Bonhoeffer was called to serve as the director of a Confessing Church seminary, first at Zingst and then at Finkenwalde, the Berlin theologian developed this theme into lectures for the seminarians, which were incorporated into the published book.[48] Although Bonhoeffer's friend and authoritative biographer Eberhard Bethge sees "both the theme and the underlying thesis" of *Discipleship* as "fully evolved before 1933,"[49] *Discipleship* must be understood within the political and ecclesiological context of the Confessing Church and National Socialism, the German church struggle, rather than Bonhoeffer's personal development.[50]

The church struggle (*Kirchenkampf*) was an ecclesiological conflict between the German Christian movement and the confessing church for control over the Protestant church in Germany.[51] The German Christians sought to fuse Germanness into the Protestant church, and create a church fully supportive of the Führer and Nazi policies.[52] Even so-called "neutrals," those like Paul Althaus who were neither German Christians nor part of the confessing church, severed the church as a *Christian* community from the public, political sphere, asserting that the government controls public matters of law and order and the church can only support the government.[53] In this perspective, the church, baptism, and the sacraments were set "into an ahistorical place 'before God,' which is to be marked off carefully from any location within earthly historical common life."[54] Bonhoeffer's *Discipleship* rejects such an invisible or spiritual understanding of the church, focusing on the Christ-church relation and placing the church in the story of the Lord Jesus in the Scriptures rather than the story of the German Christians.

Discipleship begins with a polemic against cheap grace.[55] Cheap grace allows the church to claim Christianity for itself, absent an encounter with the Lord Jesus and the marks of his lordship. Bonhoeffer argues that cheap grace, in contrast to costly grace, is a mere idea under human control. Cheap grace is a principle or a concept that can be presumed rather than the concrete grace of Christ that confronts and transforms people.[56] Cheap grace, then, isolates people from encountering the Lord, severing the church from true repentance, discipleship, and obedience. In contrast, true grace is the authoritative Word and call of the Lord Christ.[57] Grace is the encounter with Jesus wherein the Lord calls people to trust in him and follow him in obedience.[58] Without an encounter with the Lord, cheap grace eliminates the distinction between church and world, sanctifying sin without transforming sinners.[59] In the perspective of cheap grace, Christians live in the world and *like the world*, merely "going occasionally from the sphere of the world to the sphere of the church, in order to be reassured there of the forgiveness of my sins."[60] Whereas the true grace of the Lord Jesus renews sinners for faith and discipleship, Bonhoeffer believes that cheap grace dissolves Christian identity into the social and economic identity of the *Volk*.

To combat the Lutheran tendency to bypass the Lord's commands by making grace cheap,[61] the Berlin theologian brings faith and obedience together: "*only the believers obey*, and *only the obedient believe*."[62] Bonhoeffer's point is not to put faith before obedience or obedience before faith, but to unite them as close as possible, both dependent on Christ and his call.[63] Just as

Jesus called Levi directly in the Gospels,[64] the Lord today calls sinners by his Word, transforming them by faith and leading them to obedient discipleship.[65] Bonhoeffer observes how the church in Germany has evaded obedience to Jesus through principles and ideas, justifying the status quo and their bourgeois status. Bonhoeffer points the eyes of the church away from scholarship that rationalizes Christ's call and directs Christians to the Lord Jesus who is known in the Bible. "We cannot and may not go behind the word of scripture to the actual events. Instead, we are called to follow Christ by the entire word of scripture."[66] Jesus issues his call to the church today to follow him through preaching, and Bonhoeffer expects the church to simply obey.[67] Jesus is the living Lord, and his Word is heard in the church, which is to be trusted and followed.

The first part of *Discipleship* places Christians in the story of the Lord Jesus, who speaks the authoritative Word of life that creates faith anew, transforms sinners into disciples, and brings them to obey in community with the Lord. In the second part of the book, Bonhoeffer focuses on the contemporary church-community as part of the same story of the Lord Jesus. According to Bonhoeffer, "What the Synoptics describe as hearing and following the call to discipleship, Paul expresses with the concept of *baptism*."[68] By connecting Christ's call to the Word of Jesus in the church, Bonhoeffer resists a sharp distinction between the Twelve and the contemporary church.[69] Because Christ is present in the church as the crucified and risen one, the call of the Lord in baptism is not substantially different from his call to the apostles. The same Lord speaks the same powerful Word to recreate his people, giving them faith and bringing them to himself. Just as the apostles were distinguished from the crowds through the Word of Jesus, baptism too "implies a *break*. Christ invades the realm of Satan and lays hold of those who belong to him, thereby creating his church-community."[70] The Lord Jesus creates the church through baptism, demarcating his people from the fallen world, and making them new as his body.

Although the Lord calls his people away from sin to trust in him and follow in obedience,[71] the church that lives by the story of the Lord does not leave the world. Instead, the church takes up physical space *in* God's creation, as *part* of it, and called *to* it in Christ's mission.[72] For Bonhoeffer, the community of Jesus is a community within the creation, just as visible as the incarnate Son of God: "The body of the exalted Lord is likewise a visible body, taking the form of the church-community."[73] Bonhoeffer's point is not that the church is visible *in toto*; rather, as William Cavanaugh opines, "just because the boundaries of the church are invisible, it does not mean that the center is invisible as well."[74] For Bonhoeffer, this center is the Word of God preached and visible in the sacraments, consistent with the marks of the church in Luther's theology.[75] These marks must be visible, and in these marks the church takes space on earth. Although the institutional form of the church is not irrelevant,[76] most importantly for Bonhoeffer, the church must make space for proclamation, for witness to Jesus Christ in preaching and the sacraments. In proclamation, Jesus creates and sustains his church, giving identity in him by faith and sending his people on his mission in obedience.[77]

After describing the visibility of the church in terms of these distinctive church practices, Bonhoeffer emphasizes the life of the church *in the world* following the Lord. Because the Lord Jesus is the *incarnate* God, who is the Lord of all things, Bonhoeffer reasons,

> Jesus' community with his disciples was all-encompassing, extending to all areas of life. The individual's entire life was lived within this community of the disciples. And this community is a living witness to the bodily humanity of the Son of God. The bodily presence of the Son of God demands the bodily commitment to him and with him throughout one's daily life. With all of our bodily living existence, we belong to him who took on a human body for our sake.[78]

The church that lives in community with the Lord Jesus and by his story does not leave the world behind. Rather, the incarnation of the Son of God entails a bodily lordship and a bodily church. In other words, the human Jesus is Lord of life, *body* and soul, and his church is called to obedience and faithfulness not only in spiritual things, but also in the world in social, political, and bodily matters.[79] Christians are called into the world to witness and serve God's world not on the world's terms, but *as Christians*, living out their "secular" vocations in the world within "very definite *limits*," which are defined by Christ and the church.[80] The incarnate Christ calls his church to live in God's creation, looking different from the world even while participating in the goodness of the natural, created world, and witnessing to it of the hope of the risen Lord.[81] Although Bonhoeffer starkly divides the church from the world in Nazi Germany,[82] Bonhoeffer's understanding of the visible church that follows Christ the Lord requires the church to love justice, proclaim Christ's lordship, and pursue his way in the world.

For the Confessing Church and all Christians in Germany who were faced with the choice of joining the oppressors or being oppressed,[83] Bonhoeffer's *Discipleship* grounds the church in Jesus, the one who works through the Word—written, oral, and tangible—to create a people for himself and call them to follow in obedience by his Spirit. Bonhoeffer stresses that Christians are not good Germans or spiritual gurus or even those who believe in grace. Christians are those encountered by the Lord Jesus, called to trust in him and follow him in real life in the world. Jesus acts as Lord not in an ephemeral, spiritual realm, but on earth in the church through preaching, sacraments, and the church's life.

Conclusion

The story of the Lord first calls the church to repent of all that ways that it has ignored Christ's Word and failed to trust and follow. And the American church has much for which to repent! As evidenced by the individualism of American Christianity as well as the inadequacy of so many Christians and churches to stand up for people of color and do justice in local neighborhoods, most congregations are more concerned about their own members and their own needs than the story and mission of the Lord Jesus. As a sinful community that acknowledges its sin, the church must be a community of repentance, turning away from power, privilege, and other sins.[84] The Spirit effects such repentance through the story of the Lord Jesus, as the Word opens the church's ears to, for instance, hear Christ's commands anew to proclaim the gospel to *all nations*, know itself as sinful and broken along with the world, and learn service to the least of these, the poor and the vulnerable. Through the story of the Lord, the Spirit calls the church to turn from ways of sin and power, attend to the Word of Christ in the Scriptures, trust in him, and follow in his mission. The church may not choose for itself what works to do, determine whom it wishes to serve, or decide what message to proclaim. Turning away from all self-chosen or merely culturally acceptable ways and works, the church receives its identity and its purpose from the Lord Christ and lives continually in his way by the Word. The story of the Lord Jesus calls the church to know itself in Christ, listen to him, and be formed by the Spirit into his mission.

As the church is identified completely in the Lord Jesus and called to repentance, faith, and obedience, the church is distinguished from the world. As I discussed in the prior chapter, the church-world distinction is part and parcel of the Christ-church relation. For David Gides, however, an ecclesiology that distinguishes church and world, like the one in *Discipleship*, is problematic because it entails political quietism. Gides argues that Bonhoeffer's stance in *Discipleship* represents an "apolitical church-against-world stance."[85] By emphasizing the difference between the church and the world, Gides contends that Bonhoeffer "removes the necessary foundations for meaningful interaction [between church and world], leading to a vision of the church that appears unconcerned with happenings in the political realm."[86] For Gides, Bonhoeffer's emphasis on the church's relationship to the Lord separates the church from the world and makes it difficult for the church to positively influence the world.

Does an unwavering identification of the church with Christ the Lord create a sect that cannot speak to the world? I suggest that the opposite is in fact the case. The church only speaks the truth of the *gospel* and embodies the *gospel* in the world when it knows itself in Christ fully and completely. After all, the church's witness is not designed primarily to make the world a better place.[87] The church's witness is about the Lord who died on the cross for the sins of the world and was raised for its justification. The church is only the church as Christ dies for it, rises from the dead, ascends to heaven, sends his Spirit to his people, preaches the Word of repentance and faith, baptizes sinners of all ages, gives his own body and blood, and calls it to his mission in the world. In other words, the church is only the church as it knows itself in the Lord Jesus. Apart from Christ, the church may be a nice group of people, even a just or kind people, but it is not God's church. The church that knows itself in the world primarily may engage in politics, but it will not do so *as the church*. To be clear, the Christ-church relation needs to be supplemented by the Christ-world relation, through the story of Christ the Servant, which will emphasize the solidarity of the church and the world, but the necessity of the other side of the dialectic does not undercut the importance of the Christ-church relation.

Bonhoeffer's *Discipleship* sought not to distinguish the church from the world first, as if to *separate* the church from the world, but Bonhoeffer located the church in Christ, who calls the community to faith in him and obedience in the world. In other words, Bonhoeffer's logic does not dichotomize church and world but realizes the church in its Christological identity and mission. Certainly, Bonhoeffer would not identify the church's public life exclusively (or primarily) in political or social terms, but that does not mean Bonhoeffer's church has no public role in society.[88] The church has a distinct calling to work publicly in the world continuing the mission of Christ in local congregations. It is political in that the church acknowledges Christ as King and seeks to embody his kingdom by word and deed, but it is not political in the sense of partisan politics. The difference of Christ's kingdom from the ways of the world can only be recognized and embodied when the church knows itself in Christ alone, confessing its story as Christ's story and living in faith and obedience to the Lord. Without its identity in Christ, the church loses its very nature as the body of Christ.

JESUS CHRIST THE SERVANT: SOLIDARITY AND MISSION IN THE CHRIST-WORLD RELATION

While the story of the Lord Jesus highlights the identity of the church in Christ mediated by God's Word, the church's obedience to Christ in the world, and the difference between the church and the world, another story is necessary to describe the Christ-world relation and its entailments for the church-world relationship. The story of Christ the servant complements the story of the Lord Jesus by illustrating the character of Christ's mission for and in the world. Furthermore, the story of Christ the Servant transforms the church to embody Christ's own cruciform mission in the world. By humility and repentance, the church follows Jesus into the world, not concerned for its own privilege or power but focused on being with the world and for it on Christ's mission.

The story of Jesus the Servant begins with the manner of his incarnation. The one who is very God of very God, of one substance with the Father, laid down his privilege, power, and glory to fully enter the human experience. Jesus could have become a man in glory, more powerful than any other king, but instead the Son of God came into the flesh under the confines of the law and in the likeness of sinful flesh. In Philippians 2, Paul affirms the equality of Jesus with the Father—"he was in the form of God"—yet Paul confesses that the same One "made himself nothing, taking the form of a servant."[89] From the incarnation, Jesus renounced the splendor that was due him as the Son of God, and became a human being not in the luxury and riches of a palace, but in a stable, born to poor parents with little authority or influence. All privilege, glory, and honor rightfully belong to Jesus, but he gave it up for the sake of the world in his incarnation and concomitant humiliation.

The story of Christ's servanthood is not confined to Philippians 2, but is "Paul's master story."[90] Throughout his letters,[91] Paul testifies to Christ's servanthood and calls the church to live in the same story.[92] Jesus enters into human history "in the likeness of *sinful* flesh," not in the likeness of perfect humanity.[93] He exercises his lordship through service, bearing sin for the world's sake, giving up the use of his power as Son of God, and working from a position of weakness.[94] Jesus gets his hands dirty, associating with sinners and outcasts, and being present with them in the sinful world in order that he might take humanity's place and save the world by his vicarious work of salvation.[95] Having received salvation as a gift of the Son through the Spirit by the Word, the church embodies the servant ministry of Jesus as it is led by the Spirit to continue Jesus' mission in the world. In this way, the story of Christ the servant "is a narrative to be both proclaimed and performed, or, perhaps better, proclaimed in deed as well as in word."[96]

The Necessity of the Story of the Servant in North America

Not only is the story of Christ's humiliation the foundational narrative of salvation, but the account of Christ the servant is particularly important in North America because political power has deconstructed public life.[97] Politics has become so central to the North American "social imaginary" that the mission of the church is difficult to envision void of partisan politics.[98] James Davison Hunter has shown how the North American church often succumbs to the will of power as the public manifestation of its witness. Instead of Christians actively engaging local spaces in the pursuit of justice, truth, and beauty, Christians lobby political parties and vote for their preferred ideology, fighting to take back the culture through partisan politics.[99]

The problem of power has become so acute that the credibility of the gospel itself is at stake.[100] The story of Christ the servant is a story of power subverted, how the Lord of all gives up the use of his power for the sake of others, but the narrative embodied by the church has commonly been one of *ressentiment*. *Ressentiment* is a narrative of entitlement and injury wherein the church (or another group) deserves power and glory that has been taken from it.[101] This narrative makes Christians more worried about retaining current privileges or recouping old privileges through the political process than they are concerned with witnessing winsomely to the gospel.[102]

In this light, Hunter's recommendation that churches remain silent on politics does not seem so radical: "It would be salutary for the church and its leadership to remain silent for a season until it learns how to engage politics and even talk about politics in ways that are non-Nietzschean."[103] The church needs to repent of its complicity in power politics, pray for God's forgiveness, and learn from the story of Christ the Servant how to engage the community in the way of Jesus. Once the church has learned repentance, living with the world in solidarity, doing mission from below, and putting the community first, then, perhaps the church will be able to testify to the truth of the gospel "in such a way that the world is changed and renewed."[104]

Christ the Servant: A Narrative Rendering for Ecclesiology

The ministry of Jesus begins not with a powerful miracle, an astute teaching, or an authoritative sermon but the reception of John's baptism for repentance and the remission of sins, establishing the character of Christ's mission. A number of theologians in the early church struggled to make sense of Christ's baptism, even appearing to be embarrassed by it. Both Ignatius of Antioch and Justin Martyr, for example, found it necessary to justify the need for Jesus' baptism, although it was otherwise an ancillary part of their respective theologies.[105] The main point of embarrassment concerns Jesus' relationship to sin. The beginning of Mark's Gospel announces that the Son of God receives "a baptism of repentance for the forgiveness of sins" from John the Baptist.[106] The logic is difficult to overcome: if baptism is for the remission of sins, then one who receives baptism must be a sinner.[107]

At this point of perplexity, the profundity of Jesus' person and work is revealed. The baptism of Jesus discloses how fully Jesus enters into his fallen creation. In Matthew 3, Jesus comes from Galilee to the wilderness of Judea, at the Jordan River, to be baptized by John. John had been baptizing, as New Testament scholar Jeffrey Gibbs explains, "for conversion from unbelief to faith, and for entrance into the people of God"; it was for "the lost sheep who were no longer members of the true Israel."[108] More than that, it was a baptism for all of Israel because all of Israel was sinful and separated from its proper God-ordained ruler, a king in David's line. Coming to the Jordan, Jesus entreats John to grant him this baptism of repentance, requesting to be numbered with sinners and with the true Israel in hope for the kingdom of heaven.[109] Jesus is not worried about being saved from his own sins; he is concerned about the sin of his people and the bondage to death and evil burdening Israel and the cosmos.[110] John, at first, refuses to comply: "I need to be baptized by you, and do you come to me?" After all, Matthew has described Jesus through the first two chapters as Israel's Savior, adored by kings and called out of Egypt as God's Son. Consequently, John objects, thinking that the Christ does not need such a baptism for repentance. Perhaps, John had normal expectations for the Messiah in first-century Palestine, believing that through Jesus Yahweh would renew Israel in a way similar to Maccabees or King David.[111] John's incredulity suggests that he anticipated the Messiah to be powerful and glorified according to the standards of the age.[112] Jesus was something different.

Jesus responds to John enigmatically: "Let it be so now, for thus it is fitting for us to fulfill all righteousness" (Matt. 3:15). How can being numbered with transgressors and being present with sinful Israel fulfill all righteousness? The righteousness fulfilled is not Jesus' individual ethical prowess as measured by the law; it is instead *God's* righteousness, not in the sense of God's innate holiness but in Luther's sense of God's eschatological saving deeds.[113] God had entered into the world in Jesus, and was accomplishing his salvation through this Nazarene. As Gibbs claims, this baptism of repentance fits perfectly with the eschatological saving deeds that Jesus will perform:

> It shows perfectly *how* this Jesus "will save his people from their sins" (1:21). It shows *how* the reign of heaven will come now, in an unexpected way. With John's participation, Jesus will perform "all righteousness," that is, he will enact God's saving deeds for the people by (literally) standing with sinners, taking the place of sinners, receiving from John the baptism that sinners receive. Ultimately, *all* of Jesus' ministry will come to its head as the Scriptures are fulfilled (26:54, 56) in the arrest that leads to his trial and condemnation and crucifixion. There the sinless one will offer up his own life as the ransom payment

in the place of the many. That's why it is "fitting" for Jesus to come and stand in the Jordan and be baptized, to stand (literally) *in the place of the many*.[114]

Jesus enters into the waters of baptism for repentance, standing in the place of sinful Israel—and by extension sinful humanity—embodying humanity's sinfulness through solidarity with his people.[115] Jesus fulfilled all righteousness not by differentiating himself from the sinful world nor demanding that he be recognized as the Lord through power. Instead, the Messiah came in humility, being immersed in the sinfulness of this age and being glad to be numbered among the transgressors from his baptism to his death upon the cross.[116] In this baptism of solidarity with sinners, God sends the Holy Spirit upon Jesus, confirming his identity as Servant and Son, accepting his repentance and anointing him for his mission: "This is my beloved Son, with whom I am well pleased" (Matt. 3:17).

The story of Jesus' baptism not only points forward to the crucifixion, but it also points backward to the incarnation. Jesus took "the form of a servant," came "in the likeness of sinful flesh," and accepted a status "under the law."[117] Although Jesus was fully Lord and God, he lived with sinners and among sinners, dwelling for thirty years in Nazareth.[118] Although he is the Creator of life and the Giver of all good things, the Son of God did not come into the world immune from sadness and sorrow. Instead, he was incarnate under the restrictions, boundaries, and limitations of the present age. Jesus entered so fully into the world and fallen human nature that Luther puts these words in Christ's mouth:

> For the sake of you, who were under the Law, I assumed your flesh and subjected Myself to the Law. That is, beyond the call of duty I went down into the same imprisonment, tyranny, and slavery of the Law under which you were serving as captives. I permitted the Law to lord it over Me, its Lord, to terrify Me, to subject Me to sin, death, and the wrath of God.[119]

As Luther elegantly describes, Jesus became not just a human being but a suffering servant, a slave; Jesus did not lord it over human beings or even the law. Rather, the Lord entered into human weakness and sin, became subject to the horrors of guilt, shame, and the wrath of God, and was regarded as a criminal in order to reconcile sinners to God in him.[120] Jesus' baptism thus reveals the reality of his humiliation: from the incarnation, Jesus entered into life with the creation, willingly bearing the fallen creation in his body to save the world.

This character of the humiliation—solidarity and service for others—marks the entirety of Jesus' life and ministry. In Matthew's Gospel, the Spirit immediately leads Jesus from his baptism into the wilderness to be tempted by the devil, like Adam had been tempted in the Garden and Israel in the wilderness beyond the Red Sea. Jesus' temptation was not play-acting with the outcome pre-determined. Such a view annuls the extent of the humiliation and leans toward a docetic view of Christ's person.[121] In fact, for Bonhoeffer, the temptation of Jesus was a more serious and more difficult temptation than Adam's in the Garden. "Adam bore nothing in himself that could have given the tempter any right or power over him."[122] Christ, however, "bore with him the entire burden of the flesh under the curse and condemnation."[123] Jesus carried "all covetousness and all fear of the flesh, all the flesh's condemnation by and distance from God was also in him."[124] Under this burden of sinful flesh, Jesus was weak and alone in the wilderness, yet alone Jesus came into "the deepest, most immediate bond with humanity."[125] By entering into the fullness of temptation, Jesus shows the extent of his solidarity with humanity and enacts his salvation in the place of sinners. The Gospel of Mark's short account emphasizes Christ's solidarity with the creation by adding that Jesus was *with* the wild beasts, among his creatures, becoming feeble in body and mind for the sake of the world.

In the story of Jesus' servanthood, not only is the Son of God determined to be with his creatures, he is also determined to suffer rather than seek his own glory.[126] Each of the synoptics, with more of the narrative details provided in Matthew and Mark, tells the story of James and John asking to be seated in glory with Jesus at his right and left hands.[127] Even though Jesus has been proclaiming his coming suffering and death, the disciples still see him through the lens of power. They expect Jesus to seize the throne and reign supreme over a kingdom with riches, glory, and strength. And they want to share in this splendor and wealth. Jesus, however, repudiates the premise of the question. Christ will not be glorified by acquiring a throne and presiding over a prosperous kingdom with an iron fist. Thus, Jesus directs the disciples to his cup, the cup of God's wrath, and his baptism, wherein he will suffer and die with and for criminals.[128] Just as Jesus placed himself in solidarity with sinners in his baptism, so too Jesus will be in solidarity with the fallen creation at the cross. Baptism and cross combine in the one fabric of Jesus' story as the suffering servant, wherein this baptism/cross *is* the glory of Jesus.[129]

Jesus has been leading the disciples to recognize the different ways of God's reign through parables,[130] aphorisms,[131] and other teachings,[132] but the disciples do not grasp Jesus' rebuke of James and John. They become indignant with the brothers (Mk 10:41), and Jesus spells out the way of God for them again. "The Gentiles," Jesus says, "lord it over others as ones who demand to be served. They are obsessed with status and power. But not you. You shall not demand service but shall become slaves of all. This is what I, the Son of Man, am doing for you and the world, giving my life as a ransom for many."¹³³ The world, Jesus says, concerns itself with such things as privilege and honor; its interminable pursuit of power and fame demolishes anyone in its way. Jesus, however, calls his church to a different way, his own, which is other-oriented service for the world. Jesus' death on the cross not only atones for the sins of the world, but it also indicates a new way of life for the apostles. Atonement itself calls the church away from the worldly ways of power and to the ways of the servanthood of Christ.¹³⁴

The story of Christ the Servant culminates in the events of Passion Week. On Thursday evening, while celebrating Passover with his disciples, Jesus kneels at their feet. Taking the customary place of a slave, the Lord washes his disciples' feet and calls them to do the same: "For I have given you an example, that you also should do as I have done for you."¹³⁵ After supper, they journey to Gethsemane. Alone in the garden, Jesus sweats drops of blood while praying to his Father and agonizing over the coming cup of his wrath. When the mob, led by Judas Iscariot, reaches the garden to capture Jesus, the "chain of abandonments" begins, starting with the apostles.¹³⁶ Despite his authority—his voice knocks the mob to the ground in John's Gospel¹³⁷—the Son of God allows himself to be taken captive by the religious leaders as the disciples flee. At trial, Jesus is oppressed and afflicted, but he hardly opens his mouth.¹³⁸ Pilate and Herod both despise and reject him: beating, whipping, and wounding him. For the transgressions of his people nails pierce Jesus' hands and feet as he is hung on a cross between two robbers. At this crucial moment, the Lord chooses to be with sinful humanity instead of with the Father, and Jesus is abandoned even by God: "My God, My God, why have you forsaken me?"¹³⁹ Jesus dies in one final act of solidarity with sinful humanity, making his grave with the wicked, in order that he might make many righteous by bearing their iniquities.

Embodying the Story of Christ the Servant

Although the traditional dogmatic understanding of Christ's state of humiliation ends with the resurrection, Luther and Bonhoeffer both confess the persistence of Christ's humble service to the world.¹⁴⁰ Raised from the dead and ascended to the right hand of the Father, Christ continues to be present for his creation in humility. According to Bonhoeffer, "even through the empty grave, Jesus remains incognito, in the form of a stumbling block. Jesus does not emerge from his incognito, *not even as the Risen One*. He will not lay it aside until he comes again, for the Last Judgment."¹⁴¹ Christ has been adorned with the spiritual body of the new age, yet he remains the humiliated One until the dawn of the new creation. He does not present himself in power with trumpets blaring and lightning flashing. With all authority given to him, Jesus uses his divine power to be present in the church by the humble means of the cross: feeble words, mundane water, and lowly bread and wine.

Christ's continuing servanthood exposes the church's prideful attempts to live by power and privilege rather than faith and humility. The church is not better than its Lord. Rather, the church has its unique identity in him, and its purpose also belongs to the same Christ. As such, the church is distinct from the world, as we saw above under the rubric of Christ the Lord, but it is not better or greater than the world. In fact, the church's uniqueness is not its set-apartness from the world at all, but its identity from and in the humiliated One, the Servant who refused to exploit the power that belonged to him, surrendering its use to God even to death upon the cross. The church that knows itself in the story of Christ the Servant confesses Christ's presence not as an exclusive possession but as a gracious gift for the world. Recognizing the world as intended recipient of God's salvation, the church also follows Christ's way of humility in and with the world of which it is one in the story of God.

As the church declines in power in North American society, many churches have tried political, institutional-sustaining solutions to retain their old privilege, but the story of Christ the Servant calls the church to mission in the world in a different way. Jesus transforms the church by his presence, first, to humble witness in solidarity with the world, participating in his mission from below. Consequently, the church that follows Christ the Servant is, second, outward-focused, the church *for others*, as Bonhoeffer asserts in *Letters and Papers from Prison*, not concerned for its own preservation but for the welfare of the world. Through solidarity with the world and working for its welfare from below, the church relates to the world, third, in repentant humility, which will be explored in conversation with Bonhoeffer's *Ethics*.

Too often, churches conceive of themselves as sacred spaces set apart from a hostile world.[142] In this understanding, the church identifies itself overagainst the sinful world, seeking to prevent the church from being stained with sin or evil. Some versions focus on the spiritual or heavenly nature of the church while other versions emphasize the church's different life and culture. In all versions, the church is God's own people, in God's hands, and the world is fallen, sinful, and in need of God's salvation. Such an understanding of the church-world relation fits with the Western pathos—though it does not correspond to the story of Christ the Servant—construing the world in terms of haves and have-nots.[143] This problematic perspective pervades Christian notions of justice and evangelism. Christians see themselves as the ones with power and knowledge, ready to dole out gifts to others in mercy.[144] The church has; the world does not.

The story of Christ the Servant, however, recognizes the world as a proper object of Christ's love and a fellow participant with the church in the gospel. In the incarnation, the Son of God dwells in the world, taking residence in the flesh, under human constraints. Jesus does not immediately save his people like a superhero from above, but gives up the use of his power and resides in his creation, abiding in Nazareth for decades.[145] Following Christ the Servant, then, the church does not envision its mission first as "working for" the world that is in need of the church but as "being with" the world that is paramount to the mission and work of God.[146] By being present with people in their community, listening to their stories, and receiving from them, congregations construe the world as part of its same story, the mission of God. Instead of regarding unchurched people by what they lack, they are recognized as truly human, made in God's image, part of the creation and redemption of God in Christ by the Spirit.[147]

Solidarity may not seem valuable, but, through prayer and presence, the church inhabits the story of Jesus who entered into life with sinful humanity as a servant, surrendering the divine prerogative in order to reconcile the world to the Father. Through its members, the church follows Jesus into life with "outsiders," receiving others, especially the vulnerable and the disadvantaged, as fellow creatures of God, redeemed by Christ, and sought by the Spirit. By entering into life with the world, congregations witness to those outside of its membership that no one is outside of the mercy of God or the love of Christ's body. Such a witness does not come with ready-made answers, but is fully present with broken people and vulnerable communities, slow to talk and quick to listen.[148] The goal of solidarity is not to get things done so that a congregation can feel better about itself by posting on social media about its accomplishments. Such "ministry" trades in power and privilege by generating a favorable image. Instead, the congregation's goal is to enter into life with people, serving the community from within. This will undoubtedly lead to working with and for the community, but fundamentally being with people treats them as valuable persons created and redeemed by God, who have something to give.

A congregation that lives in solidarity with its community will also live its mission differently: from below.[149] Embodying the servanthood of Christ means giving up on Christendom dreams of power and privilege and focusing instead on the ministry of Jesus, serving those on the margins in word and deed. In doing mission from below, churches should not primarily focus on getting more people into pews or even converting lost souls. Instead, congregations should be focused on being present with their communities, listening to the people, and serving them. To be clear, my point is *not* that the church ought to focus on social justice at the expense of proclaiming the gospel.[150] Verbal witness and social justice are not mutually exclusive options.[151] My point, rather, is that the story of Christ the Servant situates evangelism and justice within the context of a congregation's solidarity with the world. The church should not storm into a community preaching or doing justice without entering into life with it and investing itself in the neighborhood and its people. Mission from below means that the congregation first recognizes how it is part of the local community, learns from other community members, considers itself responsible for the community, and lives credibly in it before expecting the gospel of Jesus to gain a hearing.[152]

Faithful mission in the vein of Christ's servanthood never comes from a position of power, from the perspective of one who explains "the way things really are." Instead, mission from below either comes from the local community or partners with local people, showing that the project is not about assuaging guilt but serving people who matter to Jesus and to his church. Mission is never "our mission to them," where mission reinforces the boundaries between the church and the world. Rather, continuity and partnerships are key virtues for mission so that local people are honored, real needs understood, true justice pursued, and the gospel proclaimed by those with credibility. Only by developing relationships over time can an outside congregation truly begin to be with and work with a local people in service instead of primarily doing charity from a position of power.

Second, if the church is going to live in solidarity with the world and do mission from below, it must also give up its aspirations for privilege, power, and glory and focus on the welfare of the world. As the church declines in privilege in post-Christendom, the temptation to self-preservation looms large. Building endowments, sustaining institutions, and regaining political power appear more viable than the witness of the gospel. Bonhoeffer noticed this already taking place in Germany: the Confessing Church stood up for the cause of the church but without commitment to Jesus and his way.[153] The church only cared about "defending itself," strengthening its own power, and trying to retain its status in the world, while refusing to take risks for others.[154] Similarly, the contemporary North American church often shores up its strength, trying not to lose ground morally, politically, or ideologically rather than working for the sake of the world.[155]

This focus on self-preservation is not merely a practical problem—churches not practicing God's mission—it is deeply theological. Ecclesial self-preservation is institutional *cor curvum in se*, the heart curved in upon itself, hiding under the guise of religion, and is correlated with a misunderstanding of God.[156] The most common apologetic move for the church losing its privilege, Bonhoeffer argues, is to secure a safe space for religion. "So-called ultimate questions," like death, guilt, or the individual psyche, are placed into a special Christian sphere, where they are safe from scientific and political arguments.[157] Then, Christians try to convince people they are "in reality miserable and desperate," in need of God as their "guardian" and the Christian faith as their savior.[158] This method of apologetics attempts to create a religious problem by revealing people's weakness which Christianity can solve by its strength.[159]

Bonhoeffer believes, however, that such a method aimed against "the world that has come of age" is misguided.[160] For one thing, when Christianity is walled off into a separate sphere, triumphalism rears its ugly head since the church alone has access to the truth. As the only light and truth, the church convinces itself that it is morally better than and intellectually superior to the world, thereby repudiating its own story of sin and God's salvation. Another unintended consequence is that the church makes itself an expert in one sphere, but alienates itself from all others.[161] And, in Bonhoeffer's words, "God should not be smuggled in somewhere in the very last, secret place that is left. . . . Instead, [the Word of God] reigns."[162]

Worse yet, these attempts to convince the modern world that it needs God conceive of the deity in Greek philosophical terms rather than the reality of the God of the Bible.[163] The attempt to expose the weakness of the world—in its psychological need, debilitating guilt, or impending death—assumes the existence of an omnipotent deity who saves the weak world by strength and might. The true God, however, is not the God of abstract power, but the God of the cross.[164] The cross is the heart of God's own identity where God's strength is manifested in the weakness of suffering, and the greatest glory of God is in the shame of a man hanging dead upon a tree.[165] Bonhoeffer muses,

> God consents to be pushed out of the world and unto the cross; God is weak and powerless in the world and in precisely this way, and only so, is at our side and helps us. Matt. 8:17 makes it quite clear that Christ helps us not by virtue of his omnipotence but rather by virtue of his weakness and suffering! This is the crucial distinction between Christianity and all religions. Human religiosity directs people in need to the power of God in the world, God as *deus ex machina*. The Bible directs people toward the powerlessness and suffering of God; only the suffering God can help.[166]

The true God is not the deity of power, glory, or knowledge, as defined by human philosophy. The true God is clothed in the flesh of Jesus Christ, and reveals himself as this man, who is the Lord and suffering Servant.

Bonhoeffer proclaims Jesus as God in the flesh *pro aliis*, for others, in order to turn the church away from its sinful introspection, reinforced by false theology.[167] Immersed "in Jesus' life, his sayings, actions, suffering, and dying,"[168] the church is changed into the likeness of the same Lord, who deigned to become the Servant. After all, the church is only the church as Christ is present in it. Since the Christ present in the church is the same Lord who is the Servant, the church is called to serve the world with the same attitude as that of Christ Jesus: "The church is church only when it is there for others."[169] Such a church, Bonhoeffer says, should give away property to those in need, and pastors should live solely on free-will offerings while serving in other vocations.[170] Such a church should stop fighting for political power and lobbying for its interests, and focus on the welfare of the local community. Such a church should be less concerned with enforcing its morality by law, concentrating more on living the way of Christ in its preaching and work of justice locally. The church's proper mission rejects the power and privilege of North American politics and enacts Christ's service for the world.

Third, as the church embodies the story of Christ the servant, it recognizes the world as one story with it, living in repentant humility. After all, in God's story, the church is as broken and sinful as the world. All people are guilty of acting like their own gods, trying to become their own "self-creator, self-judge, and self-renewer."[171] Rather than claiming innocence, the church embodies the servanthood of Jesus by being "the place where this acknowledgement of guilt becomes real."[172] In worship, the church prays for forgiveness not only for itself but for the world, thereby taking responsibility before God of the world and recognizing itself as truly in the world.[173] In Bonhoeffer's words,

> The church-community of Jesus Christ is the place in which Christ is believed in and obeyed as the salvation of the whole world. Thus, from the beginning and by virtue of its very nature, the church-community stands in a place of responsibility for the world that God in Christ has loved. Wherever the church-community does not perceive this responsibility, it ceases to be a church-community of Christ.[174]

The church recognizes its responsibility to the world first by seeing the world as part of the story of Jesus Christ, and then living out that responsibility for the world in confession and prayer before God and in mission that serves the world.

Reflecting upon the Ten Commandments, Bonhoeffer called the church of his day to repentance, confessing not only its own sins vis-à-vis God but also the sins of the world, even "the Western world's falling away from Jesus Christ as guilt toward Jesus Christ."[175] The church stands guilty of "apostasy from Christ" as it has failed to bear witness to the truth of the gospel in a responsible way.[176] Bonhoeffer explains how the Decalogue details the church's sins vis-à-vis the world: its failure to proclaim God and his mercy to the despised, its condoning of injustice, its divinizing of youth, its silence in the face of murder, hate, and exploitation, and its preference for power and peace.[177] The church is guilty of plenty of its own sins, but Bonhoeffer goes further to contend that the church needs to repent also for the world's sins. The church has failed to embody Christ and his servanthood in the world, and it has given up on its proper mission in the world. In doing so, the church "became guilty for the loss of responsible action in society, courageous intervention, and the readiness to suffer for what is acknowledged as right. It is guilty of the government's falling away from Christ."[178]

Bonhoeffer's call for ecclesial repentance for society and the world may seem extreme, and in contemporary North America it may even seem like some Christianized version of political liberalism. Bonhoeffer, however, grounds the church's repentance in the cross of Christ and his humiliation as characteristic of his ministry. The church needs to repent because "confession of guilt is not something that one can take or leave; it is the form of Jesus Christ breaking through in the church," the form of the one who bore the sins of the world.[179] In confession of guilt the church is drawn into the cross, and begins to embody the servanthood of Jesus.[180] This is not about being a church that is relevant to the world, which, for instance, may be more interested in social justice than the gospel; rather, confession of guilt flows from the story of Christ's humiliation, which the church is formed to embody by the Word and Spirit.[181]

Trusting in Jesus and empowered by his Spirit through Word, the church takes responsibility before God for sin: its own sin and the sin of the world. In so doing, it follows the pattern of Christ who took the form of a servant and made himself nothing, serving the world and bearing its sin in order to bring reconciliation with the Father. The church thus accepts responsibility for the world before God, recognizing the world as proper object of Christ's salvation with the church. This confession and repentance compels the church to be in true solidarity with the world and thus also to engage the world in witness and service. When the church takes responsibility for the world in prayer and repentance, it cannot do mission from a position of power as if the world were less than the church. Instead, the church that knows itself from the cross acknowledges its true solidarity with the world in the one story of God. The church lives in repentant humility as it knows itself and the world only in Jesus, the Lord who served the cosmos to death upon a cross.

Conclusion

The story of Christ the Servant is counter not only to the ways of the world but also to the natural inclinations of the church in this age. Even justified and empowered by the Spirit, the church often does not consider the world as part of its same story, live in solidarity with its local community, doing mission from below, put the welfare of the community first, or take responsibility for others in repentant humility. Because of the persistence of sin, the whole life of the church is properly a life of repentance, not only vis-à-vis the Lord, but also in its relationship to the world. The church embodies the humiliation of Christ and the story of his servanthood not by bearing the sins of the world, but by abiding in and with the world, treating community members as partners in creation, and taking responsibility for the world as part of the same reality of God. Repenting of Christendom dreams of power and prestige, the church participates in Christ's mission with the world and for it.

LORD AND SERVANT: CHRIST-CHURCH-WORLD

The church-world relationship is not lived apart from the Lord or his Word but is properly situated in Christ: Christ-church-world. The stories of the Lord Jesus and Christ the Servant offer two ways to read the Scriptures to locate the church's identity and mission in Christ, and shape it for faithfulness in the world. These stories are not merely true narratives; they are self-involving, as the Spirit brings congregations to recognize themselves in these stories and forms them by the Word into the character of Christ. Bonhoeffer himself uses these two perspectives at different times to call the church to repentance, faith in Jesus, and faithfulness to Christ's mission.

Bonhoeffer shifts the focus of his theology from the Christ-church relation in *Discipleship* to the Christ-world relation in *Letters and Papers* (and some of the *Ethics* manuscripts) while both are concerned with the church-world relation at the same time. In the story of the Lord Jesus, as this chapter has recounted it, the Christ-church relation comes to the forefront as Jesus is recognized as the creator, sustainer, and transcendent Lord of the church, and the church receives its identity and purpose from him. The church is the people of God, the body of Christ, and the temple of the Holy Spirit because of the Word and presence of the crucified and risen Jesus within it. The church that loses its bearings in Jesus substitutes its proper identity and mission in Christ with worldly ways, becoming entangled in the powerplays of politics and privilege, which is what happened in Germany during the *Kirchenkampf*. To fight against these sinful temptations, the church needs to read the Scriptures against itself, hearing the living Word of God calling it to repentance and renewing its faith in the Lord by the Spirit.[182] The story of the Lord Jesus binds congregations to Christ and his ways, calling it to believe in and follow Jesus and nothing else.

In the story of Christ the Servant, the Christ-world relationship is paramount. Christ took upon himself not only human flesh but human sinfulness, coming into the world under the law, even though he is the sinless Lord of all. Christ bore the sins of the world "from his holy birth until his death,"[183] saving the world by assuming its sin, death, and evil into himself. Christ thus served the world, working *for others* and redeeming them by being fully present in their midst. By identifying the world in the mission of God as created, sinful, and redeemed, the story of Christ the Servant confesses the world as an equal participant with the church in the work of God. The church does not stand over the world, nor does the church have special privileges vis-à-vis God. Instead, the church stands in solidarity with the world as a fellow community of sinners for whom Christ bore sin and gave up his life. In this perspective, the church embodies the mission of Christ as it relinquishes visions of power and serves its communities locally from below. A Christian congregation repents not only of its own sins but the sins of the world since the church, like the world, is a community of sinners that needs the forgiveness of God in Christ, and the church is called to take responsibility for the world in humility. At the same time, such a congregation also prays for the world to join in its repentance and reception of God's grace and justice through his Word.

The narratives of Christ the Lord and Christ the Servant work together dialectically to bring the church to repent for not attending to the Word of God, following Christ's mission in obedience, or accepting its true solidarity with the world. Whether a congregation has overinflated itself as a sacred sanctuary separate from the sinful world or it has overidentified itself as part of the world's projects, the stories of Christ the Lord and Christ the Servant indicate where congregations have failed to embody the mission of Christ, call them to repentance and faith in Jesus, and grant them new eyes to see the world in Jesus. By preaching and teaching the gospel directed to the concrete circumstances of local congregations, the church lives by and in the Word, which not only creates it as the people of God but forms it to embody the mission of Christ in his world.

NOTES

1. Methodologically, I see my work paralleling the first two parts of the fourth volume of *Church Dogmatics* where Karl Barth describes "Jesus Christ, the Lord as Servant" (IV/1) and "Jesus Christ, the Servant as Lord" (IV/2). One difference is that Barth tends to cast these ways of speaking about Jesus in terms of the two-nature doctrine whereas my focus is on the Christ-church and Christ-world relations, though these cannot be strictly separated (as Barth also affirms). For a summary of the first three part-volumes, see Karl Barth, *Church Dogmatics*, vol. 4, part 1, ed. G.W. Bromiley and T.F. Torrance (1956; reprint, Peabody, MA: Hendrickson, 2010), 128–54.

2. See, for example, Richard A. Burridge, "From Titles to Stories: A Narrative Approach to the Dynamic Christologies of the New Testament," in *The Person of Christ*, ed. Stephen R. Holmes and Murray A. Rae (London: T&T Clark, 2005), 37–60.

3. The lordship of Jesus over the world is true, relevant, and necessary, but that will not be my focus in this chapter, following *Discipleship* in particular.

4. As with Christ's lordship, the humiliation of Christ in Word and sacraments is also essential to the Christ-church relation, but my focus will be the Christ-world relation, following *Letters and Papers from Prison* especially.

5. My work shares some similarities with the recent "homiletical theology." Michael Pasquarello argues that Bonhoeffer himself is a "homiletical theologian" who unites "faith, doctrine, character, and a concrete way of life shared by a community that is attentive and receptive to God, who speaks in the person of Christ." Michael Pasquarello III, *Dietrich: Bonhoeffer and the Theology of a Preaching Life* (Waco, TX: Baylor University Press, 2017), v.

6. J.N.D. Kelly, *Early Christian Creeds*, 3rd ed. (New York: David McKay Company, 1972), 14–15.

7. C. Kavin Rowe, *Early Narrative Christology: The Lord in the Gospel of Luke* (Berlin: de Gruyter, 2006), esp. 1–30.

8. On the Gospels as rendering the identity of Jesus, see Hans W. Frei, *The Identity of Jesus Christ: The Hermeneutical Bases of Dogmatic Theology* (Philadelphia: Fortress, 1975).

9. Rowe, *Early Narrative Christology*, 27.

10. Rowe, *Early Narrative Christology*, 27n.94.

11. Compare N.T. Wright, *Paul and the Faithfulness of God*, book I (Minneapolis: Fortress, 2013), 517–37, who speaks of the "back-story" to Paul's story of Jesus, contending for a "triple narrative" of Jesus the Messiah, Israel in person and the truly human one (p. 521). As I narrate these two stories of Christ, there is a danger of overlooking Christ as Israel in person and displacing Israel and Judaism. As a reminder to the reader, my two stories are heuristic, not comprehensive. I try to locate Jesus within the broader biblical story even though this book is not the place for a discussion of Christ's relationship to Judaism. For a helpful discussion of religious dialogue from a Lutheran perspective using Bonhoeffer, see Eva Harasta, "Bonhoeffer's Lutheran Ecclesiology and Inter-Religious Dialogue: A Dogmatic Reading of Bonhoeffer," in *Bonhoeffer and Interpretative Theory: Essays on Methods and Understanding*, ed. Peter Frick (Frankfurt am Main: Peter Lang, 2013), 239–50.

12. N.T. Wright, *Creation, Power, and Truth: The Gospel in a World of Cultural Confusion* (London: SPCK, 2013), 48–57. See also Jeffrey Kloha, "Making Christ's Reign Known: Church in the New Testament," in *Inviting Community*, ed. Robert Kolb and Theodore J. Hopkins (St. Louis: Concordia Seminary Press, 2013), 40–42. For a discussion of the social and political consequences for the earliest Christians, see Larry W. Hurtado, *How on Earth Did Jesus Become a God? Historical Questions about Earliest Devotion to Jesus* (Grand Rapids, MI: Eerdmans, 2005), 56–82.

13. Wright, *Creation, Power, and Truth*, 49.

14. Wright, *Creation, Power, and Truth*, 49.

15. Wright, *Creation, Power, and Truth*, 49.

16. Wright implicates modern imperialism in Caesar's kingdom in Wright, *Creation, Power, and Truth*, 35–65. For discussions of empire and the church today, see also Karen L. Bloomquist, ed., *Being the Church in the Midst of Empire: Trinitarian Reflections* (Minneapolis: Lutheran University Press, 2007), and Wes Avram, ed., *Anxious about Empire: Theological Essays on the New Global Realities* (Grand Rapids, MI: Brazos, 2004).

17. Cheryl M. Peterson, *Who Is the Church? An Ecclesiology for the Twenty-first Century* (Minneapolis: Fortress, 2013), 24–27.

18. For my account, see my "Narrating the Church at the Dusk of Christendom: How the Loss of Predominance Affects Congregations," *Concordia Journal* 43, no. 4 (2017): 29–41; and "Theology in a Post-Christian Context: Two Stories, Two Tasks," *Concordia Theological Journal* 4, no. 2 (Spring 2017): 43–57.

19. Robert N. Bellah et al., *Habits of the Heart: Individualism and Commitment in American Life*, Updated ed. (Berkeley, CA: University of California Press, 1996). See also Kenda Creasy Dean, *Almost Christian: What the Faith of Our Teenagers is Telling the American Church* (Oxford: Oxford University Press, 2010).

20. See Peterson, *Who Is the Church*, 24–32.

21. The importance of this difference is intensified in that the therapeutic matrix incorporates certain elements of the Christian story. See Eva Illouz, *Saving the Modern Soul: Therapy, Emotions, and the Culture of Self-Help* (Berkeley, CA: University of California Press, 2008), 184.

22. See Douglas John Hall, *The End of Christendom and the Future of Christianity* (Valley Forge, PA: Trinity Press International, 1997). See also Peterson, *Who Is the Church*, 1–32.

23. Rowe, *Early Narrative Christology*, 10. Richard Hays also emphasizes the narrative character of Luke's Christology, portraying Jesus as Lord: "To understand Luke's portrayal of Jesus, our reading must be attuned to Luke's subtle narrative art, for the identity of a character is best understood through the unfolding of events in a story." Richard B. Hays, *Echoes of Scripture in the Gospels* (Waco, TX: Baylor University Press, 2016), 224. Hays thus argues that Luke describes Jesus (among other things) "as Lord and God of Israel" (243–62).

24. Rowe, *Early Narrative Christology*, 39: "With [the words of Elizabeth in Luke 1:43,] Jesus himself appears in the narrative for the first time: ὁ κύριος in the womb."

25. N.T. Wright, *Jesus and the Victory of God* (Minneapolis: Fortress, 1996), 204.

26. I. Howard Marshall, "Political and Eschatological Language in Luke," in *Reading Luke: Interpretation, Reflection, Formation*, ed. Craig G. Bartholomew, Joel B. Green, and Anthony C. Thiselton (Grand Rapids, MI: Zondervan, 2005), 158: "The language is the language of political and military deliverance, the kind of things that might be done by a mighty king."

27. Joel Green notes the "eschatological anticipation" that pervades Luke 1:5–2:52. Joel B. Green, *The Gospel of Luke*, The New International Commentary on the New Testament Series (Grand Rapids, MI: Eerdmans, 1997), 59.

28. Rowe, *Early Narrative Christology*, 78, including n.1.

29. Rowe, *Early Narrative Christology*, 81: "Through the Spirit's anointed (4:18), Jesus' public debut and the inauguration of God's jubilee year coincide (4:19). In this way it is through the mission and life of Jesus that the Spirit of the Lord (4:18) makes possible the year of the Lord's favor (4:19)."

30. Joel Green emphasizes Jesus' initiative in the text: "at every step in his address at Nazareth he asserts the universal embrace of God's salvific purpose." Green, *Gospel of Luke*, 208.

31. Compare Rowe, *Early Narrative Christology*, 82.

32. James D.G. Dunn, *Jesus and the Spirit: A Study of the Religious and Charismatic Experience of Jesus and the First Christians as Reflected in the New Testament* (1975; reprint, Grand Rapids, MI: Eerdmans, 1997), 61. Compare Marshall, "Political and Eschatological Language in Luke," 161: the mission of Jesus is "'political' but . . . 'not as we know it.'"

33. Rowe, *Early Narrative Christology*, 82: "the larger concern in this passage is ecclesiological."

34. Compare Rowe, *Early Narrative Christology*, 82–89. For the significance and grammatical ambiguity of κύριε, see pp. 85–88.

35. "Jesus' being as Lord and Peter's being as a sinner are objectively correlated" (my translation). Rowe, *Early Narrative Christology*, 88: quoting Wolfgang Dietrich, *Das Petrusbild.der lukanischen Schriften* (Stuttgart: Kohlhammer, 1972), 51.

36. Compare Green, *Gospel of Luke*, 230: "The initial purpose of this episode is to secure for Luke's audience the nature of appropriate response to the ministry of Jesus."

37. Martin Luther's notion of repentance in connection to baptism in the Large Catechism shows how such repentance plays a daily role in the Christian life even in situations without persecution. Robert Kolb and Timothy J. Wengert, eds., *The Book of Concord: The Confessions of the Evangelical Lutheran Church* (Minneapolis: Fortress, 2000), 464–66.

38. Compare Green, *Gospel of Luke*, 400: "The primary emphasis on the formation of a people who embody the word of God . . . is not discarded but heightened with the onset of the journey narrative."

39. DBWE 4, 60: "The *first* disciple took the initiative to follow Jesus. He was not called."

40. On the textual questions related to κύριε and an argument to retain it in 9:59, see Rowe, *Early Narrative Christology*, 127–28.

41. DBWE 4, 61.

42. Compare Rowe, *Early Narrative Christology*, 131n.23, quoting E.P. Sanders, *Jesus and Judaism* (London: SCM, 1985), 254: "Jesus *consciously* requires disobedience of a commandment understood by all Jews to have been given by God." Emphasis original.

43. Rowe, *Early Narrative Christology*, 132: "No explanations for the demand are given, and there is no attempt at persuasion in light of the cost."

44. DBWE 4, 60.

45. John Howard Yoder, *The Politics of Jesus: Vicit Agnus Noster*, 2nd ed. (Grand Rapids, MI: Eerdmans, 1994), 39.

46. Compare Rowe, *Early Narrative Christology*, 181:

> In general terms, Jesus' identity as κύριος as displayed in these two Lukan passages [22:38 and 22:49] deconstructs the normal association of power (Lordship) with violence. The nature of Jesus' Lordship is radically misunderstood if interpreted as the power to destroy opponents by means of the sword.

47. I am reading *Discipleship* (DBWE 4) ecclesiologically whereas some read it more narrowly in terms of sanctification. Doing so, however, misses the fact that the second half of the book is epistemologically prior to the first half. The Christian listens to Jesus *because* she has been incorporated into his body by baptism. As Florian Schmitz notes, "From a structural point of view . . . the whole of the first part of *Discipleship* [receives its] right to actualization from the theology developed in the second main part of the book." Florian Schmitz, "'Only the believers obey, and only the obedient believe.' Notes on Dietrich Bonhoeffer's Biblical Hermeneutics with Reference to *Discipleship*," in *God Speaks to Us: Dietrich Bonhoeffer's Biblical Hermeneutics*, ed. Ralf K. Wüstenberg and Jens Zimmermann (Frankfurt am Main: Peter Lang, 2013), 182. Furthermore, much of *Discipleship* is explicitly directed toward the church-community. For instance, the preface names the present as a time of "church renewal," and the headings include "Visible Church Community," "Community of Disciples Is Set Apart," and the entire Part II on the Body of Christ. I would thus suggest that *Discipleship* is closer to a prophetic ecclesiology than a manual of sanctification, and sanctification is part of the life of the church.

48. Eberhard Bethge, *Dietrich Bonhoeffer: A Biography*, rev. ed., ed. Victoria J. Barnett (Minneapolis: Fortress, 2000), 450–51.

49. Bethge, *Bonhoeffer*, 457.

50. David S. Yeago, "The Church as Polity? The Lutheran Context of Robert Jenson's Ecclesiology," in *Trinity, Time, and Church: A Response to the Theology of Robert W. Jenson*, ed. Colin E. Gunton (Grand Rapids, MI: Eerdmans, 2000), 214–18.

51. See Victoria Barnett, *For the Soul of the People: Protestant Protest Against Hitler* (New York: Oxford University Press, 1992). For a perspective on the German church struggle as it was happening, see Karl Barth, *The German Church Conflict* (Richmond, VA: John Knox, 1965).

52. A good example of fusing Germanness in the church is the so-called "Aryan paragraph," that required proof of "pure" Aryan descent for one to be a pastor in the Protestant church. On the ideology of the German Christians and what kind of church they wanted to construct, see Doris Bergen, *Twisted Cross: The German Christian Movement in the Third Reich* (Chapel Hill, NC: University of North Carolina Press, 1996).

53. If it seems contradictory to be pushing German Christian ideology in the church while claiming to remain apolitical, Althaus seemed to believe that National Socialism was more movement than politics, part of the spirit of the times to which the church needed to adapt. Robert P. Ericksen, *Theologians Under Hitler: Gerhard Kittel, Paul Althaus, and Emanuel Hirsch* (New Haven, CT: Yale University Press, 1985), 85–86.

54. Yeago, "Church as Polity," 218.

55. DBWE 4, 43–56.

56. DBWE 4, 52–53. To understand Bonhoeffer's distinction of cheap and costly grace within the Lutheran understanding of justification, see Jonathan D. Sorum, "Cheap Grace, Costly Grace, and Just Plain Grace: Bonhoeffer's Defense of Justification by Faith Alone," *Lutheran Forum* 21, no. 3 (1993): 20–23.

57. DBWE 4, 57: "Jesus calls to discipleship, not as a teacher and a role model, but as the Christ, the Son of God."

58. Hence, Bonhoeffer's discussion of Peter: DBWE 4, 46.

59. DBWE 4, 50–51.

60. DBWE 4, 51.

61. DBWE 4, 53.

62. DBWE 4, 63. Emphases original.

63. Schmitz, "'Only the believers obey, and only the obedient believe,'" 171–75.

64. DBWE 4, 57.

65. Compare DBWE 4, 62: Jesus' call "creates existence anew."

66. DBWE 4, 82.

67. For Bonhoeffer, simple obedience is not easy, but neither is it legalism, which is often paired with biblicism. Rather, I think it is more like Luther's encouragement to Melanchthon to "sin boldly." Florian Schmitz argues that simple obedience for Bonhoeffer requires the "venture" of faith in which one behaves as if "it is exactly this behavior that is asked of him/her here and now." Schmitz, "'Only the believers obey, and only the obedient believe,'" 185.

68. DBWE 4, 207. Emphasis original.

69. DBWE 4, 202: "Christ speaks to us exactly as he spoke to them."

70. DBWE 4, 207. Emphasis original.

71. DBWE 4, 209–10.

72. DBWE 4, 225: "The Body of Christ takes up physical space here on earth."

73. DBWE 4, 226.

74. William T. Cavanaugh, *Migrations of the Holy: God, State, and the Political Meaning of the Church* (Grand Rapids, MI: Eerdmans, 2011), 152. Cavanaugh sees canonization of both texts and people as examples of visibility, consistent with Roman Catholic theology, but his point applies well to Bonhoeffer even though Bonhoeffer uses the Lutheran notion of the marks of the church.

75. DBWE 4, 226–32: preaching, baptism and the Lord's Supper, and the ordained office are the first marks named by Bonhoeffer. Bonhoeffer mentions church order right before the preaching office but primarily to state (against German Christian intrusion) that church order belongs to the purpose and mission of the church, not to be changed from the outside (pp. 230–31). For Luther's understanding of the marks of the church, see Martin Luther, "On the Councils and the Church," in vol. 41 of *Luther's Works* (Philadelphia: Fortress, 1966), 148–67; and Bernhard Lohse, *Martin Luther's Theology: Its Historical and Systematic Development* (Minneapolis: Fortress, 1999), 283–85.

76. DBWE 4, 230: "The order of the church-community is of divine origin and character." Church order was particularly important during Bonhoeffer's time because German Christians had taken numerous leadership roles in the Protestant

church. Hence, Bonhoeffer mentions that church order can be modified, but not from outside the church (p. 231).

77. Compare DBWE 4, 202: "It is within the church that Jesus Christ calls through his word and sacrament. The preaching and sacrament of the church is the place where Jesus Christ is present."

78. DBWE 4, 232.

79. Compare Wright, *Creation, Power, and Truth*, 47: The truth of the gospel is not a private truth but a "public truth for the public world" since "the risen Jesus is Lord of earth as well as heaven."

80. DBWE 4, 245. Emphasis original.

81. DBWE 4, 249-50.

82. David Gides is right to point out the starkness of the church-world divide in *Discipleship*. David M. Gides, *Pacifism, Just War, and Tyrannicide: Bonhoeffer's Church-World Theology and His Changing Forms of Political Thinking and Involvement* (Eugene, OR: Pickwick, 2011), 250-56. Against Gides, however, I believe the starkness of the church-world divide is secondary to the logic of the Christ-church relation, which enables Bonhoeffer's *prophetic* critique of the church in *Discipleship*. The logic enables different kinds of critiques in different contexts, which accounts for Bonhoeffer's different tone with nearly identical logic in *Ethics*.

83. Perhaps, this alternative underlies Bonhoeffer's comments on slavery in *Discipleship* (DBWE 4, 235-47). If these are the options, it is better to be oppressed than to be an oppressor. Bonhoeffer might seem to justify the status quo, but such a reading does not correspond well with the broader prophetic call of the book.

84. The theme of the church's sinfulness has also been emphasized by Cavanaugh, *Migrations of the Holy*, 141-69; and Michael Mawson, "The Spirit and the Community: Pneumatology and Ecclesiology in Jenson, Hütter, and Bonhoeffer," *International Journal of Systematic Theology* 15, no. 4 (2013): 453-68.

85. Gides, *Pacifism, Just War, and Tyrannicide*, 270.

86. Gides, *Pacifism, Just War, and Tyrannicide*, 208-9.

87. Compare Stanley Hauerwas, *Performing the Faith: Bonhoeffer and the Practice of Nonviolence* (Grand Rapids, MI: Brazos, 2004), 56: "the first task of the church is not to make the world more just but to make the world the world."

88. For Gides it seems as if the church *qua church* is ruled out as a political community *apriori*. It is only in relationship to the state that the church can act politically, according to Gides. This can be seen in Gides' understanding that the church's difference from the secular is already apolitical (*Pacifism, Just War, and Tyrannicide*, 256) and in his reference to the church as sect (p. 209), following Ernst Troeltsch's typology. For analysis and critique of Troeltch and this typology, see Nathan R. Kerr, *Christ, History and Apocalyptic: The Politics of Christian Mission* (Eugene, OR: Cascade, 2009), 23-62.

89. Phil. 2:6-7.

90. Michael J. Gorman, "'Although/Because He Was in the Form of God': The Theological Significance of Paul's Master Story (Phil 2:6-11)," *Journal of*

Theological Interpretation 1, no. 2 (2007): 150; Michael J. Gorman, *Becoming the Gospel: Paul, Participation and Mission* (Grand Rapids, MI: Eerdmans, 2015), 108.

91. Rom. 15:1–4; Gal. 6:2; Col. 3:13, as just a few examples.

92. Gorman, *Becoming the Gospel*, 109: "Paul's master story is both a narrative about Christ and a narrative about the church."

93. Rom. 8:3. Emphasis added. See also DBWE 12, 355–57.

94. Compare Gorman, "'Although/Because He was in the Form of God,'" 161: "Although Christ was in the form of God, which leads us to certain expectations, he subverted and deconstructed these expectations when he emptied and humbled himself, which he did *because* he was the *true* form of God." Emphases original.

95. "Vicarious representative action," *Stellvertretung*, is important in Bonhoeffer's corpus. Clifford Green notes the Christological root and the connection to responsibility: "In 1942, having defined 'life' by Jesus, Bonhoeffer argues that the life of Jesus is not the isolated individual seeking personal perfection but that of the One who lives in vicarious representative action for humanity; he is 'the responsible person par excellence.'" Clifford J. Green, *Bonhoeffer: A Theology of Sociality*, rev. ed. (Grand Rapids, MI: Eerdmans, 1999), 313. Green is citing Bonhoeffer's *Ethics*. See also DBWE 6, 231–36.

96. Gorman, *Becoming the Gospel*, 116.

97. James Davison Hunter, *To Change the World: The Irony, Tragedy, and Possibility of Christianity in the Late Modern World* (Oxford: Oxford University Press, 2010), 168: "Politics is the way in which social life and its problems are imagined and it provides the framework for how Christians envision solutions to those problems." Compare William T. Cavanaugh, *Theopolitical Imagination* (London: T&T Clark, 2002), 3.

98. "Social imaginary" refers to "the way that we collectively imagine, even pretheoretically, our social life in the contemporary Western world." Charles Taylor, *A Secular Age* (Cambridge, MA: Belknap Press of Harvard University Press, 2007), 146. More specifically, a social imaginary "is something much broader and deeper than the intellectual schemes people may entertain when they *think* about social reality in a disengaged mode. I am thinking rather of the ways in which they imagine their social existence, how they fit together with others, how things go on between them and their fellows, the expectations which are normally met, and the deeper normative notions and images which underlies these expectations" (171). I was pointed to this definition by James K.A. Smith, *How (Not) to Be Secular: Reading Charles Taylor* (Grand Rapids, MI: Eerdmans, 2014), 143.

99. Hunter, *To Change the World*, 111–49.

100. Bonhoeffer recognizes the importance of credibility to relevant preaching and teaching. From student notes at the end of "Contemporizing New Testament Texts," DBWE 12, 433: "The real offense of the [or with regard to] the world, no longer found comprehensibility, in the cross, but in credibility. . . . Contemporizing: as much as we can, make credible."

101. Hunter, *To Change the World*, 107–9.

102. The response of some Christians during the COVID pandemic of 2020 is an illustration of the will to power, manifested in a narrative of victimhood and *ressentiment*. Public health policy was far too readily interpreted as oppression.

103. Hunter, *To Change the World*, 186.

104. DBWE 8, 390. Earlier in the same sermon, Bonhoeffer posits a similar suggestion to Hunter's for silence (p. 389),

> Our church has been fighting during these years only for its self-preservation, as if that were an end in itself. It has become incapable of bringing the word of reconciliation and redemption to humankind and to the world. So the words we used before must lose their power, be silenced, and we can be Christians today in only two ways, through prayer and in doing justice among human beings. All Christian thinking, talking, and organizing must be born anew, out of that prayer and action.

105. Kilian McDonnell, *The Baptism of Jesus in the Jordan: The Trinitarian and Cosmic Order of Salvation* (Collegeville, MN: The Liturgical Press, 1996), 19.

106. Mark 1:4.

107. Compare this with the fictitious debate between the bishop Archelaus and a disciple of Mani, the Manichean, from the fourth century. McDonnell, *Baptism of Jesus*, 20.

108. Jeffrey A. Gibbs, *Matthew 1:1–11:1*, Concordia Commentary Series (St. Louis: Concordia, 2006), 178.

109. Compare McDonnell, *Baptism of Jesus*, 17: "The baptism of Jesus is related not only to his own righteousness, but to that of the whole people."

110. This is not to say that Jesus' baptism was not meaningful for him. It is a central event of the unfolding of his mission and "creates something new in Christ's spiritual itinerary." Raniero Cantalamessa, *The Holy Spirit in the Life of Jesus: The Mystery of Christ's Baptism*, trans. Alan Neame (Collegeville, MN: The Liturgical Press, 1994), 12.

111. Wright, *Jesus and the Victory of God*, 482–83.

112. No monolithic view of the Messiah existed, but the focus was power and glory. Wright, *Jesus and the Victory of God*, 484–85.

113. Gibbs, *Matthew*, 180. My reference to Luther is to his later recounting of his "evangelical breakthrough" by which he came to know the righteousness of God in Romans 1:17 in a new way. In the 1545 preface to his Latin writings, Luther recalls his breakthrough as recognizing that God's righteousness is not his ontological holiness by which he judges, but his saving deeds by which he makes his creatures righteous, which is received passively by faith. See Robert Kolb, *Martin Luther: Confessor of the Faith* (Oxford: Oxford University Press, 2009), 64–68.

114. Gibbs, *Matthew*, 181. Emphases original.

115. See Wright, *Jesus and the Victory of God*, 477–539, for more on how Jesus identifies himself in Israel's history and as Israel's Messiah.

116. Compare FC, SD, 3, 58: "Therefore, faith looks to the person of Christ, as this person submitted to the law for us, bore our sin, and in going to his Father performed complete and perfect obedience for us poor sinners, *from his holy birth to his death*." Kolb and Wengert, eds., *Book of Concord*, 572. Emphasis added.

117. Phil. 2:7, Rom. 8:3, and Gal. 4:4, respectively.

118. Sam Wells explores the importance of Nazareth in this regard as Jesus simply lived *with* fellow creatures. Samuel Wells, *A Nazareth Manifesto: Being with God* (Malden, MA: Wiley Blackwell, 2015), 23–27.

119. Martin Luther, *Lectures on Galatians, 1535, Chapters 1–4,* vol. 26 of *Luther's Works* (St. Louis: Concordia, 1963), 370–71.

120. Compare Luther, *Galatians,* 277: "Christ was not only found among sinners; but of His own free will and by the will of the Father He *wanted to be* an associate of sinners, having assumed the flesh and blood of those who were sinners and thieves and who were immersed in all sorts of sin." Emphasis added.

121. This is not to say that Jesus could have sinned, which is also a dangerous affront to the church's confession. As Robert Jenson argues, Christological dogma rules out both the reading that Jesus *could not* have sinned by choosing his own desires instead of the Father's and that Jesus *could* have done so. This tension flows from the Christological dogma that Jesus is true man, distinct from the Father, and one with the Father as One of the Trinity. How, then, should one read the story of temptation or the agony in the Garden? "It would appear that the only answer that preserves the narrative integrity both of the pericope itself and of the story of which it is one incident is that he could have fled and that this too, if it had occurred, would have belonged to the divine necessity that determined his life." Jenson, "Identity, Jesus, and Exegesis (2008)," in *Theology as Revisionary Metaphysics,* 86.

122. DBWE 15, 392.

123. DBWE 15, 392.

124. DBWE 15, 392.

125. DBWE 1, 145. Bonhoeffer is speaking generally about sin. For context:

> The reality of sin . . . places the individual in a state of utmost solitude, a state of radical separation from God and other human beings. . . . But the reality of sin places the individual at the same time, both subjectively and objectively, into the deepest, most immediate bond with humanity, precisely because everybody has become guilty.

I was reminded of Bonhoeffer's understanding of sin as isolation by Michael Mawson, *Christ Existing as Community: Bonhoeffer's Ecclesiology* (Oxford: Oxford University Press, 2018), 103.

126. This too is an essential point of the temptation account. Jesus refuses to use power for himself but is determined to be obedient to his Father and to his mission to death upon the cross.

127. Mark 10:35–45 and Matt. 20:20–28.

128. On the meaning of cup and baptism, see R.T. France, *The Gospel of Mark: A Commentary on the Greek Text* (Grand Rapids, MI: Eerdmans, 2002), 416–17.

129. Notice the same logic as Philippians 2:5–11. As Richard Bauckham summarizes, "Only the Servant can also be the Lord." Richard Bauckham, *God Crucified: Monotheism and Christology in the New Testament* (Grand Rapids, MI: Eerdmans, 1998), 61.

130. A paucity of parables pervades Mark's Gospel, but Mark 4:30–32 may be an example. In the other synoptics, plenty of parables subvert the normal ways of the world, such as Luke 14:12–24, the three parables of Luke 15, 16:19–31, and 18:9–14, and Matt. 20:1–16.

131. For example, Mark 10:31: "The last shall be first and the first last."

132. For example, Mark 8:34–38, 9:32–37, and 10:13–16.

133. This is my own paraphrase of Mark 10:42–45.
134. Wright, *Creation, Power, and Truth*, 52–53.
135. John 13:15.
136. Wells, *Nazareth Manifesto*, 80.
137. John 18:6.
138. Much of the remainder of this paragraph echoes Isaiah 53.
139. Mark 15:34. This is profoundly proclaimed by Sam Wells, *Nazareth Manifesto*, 82:

> At the central moment in history, Jesus, the incarnate Son of God, has to choose between being with the Father and being with us. And he chooses us. At the same time the Father has to choose between letting the Son be with us and keeping the Son to Himself. And he chooses to let the Son be with us. That is the choice on which our eternal destiny depends. That is the epicenter of the Christian faith and our very definition of love.

The whole chapter "The Story of Jesus" (pp. 67–85) presents the solidarity of Christ with his creatures far better than I ever could.

140. So Luther: "For Christ is emptied even after the ascension, according to Luther. Christ has gone into glory as the emptied one; he is still found sitting at the right hand of God in the state of humility." Johann Anselm Steiger, "The *Communicatio Idiomatum* as the Axle and Motor of Luther's Theology," *Lutheran Quarterly* 14, no. 2 (2000): 136.

141. DBWE 12, 360. Emphasis added.

142. For example, Joel Biermann, "Sanctuary: The Congregation as Haven in a Hostile World," in *Inviting Community*, ed. Robert Kolb and Theodore J. Hopkins (St. Louis: Concordia Seminary Press, 2013), 195–207.

143. Wells, *Nazareth Manifesto*, 100–1.

144. The common Lutheran Church—Missouri Synod translation of *diakonia* as "mercy" may reflect this. The common trope among conservative Christians of doing evangelism because people will go to hell if you do not is another example. The haves have the gospel and the have nots need the gospel. Such is a common logic of evangelism.

145. On Nazareth and its importance, see Wells, *Nazareth Manifesto*, 23–27.

146. Using elements of the typology of doing justice from Samuel Wells and Marcia A. Owens, *Living Without Enemies: Being Present in the Midst of Violence* (Downers Grove, IL: IVP, 2011), 23–26.

147. Compare Wells, *Nazareth Manifesto*, 102.

148. For three stories that illustrate "being with" at the heart of Christian discipleship, see Wells, *Nazareth Manifesto*, 169–227.

149. Bonhoeffer himself used this category. Compare DBWE 8, 52: "We have for once learned to see the great events of world history from below, from the perspective of the outcasts, the suspects, the maltreated, the powerless, the oppressed and reviled, in short from the perspective of the suffering."

150. I agree with Dietrich Bonhoeffer: "The Bible teaches, however, that the *proclamation* and the conduct of the congregation occur in responsibility for the world.

There is absolutely no evasion of this responsibility; for God loved the world and desires that all people be helped." DBWE 16, 598. Emphasis added.

151. Too often evangelism is considered to be a form of power whereas justice can be done from below. Compare Brian K. Peterson, "Being the Church in Philippi," *Horizons in Biblical Theology* 30 (2008): 178,

> The language Paul uses for the mission of the church and what it is doing in the world is not the language of growth, or even the language of converting the world. It is the language of a communal life that stands against the death dealt by empire. The church is the beginning of God's new creation in concrete ways by gathering, by sharing meals, by breaking down ethnic-social barriers that keep empire stable, and by doing good for all.

For a helpful corrective of Peterson, see Gorman, *Becoming the Gospel*, 125–29.

152. On the importance of credibility in the linking of life and preaching, compare DBWE 14, 433: "Ask ourselves whether through our own lives we have not already robbed [the] scriptural word of credibility." I have adjusted the student notes for clarity.

153. DBWE 8, 500.

154. DBWE 8, 500.

155. See Hunter, *To Change the World*.

156. Compare DBWE 8, 478: "There is no such way back [to the intellectual roots of medieval Christendom]—at least not by willfully throwing away one's inner integrity, but only in the sense of Matt. 18:3, that is, through *repentance*, through *ultimate honesty!*" (First emphasis added; second is original.) Bonhoeffer goes on to speak of the God who empowers such repentance as the God of the cross: "The same God who is with us is the God who forsakes us" (478–79).

157. DBWE 8, 427.

158. DBWE 8, 427. I see a dangerous foundationalism at work in apologetics like this that assumes guilt is universally felt and experienced because it is universally valid. Those who do not feel guilt are assumed to be bad or stupid (e.g., delusional or self-deceptive). To be clear, Christians believe that humanity is universally guilty, but such guilt is a matter of God's judgment, not uninterpreted human experience. In other words, human guilt makes sense within a story, not outside of a frame of interpretation.

159. Compare DBWE 8, 450–51.

160. For the first use of the phrase, see DBWE 8, 424–31. On the meaning of the term, Ernst Feil, *The Theology of Dietrich Bonhoeffer*, trans. Martin Rumscheidt (Philadelphia: Fortress, 1985), 185–91:

> Being of age is not a category primarily of individual maturation but one of epochal social emancipation. Such emancipation causes people to cope with their problems, be they scientific, ethical, cultural, or religious, without God; they no longer live in the heteronomy of a certain world view and its corresponding understanding of God. (186)

161. Hence, Bonhoeffer's continual focus on worldliness within the prison letters. For example, DBWE 8, 480–82. The clear example of this triumphalism in

contemporary North American Christianity is creation science, which is so convinced of its truth that the only people listening are in its own echo chamber.

162. DBWE 8, 457.

163. DBWE 8, 426–28.

164. Compare Bonhoeffer's poem "Christians and Heathens" (DBWE 8, 460–61): "People go to God when they're in need/ plead for help, pray for blessing and bread/ for rescue from their sickness guilt, and death. So do they all, all of them, Christians and heathens." Stanzas 2 and 3 go on to speak of Jesus, the God of the cross, "poor, reviled, without shelter or bread," "devoured by sin, weakness, and death," who yet "forgives . . . both" Christians and heathens by his death.

165. DBWE 8, 514–15: "What we imagine a God could and should do—the God of Jesus Christ has nothing to do with all that."

166. DBWE 8, 479.

167. DBWE 8, 501.

168. DBWE 8, 515.

169. DBWE 8, 503.

170. DBWE 8, 503.

171. DBWE 6, 134.

172. DBWE 6, 135.

173. Compare DBWE 1, 214: "In the church, as in any other community, people repent both for their own sin and for that of the collective person of the community." When the church repents for the world, it considers itself part of the "collective person" of the world—part of the same story in my language. On the connection of responsibility and guilt in Bonhoeffer, see also Christine Schliesser, *Everyone Who Acts Responsibly Becomes Guilty: Bonhoeffer's Concept of Accepting Guilt* (Louisville, KY: Westminster John Knox, 2008), 174.

174. DBWE 16, 543.

175. DBWE 6, 135.

176. DBWE 6, 140.

177. DBWE 6, 138–40.

178. DBWE 6, 141.

179. DBWE 6, 142.

180. DBWE 6, 142.

181. Jennifer M. McBride, "Thinking within the Movement of Bonhoeffer's Theology: Towards a Christological Reinterpretation of Repentance," in *Religion, Religionlessness and Contemporary Western Culture: Explorations in Dietrich Bonhoeffer's Theology*, ed Stephen Plant and Ralf K. Wüstenberg (Frankfurt: Peter Lang, 2007), 107: the church "vicariously represents Christ to the world by taking the crucified Christ's form of confession unto repentance," witnessing to the world in the same manner as the humiliated Christ.

182. DBWE 11, 377–78: "We prefer our own thoughts to those of the Bible. We no longer read the Bible seriously. We read it no longer against ourselves but only for ourselves."

183. FC, SD, 3, 58. Kolb and Wengert, eds., *Book of Concord*, 572.

Conclusion

If ecclesiology rightly attends to the interrelations of Christ, church, and world—as I have argued throughout—ecclesiology is not primarily a matter of theological theory but of preaching and teaching the Scriptures faithfully and the local congregation's response in word and deed in the world. In other words, the identity and mission of the church come from listening to the Bible and scriptural preaching, receiving Christ and his forgiveness in Word and Sacrament, and then living in the story of Christ with and in the world. Christ is present in his church as God's law and gospel are proclaimed, baptism is administered, the body and blood of Jesus are offered and received, sins are confessed and forgiven, the Scriptures are faithfully taught, prayers are offered for the world, and the church suffers in solidarity with the poor and the vulnerable as it works to enact God's justice and embody Christ's loving service.[1] Such practices embody the stories of Christ the Lord and Servant because in them the Lord Jesus gives himself to his people and these practices participate in his coming kingdom. Through the same, the church is formed into Christ's likeness and called to live into his mission.

One challenge of my approach to ecclesiology is that I have given no simple definition for what the church is, focusing instead on the Christ-church-world triad. I suppose that I could define the church this way: The church is the creature of God's Word, inhabited by the Christ through the Spirit, that has been brought into the mission of God to be lived in the world. Such a definition is true as it stands, but it obscures as much as it illumines. For instance, these questions remain: Who is this God, Christ, and Spirit? What is the content of this Word of God? How should the world be understood? The dialectics of the Christ-church-world triad may not be as simple as a definition, but the triad avoids the inherent oversimplifications of simple definition by recognizing the relational dimensions of the church's identity and mission. Moreover, the content of what one says about Christ is just as important for shaping the church as the fact that the church is defined in relationship to Christ. The same holds true for the world. The church needs not only to be defined in terms of Christ and the world, but both Christ and the world must also be biblically and narratively portrayed in order to describe the church accurately.

To this end, I have narrated the scriptural accounts of Christ the Lord and Christ the Servant to depict the church and the world in relation to the incarnate Son of God and bring about a reorientation of the church to the God who so sent his Son into the world in the power of the Spirit. This understanding of the church is neither simple nor static. The point is not to define the church by a particular model or a few propositions—although propositions are certainly involved. The point is to see the church in the narrative of the Scriptures, the story of God who created all things and reconciled the entire cosmos to himself through his Son. In this story, the church does not find itself alone, but in relationship to the triune God and the world that God created but does not know its true identity as God's world. In Christ, the church comes to know itself and the world, and is formed by the Spirit into his mission.

The church gains the mind of Christ, a Christian imagination, by inhabiting the Bible, reading the stories of Christ the Lord and Christ the Servant not as mere information or doctrine but as a reality that is lived in the real world. Trusting in Christ and living in his story, the church embodies the basic Christian conviction—eroded away in modernity—that in light of the risen Christ, "*sub specie resurrectionis*, everything looks different."[2] In this new reality, the church learns to read, interpret, and dwell in the world, believing that Christ is present and active and attending to God's Word to be sculpted into faithful witnesses and doers of God's justice for others. As part of this formation into the story of Christ, the church also learns to regard the world as God's own. In recognizing the world as part of God's story with inherent God-given value, the church is enabled to partner with what is good, just, and right in the world, listen to fellow creatures, and serve it from below. Thereby, the church testifies to its conviction that the world is God's creation, redeemed in Christ, and waiting to be filled with the Spirit to the brim in the eschaton. As God's people wait for the consummation of the age, the church delivers the justice of the new age in God's Word of justification and prefigures the shalom of God's justice in deeds of service with the world. In Christ, the church lives in and with the world on his mission.

LUTHERAN ECCLESIOLOGY

I am afraid that some will finish this book exasperated that I have not written an ecclesiology at all. Perhaps, they will think, this is missiology or social ethics or Christology or hermeneutics, or some weird mix of all four. Whatever it is, this is not an ecclesiology. After all, I have not even attempted to address fellowship, ecumenism, church structure, or ordination and ministry. The criticism hits home to a point. I have not addressed many of the questions that a typical ecclesiology confronts. Nevertheless, I believe that I have tackled the most important questions faced by congregations: How does Christ relate to his people that he has created for himself? How should the church view the world in which it is placed? What is the church's mission to the world and how does the Spirit shape it for God's own mission? Ecclesiology in the Christ-church-world triad reforms the most important questions of ecclesiology to be closer to the inquiries of the early church, for example, "How does the church embody Christ in the world?" rather than, "How does ecclesiology fit into a theological system?"

Although I have not concentrated on the typical questions of ecclesiology, my storied ecclesiology of the Christ-church-world triad does correspond to the formulations of Nicaea: one, holy, catholic, and apostolic. The church is *one*, as the people are called by the one gospel and inhabited by the one Lord through the one Spirit into various congregations, instantiations of the *una sancta*. What makes the church *one* is the presence of Christ Jesus in it by Word and Sacrament and his one mission to which he has called his church. This perspective certainly reveals the travesty of the church's divisions, but in the Christ-church-world triad the oneness of the church also points to the goal of Christ's mission. The world is not one with the church by faith right now, but it is ultimately one, both eschatologically in hope and as part of the one story of God in Christ which gives all things their true ontology as created, sinful, and redeemed. The church is *holy*, as it is set apart from the world, distinct in the Christ-church relation. Such a perspective does not annul the church's sinfulness nor its solidarity with the world, but the church's holiness does underscore Christ's presence in his church, making it his own body, and emphasizes how Jesus gave the church his own mission to the world. The church is *catholic*, as it embodies and lives in the true story of the *whole* world. Not only is the church one church throughout the world, but its catholicity also recognizes the world as the object of Christ's mission and a fellow participant in Christ's story. Finally, the church is *apostolic*, as it stands on the witness of the apostles and their doctrine to confess the identity of Jesus as One of the Trinity who has come into the flesh, to proclaim the gospel of forgiveness of sins in Jesus, and to receive Christ's Word that sends the church on his mission, following the apostles as they followed Christ. If the Christ-church-world triad is at all helpful in identifying the church, much more needs to be said to fill out these marks and address other typical questions of ecclesiology.[3] For now, it is enough to demonstrate that my

Christ-church-world ecclesiology remains within the church's confession of the Nicene Creed.

Although my project may not seem like a typical ecclesiology, it does follow the trajectory of the Lutheran ecclesiology of the Word in focusing on preaching more than structure. In fact, one of the reasons that my ecclesiology has not addressed traditional questions of the church is because of my indebtedness to the logic of the Lutheran ecclesiology of the Word. I agree with the Lutheran ecclesiology of the Word that the most important way that Jesus creates and forms his church is through preaching, and preaching takes precedence over polity.[4] I follow this logic in highlighting the relationships of Christ to the church and the world that are known in and formed by preaching and teaching the gospel. Consequently, my goal has not been to describe the church as an institution but to provide resources to read the Scriptures ecclesiologically, recognizing church and world as proper characters in the story of the Bible and proclaiming Christ, church, and world together in one story to form the church for God's mission.

In this way, the gospel is the center of the church, and the church is a creature of the Word, as the Lutheran Confessions assert, but God's Word is more than just the origin of the church. God's Word forms the church's identity and being, sustains its life, gives it its mission, and propels it to faithfulness in the world. The church needs theological description not only for its origin and being but also for how the Spirit forms its life in Christ for visible faithfulness in the world. Following Bonhoeffer's Christology, the church stands rooted in the Christ who justifies *extra se*, but it also must recognize the world in Jesus, and live out its relationship in the world on the basis of Christ the Lord and Servant. Such a perspective needs concrete preaching and teaching, calling congregations to repentance for their complicity in partisan politics and therapeutic individualism, recognizing Christ's presence in the means of grace, painting a picture of the world in Christ, and helping congregations to follow Jesus in their local communities.

DIETRICH BONHOEFFER'S THEOLOGY

Although the primary goal of this book is to repair Lutheran ecclesiology, Dietrich Bonhoeffer has been my main resource and interlocutor throughout the project, and I have outlined the Christological logic of his thought. Although every scholar agrees that Bonhoeffer's work is Christological, his theology has been used to ground everything from conservative evangelicalism to liberal movements like the death of God theology.[5] Abstracted from the Christ-church-world triad in which I contextualized Bonhoeffer's understanding of both the Christ-church and the Christ-world relations, such divergent interpretations of Bonhoeffer begin to make sense. When the world is forgotten from the triad, the Christ-church relation can be construed quite easily in terms of personal faith, especially for those steeped in evangelicalism. In a similar way, scholars who ignore the Christ-church relation emphasize social justice and politics, mining Bonhoeffer for insights into social ethics in a secular world but losing the importance of the Word and the sacraments in Bonhoeffer's thought.[6] To be clear, many of Bonhoeffer's works emphasize one relation of the Christ-church-world triad in order to call the church to repentance and faithfulness, but Bonhoeffer never obliterates the triad. The logic of the triad is explored in his Christology lectures and is present throughout his corpus.[7]

In light of the Christ-church-world triad, Bonhoeffer's infamous comment in the prison letters on *Discipleship* comes into sharp relief: "Today I clearly see the dangers of that book [*Discipleship*], though I still stand by it."[8] Bonhoeffer admits that he was overly focused on the church's obedience to Christ in *Discipleship*, marginalizing the Christ-world relation that also needs to shape the church and the Christian life. Hence, in the later works, Bonhoeffer establishes the Christ-world relation to balance the triad, but he could never reject the centrality and place of the Christ-church relation, as accentuated in the Finkenwalde period. *Discipleship*'s perspective may be off-kilter, but it could never be simply wrong since it was constructed on Christ.

Although I have begun to explore Bonhoeffer's Christological logic, much remains to be done. While I have offered some evidence for how the Christ-church relation functions in Bonhoeffer's later works, I have not answered most of the questions or issues that persist in Bonhoeffer's theology. I believe that the dialectics of the Christ-church-world triad illuminates the provocative mix of traditional and revolutionary in Bonhoeffer's corpus, but I have not shown this extensively or even deeply. In addition, I have interpreted Bonhoeffer as a kind of Lutheran pragmatist, who employs theological dialectics to call to repentance and construct the church in Christ.[9] To be clear, Bonhoeffer never shied away from theory or doctrine—criticizing a Jamesian pragmatism that only worries about what works[10]—but he also employs a pragmatic approach that is concerned for how theology is actually lived.[11] Although my interpretation of Bonhoeffer may be evidence that a pragmatic reading of Bonhoeffer works, Bonhoeffer's pragmatism—also in light of his reading of William James at Union Theological Seminary[12]—needs to be explicitly explored, especially as Bonhoeffer's thought relates to Lutheran theology.[13]

Christ, church, and world: until Christ's return, the church will not cease to be the body of Christ in, with, and called to the world on Christ's mission. Whether facing the post-Christendom challenges of today or whatever tomorrow may bring, the stories of Christ the Lord and Christ the Servant give the church its foundation in the transcendent Christ who stands over his body and is fully present in it, and they open the church's eyes to see the world in light of Christ and propel it to faithful mission with the world. The dynamic of Christ-church-world will not cease until the new age dawns, and it is ecclesiology's task during the interim to inform Christian preaching and teaching so that the church is formed into Christ by his Spirit for the mission of God in every time and place.

NOTES

1. These are Luther's seven marks of the church—though I have reduced ordination to aptitude (*faithful* preaching and teaching)—but as a conclusion to my Christological understanding of the church rather than a presupposition. For the marks, see Martin Luther, "On the Councils and the Church," in vol. 41 of *Luther's Works* (Philadelphia: Fortress, 1966), 148–67.

2. John Webster, *Word and Church: Essays in Christian Dogmatics*, Cornerstones (London: Bloomsbury T&T Clark, 2016), 2.

3. Note that earlier in the conclusion I identified Luther's seven marks of the church within my account of the church as well.

4. Lutherans have structured themselves in many ways. Philip Melanchthon, in his subscription to the *Smalcald Articles*, was even willing to accept papal rule as long as the Pope's authority was acknowledged *iure humano*, and preaching of the gospel was given free rein. Robert Kolb and Timothy J. Wengert, eds., *The Book of Concord: The Confessions of the Evangelical Lutheran Church* (Minneapolis: Fortress, 2000), 326.

5. See Stephen R. Haynes, *The Bonhoeffer Phenomenon: Portraits of a Protestant Saint* (Minneapolis: Fortress Press, 2004).

6. This seems to have happened in some recent Bonhoeffer scholarship. For instance, many of the recent topics in Bonhoeffer conferences have been more political than theological.

7. I am not yet convinced about *Sanctorum Communio*, DBWE 1. Parts of the logic are definitely present, but I have yet to decide whether Christology is truly the center of his account of the church. Michael Mawson, however, has argued that it is: *Christ Existing as Community: Bonhoeffer's Ecclesiology* (Oxford: Oxford University Press, 2018), 144–49. Michael DeJonge's analysis of *Act and Being* shows the same logic at work in Bonhoeffer's account of revelation: Michael P. DeJonge, *Bonhoeffer's Theological Formation: Berlin, Barth, and Protestant Theology* (Oxford: Oxford University Press, 2012).

8. DBWE 8, 486.

9. Compare my argument in "Luther and Bonhoeffer on the Sermon on the Mount: Similar Tasks, Different Tools," *Concordia Theological Journal* 7, no. 1 (Winter 2020): 33–58.

10. DBWE 15, 458–62.

11. On Bonhoeffer's theology as lived, see Michael Pasquarello III, *Dietrich: Bonhoeffer and the Theology of a Preaching Life* (Waco, TX: Baylor University Press, 2017) and Derek W. Taylor, *Reading Scripture as the Church: Dietrich Bonhoeffer's Hermeneutic of Discipleship* (Downers Grove, IL: IVP, 2020).

12. See Martin Rumscheidt, "The Formation of Bonhoeffer's Theology," in *The Cambridge Companion to Dietrich Bonhoeffer*, ed. John W. de Gruchy (Cambridge: Cambridge University Press, 1999), 67.

13. Lutheran theology has its own pragmatic strand. See Scott Edward Yakimow, "Proclamatory Pragmatism: An Investigation into the Lutheran Logic of Law and Gospel," (PhD diss., University of Virginia, 2014).

Bibliography

Arand, Charles P. "What Are Ecclesiologically Challenged Lutherans to Do? Starting Points for a Lutheran Ecclesiology." *Concordia Journal* 34 (2008): 157–71.
Augustine. *On Christian Teaching.* Translated by R.P.H. Green. New York: Oxford University Press, 1999.
Austin, J. L. *How to Do Things with Words.* 2nd ed. Oxford: Clarendon Press, 1975.
Avram, Wes, editor. *Anxious about Empire: Theological Essays on the New Global Realities.* Grand Rapids, MI: Brazos, 2004.
Badcock, Gary D. *The House Where God Lives: Renewing the Doctrine of the Church for Today.* Grand Rapids, MI: Eerdmans, 2009.
Barker, H. Gaylon. *The Cross of Reality: Luther's* Theologia Crucis *and Bonhoeffer's Christology.* Minneapolis: Fortress, 2015.
Barna, George. *Marketing the Church.* Colorado Springs, CO: NavPress, 1988.
Barnett, Victoria. *For the Soul of the People: Protestant Protest Against Hitler.* New York: Oxford University Press, 1992.
Barth, Karl. *Church Dogmatics.* 4 vols in 13. Edited by G.W. Bromiley and T.F. Torrance. 1936–69. Reprint, Peabody, MA: Hendrickson, 2010.
———. *The German Church Conflict.* Richmond, VA: John Knox, 1965.
———. *The Humanity of God.* Atlanta: John Knox, 1960.
———. *The Word of God and the Word of Man.* Translated by Douglas Horton. New York: Harper & Row, 1957.
Bauckham, Richard. *God Crucified: Monotheism and Christology in the New Testament.* Grand Rapids, MI: Eerdmans, 1998.
Bayer, Oswald. "Hermeneutical Theology." *Scottish Journal of Theology* 56, no. 2 (2003): 131–47.
———. *Living by Faith: Justification and Sanctification.* Translated by Geoffrey W. Bromiley. Grand Rapids, MI: Eerdmans, 2003.
———. *Martin Luther's Theology: A Contemporary Interpretation.* Translated by Thomas H. Trapp. Grand Rapids, MI: Eerdmans, 2008.

———. *Theology the Lutheran Way*. Translated and edited by Jeffrey G. Silcock and Mark C. Mattes. Grand Rapids, MI: Eerdmans, 2007.

Bellah, Robert N., Richard Madsen, William M. Sullivan, Ann Swidler, and Steven M. Tipton. *Habits of the Heart: Individualism and Commitment in American Life*. Updated ed. Berkeley, CA: University of California Press, 1996.

Bergen, Doris L. *Twisted Cross: The German Christian Movement in the Third Reich*. Chapel Hill, NC: University of North Carolina Press, 1996.

Berger, Peter L. *Facing Up to Modernity: Excursions in Society, Politics, and Religion*. New York: Basic Books, 1977.

Bethge, Eberhard. *Dietrich Bonhoeffer: A Biography*. Rev. ed., edited by Victoria J. Barnett. Minneapolis: Fortress, 2000.

Biermann, Joel D. *A Case for Character: Toward a Lutheran Virtue Ethics*. Minneapolis: Fortress, 2014.

———. "Sanctuary: The Congregation as Haven in a Hostile World." In *Inviting Community*, edited by Robert Kolb and Theodore J. Hopkins, 195–207. St. Louis: Concordia Seminary Press, 2013.

Biggar, Nigel. "Is Stanley Hauerwas Sectarian?" In *Faithfulness and Fortitude: In Conversation with the Theological Ethics of Stanley Hauerwas*, edited by Mark Thiessen Nation and Samuel Wells, 141–60. Edinburgh: T&T Clark, 2000.

Bliese, Richard H. "Dietrich Bonhoeffer (1906–1945)." In *Twentieth-Century Lutheran Theologians*, edited by Mark C. Mattes, 223–48. Göttingen: Vandenhoeck & Ruprecht, 2013.

Bloomquist, Karen L., editor. *Being the Church in the Midst of Empire: Trinitarian Reflections*. Minneapolis: Lutheran University Press, 2007.

Bonhoeffer, Dietrich. *Act and Being: Transcendental Philosophy and Ontology in Systematic Theology*. Edited by Wayne Whitson Floyd, Jr. Vol. 2 of *Dietrich Bonhoeffer Works English Edition*. Minneapolis: Fortress, 1996.

———. *Barcelona, Berlin, New York: 1928–1931*. Edited by Clifford J. Green. Vol. 10 of *Dietrich Bonhoeffer Works English Edition*. Minneapolis: Fortress, 2008.

———. *Berlin: 1932–1933*. Edited by Larry L. Rasmussen. Vol. 12 of *Dietrich Bonhoeffer Works English Edition*. Minneapolis: Fortress, 2009.

———. *Conspiracy and Imprisonment: 1940-1945*. Edited by Mark S. Brocker. Vol. 16 of *Dietrich Bonhoeffer Works English Edition*. Minneapolis: Fortress, 2006.

———. *Creation and Fall: A Theological Exposition of Genesis 1–3*. Edited by John W. de Gruchy. Vol. 3 of *Dietrich Bonhoeffer Works English Edition*. Minneapolis: Fortress, 1997.

———. *Discipleship*. Edited by Geffrey B. Kelly and John D. Godsey. Vol. 4 of *Dietrich Bonhoeffer Works English Edition*. Minneapolis: Fortress, 2001.

———. *Ecumenical, Academic and Pastoral Work: 1931–1932*. Edited by Victoria J. Barnett, Mark S. Brocker, and Michael B. Lukens. Vol. 11 of *Dietrich Bonhoeffer Works English Edition*. Minneapolis: Fortress, 2012.

———. *Ethics*. Edited by Clifford J. Green. Vol. 6 of *Dietrich Bonhoeffer Works English Edition*. Minneapolis: Fortress, 2005.

―――. *Letters and Papers from Prison*. Edited by John W. de Gruchy. Vol. 8 of *Dietrich Bonhoeffer Works English Edition*. Minneapolis: Fortress, 2009.

―――. *Life Together and Prayerbook of the Bible*. Edited by Geffrey B. Kelly. Vol. 5 of *Dietrich Bonhoeffer Works English Edition*. Minneapolis: Fortress, 1996.

―――. *Sanctorum Communio: A Theological Study of the Sociology of the Church*. Edited by Clifford J. Green. Vol. 1 of *Dietrich Bonhoeffer Works English Edition*. Minneapolis: Fortress, 1998.

―――. *Theological Education at Finkenwalde: 1935–37*. Edited by H. Gaylon Barker and Mark S. Brocker. Vol. 14 of *Dietrich Bonhoeffer Works English Edition*. Minneapolis: Fortress Press, 2013.

―――. *Theological Education Underground: 1937–1940*. Edited by Victoria J. Barnett. Vol. 15 of *Dietrich Bonhoeffer Works English Edition*. Minneapolis: Fortress, 2012.

Bowers, Diane Virginia. "Martin Luther and the Joyful Exchange Between Christ and his Christian: Implications for the Doctrine of Justification and the Christian Life." PhD diss., Graduate Theological Union, Berkley, CA, 2008.

Braaten, Carl E. *Mother Church: Ecclesiology and Ecumenism*. Minneapolis: Fortress, 1998.

―――. *That All May Believe: A Theology of the Gospel and the Mission of the Church*. Grand Rapids, MI: Eerdmans, 2008.

Bretherton, Luke. *Christianity and Contemporary Politics: The Conditions and Possibilities of Faithful Witness*. Malden, MA: Wiley-Blackwell, 2010.

Brunner, Peter. "Von der Sichtbarkeit der Kirche." In *Pro Ecclesia: Gesammelte Aufsätze zur dogmatischen Theologie*. Vol. 1, 2nd ed., 205–12. Berlin: Lutherisches Verlagshaus, 1962.

Burridge, Richard A. "From Titles to Stories: A Narrative Approach to the Dynamic Christologies of the New Testament." In *The Person of Christ*, edited by Stephen R. Holmes and Murray A. Rae, 37–60. London: T&T Clark, 2005.

Burtness, James H. "As Though God Were Not Given: Barth, Bonhoeffer, and the *Finitum Capax Infiniti*." *Dialog* 19, no. 4 (1980): 249–55.

Caenegem, R. Van. "Government, Law and Society." In *The Cambridge History of Medieval Political Thought, c. 350–c. 1450*, edited by J.H. Burns, 174–210. Cambridge: Cambridge University Press, 1988.

Cantalamessa, Raniero. *The Holy Spirit in the Life of Jesus: The Mystery of Christ's Baptism*. Translated by Alan Neame. Collegeville, MN: The Liturgical Press, 1994.

Carson, D. A. *The Gospel According to John*. Grand Rapids, MI: Eerdmans, 1991.

Carter, Craig A. *Rethinking Christ and Culture: A Post-Christendom Perspective*. Grand Rapids, MI: Brazos, 2006.

Case-Green, Karen. "Defamiliarization: Purging our Preaching of Platitudes." In *Text Message: The Centrality of Scripture in Preaching*, edited by Ian Stackhouse and Oliver D. Crisp, 145–65. Eugene, OR: Pickwick, 2014.

Cavanaugh, William T. *Migrations of the Holy: God, State, and the Political Meaning of the Church*. Grand Rapids, MI: Eerdmans, 2011.

―――. *Theopolitical Imagination*. London: T&T Clark, 2002.

Chaves, Mark. *American Religion: Contemporary Trends.* 2nd ed. Princeton, NJ: Princeton University Press, 2017.
Chemnitz, Martin. *The Two Natures in Christ.* Translated by J.A.O. Preus. Saint Louis: Concordia, 1971.
Daniel, David P. "Luther on the Church." In *The Oxford Handbook of Martin Luther's Theology,* edited by Robert Kolb, Irene Dingle, and L'ubomír Batka, 333–52. Oxford: Oxford University Press, 2014.
Dean, Kenda Creasy. *Almost Christian: What the Faith of Our Teenagers is Telling the American Church.* Oxford: Oxford University Press, 2010.
Dean, Robert John. *For the Life of the World: Jesus Christ and the Church in the Theologies of Dietrich Bonhoeffer and Stanley Hauerwas.* Eugene, OR: Pickwick, 2016.
———. "For the Life of the World: Jesus Christ and the Church in the Theologies of Dietrich Bonhoeffer and Stanley Hauerwas." PhD diss., University of Toronto, 2014.
———. "A Matter of Mission: Bonhoeffer, the Bible, and Ecclesial Formation." *Didaskalia* 28 (2017–18): 49–74.
De Gruchy, John W., Stephen Plant, and Christiane Tietz, editors. *Dietrich Bonhoeffers Theologie heute: Ein Weg zwischen Fundamentalismus und Säkularismus?* Gütersloh: Gütersloher Verlagshaus, 2009.
DeHart, Paul J. *The Trial of the Witnesses: The Rise and Decline of Postliberal Theology.* Malden, MA: Blackwell, 2006.
DeJonge, Michael P. "Between Fundamentalism and Secularism: Bonhoeffer's Negotiation of Oppositional Pairs in *Ethics* and Its Precedent in *Act and Being.*" In *Dietrich Bonhoeffers Theologie heute: Ein Weg zwischen Fundamentalismus und Säkularismus?,* edited by John W. de Gruchy, Stephen Plant, and Christiane Tietz, 75–89. Gütersloh: Gütersloher Verlagshaus, 2009.
———. *Bonhoeffer's Reception of Luther.* Oxford: Oxford University Press, 2017.
———. *Bonhoeffer's Theological Formation: Berlin, Barth, and Protestant Theology.* Oxford: Oxford University Press, 2012.
Del Colle, Ralph. *Christ and the Spirit: Spirit Christology in Trinitarian Perspective.* New York: Oxford University Press, 1994.
Doyle, Dennis M. *Communion Ecclesiology.* Maryknoll, NY: Orbis, 2000.
Dreher, Rod. *The Benedict Option: A Strategy for Christians in a Post-Christian Nation.* New York: Sentinel, 2017.
Dulles, Avery. *Models of the Church.* Expanded ed. New York: Image Books, 2002.
Dunn, James D.G. *Jesus and the Spirit: A Study of the Religious and Charismatic Experience of Jesus and the First Christians as Reflected in the New Testament.* 1975. Reprint, Grand Rapids, MI: Eerdmans, 1997.
Eriksen, Robert P. *Theologians Under Hitler: Gerhard Kittel, Paul Althaus, and Emanuel Hirsch.* New Haven, CT; London: Yale University Press, 1985.
Evanson, Charles J. "Center and Periphery in Lutheran Ecclesiology." *Concordia Theological Quarterly* 68 (2004): 231–70.
Feil, Ernst. *The Theology of Dietrich Bonhoeffer.* Translated by Martin Rumscheidt. Philadelphia: Fortress, 1985.

Finke, Greg. *Joining Jesus on his Mission: How to be an Everyday Missionary*. Elgin, IL: Tenth Power, 2014.

Fitch, David E. *Faithful Presence: Seven Disciplines that Shape the Church for Mission*. Downers Grove, IL: IVP Books, 2016.

Forde, Gerhard O. *A More Radical Gospel: Essays on Eschatology, Authority, Atonement, and Ecumenism*. Edited by Mark C. Mattes and Steven D. Paulson. Grand Rapids, MI: Eerdmans, 2004.

———. *On Being a Theologian of the Cross: Reflections on Luther's Heidelberg Disputation, 1518*. Grand Rapids, MI: Eerdmans, 1997.

———. *Theology Is for Proclamation*. Minneapolis: Fortress, 1990.

———. "The Work of Christ." In vol. 2 of *Christian Dogmatics*, edited by Carl E. Braaten and Robert W. Jenson, 5–99. Philadelphia: Fortress, 1984.

France, R. T. *The Gospel of Mark: A Commentary on the Greek Text*. Grand Rapids, MI: Eerdmans, 2002.

Franklin, Patrick S. *Being Human, Being Church: The Significance of Theological Anthropology for Ecclesiology*. Milton Keynes, UK: Paternoster, 2016.

Frei, Hans W. *The Identity of Jesus Christ: The Hermeneutical Bases of Dogmatic Theology*. Philadelphia: Fortress, 1975.

Gibbs, Jeffrey A. *Matthew 1:1–11:1*. Concordia Commentary Series. St. Louis: Concordia, 2006.

Gides, David M. *Pacifism, Just War, and Tyrannicide: Bonhoeffer's Church-World Theology and His Changing Forms of Political Thinking and Involvement*. Eugene, OR: Pickwick, 2011.

Gorman, Michael J. "'Although/Because He Was in the Form of God': The Theological Significance of Paul's Master Story (Phil 2:6–11)." *Journal of Theological Interpretation* 1, no. 2 (2007): 147–69.

———. *Becoming the Gospel: Paul, Participation and Mission*. Grand Rapids, MI: Eerdmans, 2015.

Green, Clifford J. *Bonhoeffer: A Theology of Sociality*. Rev. ed. Grand Rapids, MI: Eerdmans, 1999.

———. "Sociality, Discipleship, and Worldly Theology in Bonhoeffer's Christian Humanism." In *Being Human, Becoming Human: Dietrich Bonhoeffer and Social Thought*, edited by Jens Zimmermann and Brian Gregor, 71–90. Eugene, OR: Pickwick, 2010.

Green, Joel B. *The Gospel of Luke*. The New International Commentary on the New Testament Series. Grand Rapids, MI: Eerdmans, 1997.

Guder, Darrell L. *The Continuing Conversion of the Church*. Grand Rapids, MI: Eerdmans, 2000.

———. *The Incarnation and the Church's Witness*. Harrisburg, PA: Trinity Press International, 1999.

———. "Missional Hermeneutics: The Missional Vocation of the Congregation—and How Scripture Shapes That Calling." *Mission Focus: Annual Review* 15 (2007): 125–42.

Gustafson, James M. "The Sectarian Temptation: Reflections on Theology, the Church and the University." *Proceedings of the Catholic Theological Society of America* 40 (1985): 83–94.
Hall, Douglas John. *The End of Christendom and the Future of Christianity*. Valley Forge, PA: Trinity Press International, 1997.
Handy, Robert T. *A Christian America: Protestant Hopes and Historical Realities*. New York: Oxford University Press, 1971.
Harasta, Eva. "Bonhoeffer's Lutheran Ecclesiology and Inter-Religious Dialogue: A Dogmatic Reading of Bonhoeffer." In *Bonhoeffer and Interpretative Theory: Essays on Methods and Understanding*, edited by Peter Frick, 239–50. Frankfurt am Main: Peter Lang, 2013.
———. "One Body: Dietrich Bonhoeffer on the Church's Existence as Sinner and Saint at Once." *Union Seminary Quarterly Review* 62, no. 3–4 (2010): 17–34.
———. "The Responsibility of Doctrine: Bonhoeffer's Ecclesiological Hermeneutics of Dogmatic Theology." *Theology Today* 71, no. 1 (2014): 14–27.
Harrelson, Walter. "Bonhoeffer and the Bible." In *The Place of Bonhoeffer*, edited by Martin E. Marty, 115–39. New York: Association Press, 1962.
Harvey, Barry. "The Narrow Path: Sociality, Ecclesiology, and the Polyphony of Life in the Thought of Dietrich Bonhoeffer." In *Being Human, Becoming Human: Dietrich Bonhoeffer and Social Thought*, edited by Jens Zimmermann and Brian Gregor, 102–23. Eugene, OR: Pickwick, 2010.
Hauerwas, Stanley. *A Better Hope: Resources for a Church Confronting Capitalism, Democracy, and Postmodernity*. Grand Rapids, MI: Brazos, 2000.
———. *A Community of Character: Toward a Constructive Christian Social Ethic*. Notre Dame: Notre Dame University Press, 1981.
———. *The Hauerwas Reader*. Edited by John Berkman and Michael Cartwright. Durham: Duke University Press, 2001.
———. *The Peaceable Kingdom: A Primer in Christian Ethics*. Notre Dame: Notre Dame University Press, 1983.
———. *Performing the Faith: Bonhoeffer and the Practice of Nonviolence*. Grand Rapids, MI: Brazos, 2004.
———. *Sanctify Them in the Truth: Holiness Exemplified*. Nashville, TN: Abingdon, 1998.
———. *With the Grain of the Universe: The Church's Witness and Natural Theology*. Grand Rapids, MI: Brazos, 2001.
———. *The Work of Theology*. Grand Rapids, MI: Eerdmans, 2015.
Hauerwas, Stanley and L. Gregory Jones, editors. *Why Narrative? Readings in Narrative Theology*. Eugene, OR: Wipf & Stock, 1997.
Hauerwas, Stanley and William H. Willimon. *Resident Aliens: Life in the Christian Colony*. Nashville: Abingdon, 1989.
———. "Why *Resident Aliens* Struck a Chord." In *In Good Company: The Church as Polis*, 51–63. Notre Dame: Notre Dame University Press, 1995.
Haynes, Stephen R. *The Bonhoeffer Phenomenon: Portraits of a Protestant Saint*. Minneapolis: Fortress Press, 2004.

Hays, Richard B. *Echoes of Scripture in the Gospels*. Waco, TX: Baylor University Press, 2016.

———. "The Story of God's Son: The Identity of Jesus in the Letters of Paul." In *Seeking the Identity of Jesus: A Pilgrimmage*, edited by Beverly Roberts Gaventa and Richard B. Hays, 180–99. Grand Rapids, MI: Eerdmans, 2008.

Healy, Nicholas M. *Church, World and the Christian Life: Practical-Prophetic Ecclesiology*. Cambridge: Cambridge University Press, 2001.

———. "Communion Ecclesiology: A Cautionary Note." *Pro Ecclesia* 4, no. 4 (Fall 1995): 442–53.

———. "Ecclesiology and Communion." *Perspectives in Religious Studies* 31, no. 3 (Fall 2004): 273–90.

———. *Hauerwas: A (Very) Critical Introduction*. Grand Rapids, MI: Eerdmans, 2014.

———. "Practices and the New Ecclesiology: Misplaced Concreteness?" *International Journal of Systematic Theology* 5 (2003): 287–308.

Heil, Oliver. *Die Auslegung der Bergpredigt im Dritten Reich*. Norderstedt, Ger.: GRIN Verlag, 2011.

Helmer, Christine. "The Subject of Theology in the Thought of Oswald Bayer." *Lutheran Quarterly* 14 (2000): 21–52.

———. *The Trinity and Martin Luther: A Study on the Relationship Between Genre, Language and the Trinity in Luther's Works (1523–1546)*. Mainz: Verlag Philipp Von Zabern, 1999.

Hendrix, Scott. "In Quest for the Vera Ecclesia: The Crisis of Medieval Ecclesiology." *Viator* 7 (1976): 347–78.

Hinlicky, Paul R. *Beloved Community: Critical Dogmatics After Christendom*. Grand Rapids, MI: Eerdmans, 2015.

———. *Luther and the Beloved Community: A Path for Christian Theology after Christendom*. Grand Rapids, MI: Eerdmans, 2010.

———. "Luther's Anti-Docetism in the Disputatio de divinitate et humanitate Christi (1540)." In *Creator est Creatura: Luthers Christologie als Lehre von der Idiomenkommunikation*, edited by Oswald Bayer and Benjamin Gleede, 139–85. Berlin: de Gruyter, 2007.

———. "*Verbum Externum*: Dietrich Bonhoeffer's Bethel Confession." In *God Speaks to Us: Dietrich Bonhoeffer's Biblical Hermeneutics*, edited by Ralf K. Wüstenberg and Jens Zimmermann, 189–215. Frankfurt am Main: Peter Lang, 2013.

Holl, Karl. *The Cultural Significance of the Reformation*. Translated by Karl and Barbara Hertz and John H. Lichtblau. New York: Meridian, 1959.

———. *What Did Luther Understand by Religion?* Edited by James Luther Adams and Walter F. Bense. Philadelphia: Fortress, 1977.

Holland, Scott. "The Problems and Prospects of a 'Sectarian Ethic': A Critique of the Hauerwas Reading of the Jesus Story." *The Conrad Grebel Review* 10, no. 2 (1992): 157–68.

Holmes, Christopher R.J. "Bonhoeffer and Reformed Christology: Towards a Trinitarian Supplement." *Theology Today* 71, no. 1 (2014): 28–42.

Holze, Heinrich, editor. *The Church as Communion: Lutheran Contributions to Ecclesiology*. Geneva: Lutheran World Federation, 1997.

Hopkins, Theodore J. "How Christology Shapes Ecclesiology and Missiology." *Concordia Theological Journal* 4, no. 1 (Fall 2016): 34–45.

———. "Luther and Bonhoeffer on the Sermon on the Mount: Similar Tasks, Different Tools." *Concordia Theological Journal* 7, no. 1 (Winter 2020): 33–58.

———. "Narrating the Church at the Dusk of Christendom: How the Loss of Predominance Affects Congregations." *Concordia Journal* 43, no. 4 (2017): 29–41.

———. "Theology in a Post-Christian Context: Two Stories, Two Tasks." *Concordia Theological Journal* 4, no. 2 (Spring 2017): 43–57.

———. "Theology Is for Confession." *Concordia Theological Journal* 6, no. 1 (2018): 7–9.

Hopkins, Theodore J. and Mark A. Koschmann. "Faithful Witness in Wounded Cities: Congregations and Race in America." *Lutheran Mission Matters* 4, no. 2 (2016): 247–63.

Horton, Michael S. *Lord and Servant: A Covenant Christology*. Louisville, KY: Westminster John Knox, 2005.

———. *People and Place: A Covenant Ecclesiology*. Louisville, KY: Westminster John Knox Press, 2008.

Hunsberger, George R. "Proposals for a Missional Hermeneutic: Mapping a Conversation." *Missiology: An International Review* 39, no. 3 (2011): 309–21.

Hunter, James Davison. *To Change the World: The Irony, Tragedy, and Possibility of Christianity in the Late Modern World*. Oxford: Oxford University Press, 2010.

Hurtado, Larry W. *How on Earth Did Jesus Become a God? Historical Questions about Earliest Devotion to Jesus*. Grand Rapids, MI: Eerdmans, 2005.

Hütter, Reinhard. "The Church as Public: Doctrine, Practice, and the Holy Spirit." In *Bound to Be Free: Evangelical Catholic Engagements in Ecclesiology, Ethics, and Ecumenism*, 19–42. Grand Rapids, MI: Eerdmans, 2004.

———. "The Church as Public: Dogma, Practice, and the Holy Spirit." *Pro Ecclesia* 3 (1994): 334–61.

———. *Suffering Divine Things: Theology as Church Practice*. Translated by Doug Stott. Grand Rapids, MI: Eerdmans, 2000.

Illouz, Eva. *Saving the Modern Soul: Therapy, Emotions, and the Culture of Self-Help*. Berkeley, CA: University of California Press, 2008.

Jacobsen, Eric O. *The Space Between: A Christian Engagement with the Built Environment*. Grand Rapids, MI: Baker Academic, 2012.

Jensen, Alexander S. "Schleiermacher and Bonhoeffer as Negative Theologians: A Western Response to Some Eastern Challenges." *St. Mark's Review* 215, no. 1 (2011): 7–21.

Jenson, Robert W. "How the World Lost its Story." *First Things* 36 (1993): 19–24.

———. "Luther's Contemporary Theological Significance." In *The Cambridge Companion to Martin Luther*, edited by Donald K. McKim, 272–88. Cambridge: Cambridge University Press, 2003.

———. *Systematic Theology*. Two vols. Oxford: Oxford University Press, 1997–1999.

———. *Theology as Revisionary Metaphysics: Essays on God and Creation.* Edited by Stephen John Wright. Eugene, OR: Cascade Books, 2014.

———. *A Theology in Outline: Can These Bones Live?* Edited by Adam Eitel. New York: Oxford University Press, 2016.

Jennings, William James. "The Desire of the Church." In *The Community of the Word: Toward an Evangelical Ecclesiology*, edited by Mark Husbands and Daniel J. Treier, 235–50. Downers Grove, IL: Intervarsity, 2005.

Jinkins, Michael. *The Church Faces Death: Ecclesiology in a Post-Modern Context.* New York: Oxford University Press, 1999.

Jones, L. Gregory. "The Cost of Forgiveness: Grace, Christian Community, and the Politics of Worldly Discipleship." In *Theology and the Practice of Responsibility: Essays on Dietrich Bonhoeffer*, edited by Wayne Whitson Floyd, Jr. and Charles Marsh, 149–69. Valley Forge, PA: Trinity Press International, 1994.

Kande, Karina Juhl. "Biblical Metaphors in Dietrich Bonhoeffer's Understanding of The Church." In *God Speaks to Us: Dietrich Bonhoeffer's Biblical Hermeneutics*, edited by Ralf K. Wüstenberg and Jens Zimmermann, 123–39. Frankfurt am Main: Peter Lang, 2013.

Kelly, J.N.D. *Early Christian Creeds.* 3rd ed. New York: David McKay Company, 1972.

Kelsey, David H. *Eccentric Existence: A Theological Anthropology.* Two vols. Louisville, KY: Westminster John Knox, 2009.

Kenneson, Philip D. and James L. Street. *Selling Out the Church: The Dangers of Church Marketing.* Nashville, TN: Abingdon, 1997.

Kerr, Nathan R. *Christ, History and Apocalyptic: The Politics of Christian Mission.* Eugene, OR: Cascade, 2009.

Kliefoth, Theodor. *Einleitung in die Dogmengeschichte.* Parchim: D.C. Hinstorff, 1839.

Kloha, Jeffrey. "Making Christ's Reign Known: Church in the New Testament." In *Inviting Community*, edited by Robert Kolb and Theodore J. Hopkins, 35–50. St. Louis: Concordia Seminary Press, 2013.

Kolb, Robert. *The Christian Faith: A Lutheran Exposition.* Saint Louis: Concordia, 1993.

———. *Luther and the Stories of God: Biblical Narratives as a Foundation for Christian Living.* Grand Rapids, MI: Baker Academic, 2012.

———. "Luther on the Two Kinds of Righteousness: Reflections on his Two-Dimensional Definition of Humanity at the Heart of his Theology." *Lutheran Quarterly* 13 (1999): 449–66.

———. *Martin Luther: Confessor of the Faith.* Oxford: Oxford University Press, 2009.

———. "The Sheep and the Voice of the Shepherd: The Ecclesiology of the Lutheran Confessional Writings." *Concordia Journal* 36 (2010): 324–41.

Kolb, Robert and Timothy J. Wengert, editors. *The Book of Concord: The Confessions of the Evangelical Lutheran Church.* Minneapolis: Fortress, 2000.

Krötke, Wolf. "Dietrich Bonhoeffer and Martin Luther." In *Bonhoeffer's Intellectual Formation: Theology and Philosophy in His Thought*, edited by Peter Frick, 53–82. Tübingen: Mohr Siebeck, 2008.

———. *Karl Barth and Dietrich Bonhoeffer: Theologians for a Post-Christian World*. Translated by John P. Burgess. Grand Rapids, MI: Baker Academic, 2019.

Kuske, Martin. *The Old Testament as the Book of Christ: An Appraisal of Bonhoeffer's Interpretation*. Translated by S. T. Kimbrough, Jr. Philadelphia: Westminster Press, 1976.

Laato, Timo. "Romans as the Completion of Bonhoeffer's Hermeneutics." *JETS* 58, no. 4 (2015): 709–29.

LaCugna, Catherine Mowry. *God for Us: The Trinity and Christian Life*. San Francisco: Harper, 1991.

Lawrence, Joel. *Bonhoeffer: A Guide for the Perplexed*. London: T&T Clark, 2010.

Lehenbauer, Joel D. "The Theology of Stanley Hauerwas." *Concordia Theological Quarterly* 76 (2012): 157–74.

Lehmkühler, Karsten. "Christologie." In *Bonhoeffer und Luther: Zentrale Themen ihrer Theologie*, edited by Klaus Grünwaldt, Christiane Tietz, and Udo Han, 55–78. Velkd, 2007.

Lindbeck, George A. "The Church as Israel: Ecclesiology and Ecumenism." In *Jews and Christians: People of God*, edited by Carl E. Braaten and Robert W. Jenson, 78–94. Grand Rapids, MI: Eerdmans, 2003.

———. *The Church in a Postliberal Age*. Edited by James J. Buckley. Grand Rapids, MI: Eerdmans, 2002.

———. "Confession and Community: An Israel-like View of the Church." *The Christian Century* 107 (6 May 1990): 492–96.

———. *The Nature of Doctrine: Religion and Theology in a Postliberal Age*. Philadelphia: Westminster, 1984.

———. "The Sectarian Future of the Church." In *The God Experience*, edited by J.P. Whelan, 226–43. New York: Newman, 1971.

Linde, Charlotte. *Life Stories: The Creation of Coherence*. New York: Oxford University Press, 1993.

———. *Working the Past: Narrative and Institutional Memory*. Oxford: Oxford University Press, 2009.

Lingenfelter, Sherwood G. and Marvin K. Mayers. *Ministering Cross-Culturally: An Incarnational Model for Personal Relationships*. 2nd ed. Grand Rapids, MI: Baker Academic, 2003.

Loewenich, Walther von. *Luther's Theology of the Cross*. Translated by Herbert J.A. Bouman. Minneapolis: Augsburg, 1976.

Lohfink, Gerhard. *Jesus of Nazareth: What He Wanted, Who He Was*. Translated by Linda M. Maloney. Collegeville, MN: Liturgical Press, 2012.

Lohse, Bernhard. *Martin Luther's Theology: Its Historical and Systematic Development*. Minneapolis: Fortress, 1999.

Lundberg, Matthew D. "Repentance as Paradigm for Christian Mission." *Journal of Ecumenical Studies* 45, no. 2 (2010): 201–17.

Luther, Martin. *Luther's Works*. American Edition. 55 vols. Edited by Jaroslav Pelikan and Helmut T. Lehman. Philadelphia: Muehlenberg and Fortress; St. Louis: Concordia, 1955–86.

Luzbetak, Louis J. *The Church and Cultures: New Perspectives in Missiological Anthropology*. Maryknoll, NY: Orbis, 1988.
MacIntyre, Alasdair. *After Virtue: A Study in Moral Theory*. 3rd ed. Notre Dame: Notre Dame University Press, 2007.
Mahn, Jason A. *Becoming a Christian in Christendom: Radical Discipleship and the Way of the Cross in America's "Christian" Culture*. Minneapolis: Fortress, 2016.
———. "What Are Churches *For*?: Toward an Ecclesiology of the Cross after Christendom." *Dialog* 51, no. 1 (2012): 14–23.
Mangina, Joseph L. "Bearing the Marks of Jesus: The Church in the Economy of Salvation in Barth and Hauerwas." *Scottish Journal of Theology* 52, no. 3 (1999): 269–305.
———. "The Cross-Shaped Church: A Pauline Amendment to the Ecclesiology of *Koinōnia*." In *Critical Issues in Ecclesiology: Essays in Honor of Carl E. Braaten*, edited by Alberto L. García and Susan K. Wood, 68–87. Grand Rapids, MI: Eerdmans, 2011.
Mannion, Gerard and Lewis S. Mudge, editors. *The Routledge Companion to the Christian Church*. New York: Routledge, 2008.
Marquart, Kurt E. *The Church and Her Fellowship, Ministry, and Governance*. Vol. 9 of Confessional Lutheran Dogmatics, edited by Robert D. Preus. St. Louis: Luther Academy, 1990.
Mattes, Mark C. *The Role of Justification in Contemporary Theology*. Grand Rapids, MI: Eerdmans, 2004.
Matthews, John W. "Responsible Sharing of the Mystery of the Christian Faith: *Disciplina Arcani* in the Life and Theology of Dietrich Bonhoeffer." In *Reflections on Bonhoeffer: Essays in Honor of F. Burton Nelson*, edited by Geffrey B. Kelly and C. John Weborg, 114–26. Chicago: Covenant Publications, 1999.
Marsh, Charles. *Reclaiming Dietrich Bonhoeffer: The Promise of His Theology*. New York: Oxford University Press, 1994.
Marshall, I. Howard. "Political and Eschatological Language in Luke." In *Reading Luke: Interpretation, Reflection, Formation*, edited by Craig G. Bartholomew, Joel B. Green, and Anthony C. Thiselton, 157–77. Grand Rapids, MI: Zondervan, 2005.
Marx, Karl. "The Jewish Question." In *Karl Marx: Early Writings*. Translated and edited by T.B. Bottomore, 3–40. New York: McGraw-Hill, 1964.
Mawson, Michael. *Christ Existing as Community: Bonhoeffer's Ecclesiology*. Oxford: Oxford University Press, 2018.
———. "Christ Existing as Community: The Ethics of Bonhoeffer's Ecclesiology." PhD diss., University of Notre Dame, 2012.
———. "The Spirit and the Community: Pneumatology and Ecclesiology in Jenson, Hütter, and Bonhoeffer." *International Journal of Systematic Theology* 15, no. 4 (2013): 453–68.
McBride, Jennifer M. "Christ Existing as Concrete Community Today." *Theology Today* 71, no. 1 (2014): 92–105.
———. *The Church for the World: A Theology of Public Witness*. Oxford: Oxford University Press, 2012.

———. "Thinking within the Movement of Bonhoeffer's Theology: Towards a Christological Reinterpretation of Repentance." In *Religion, Religionlessness and Contemporary Western Culture: Explorations in Dietrich Bonhoeffer's Theology*, edited by Stephen Plant and Ralf K. Wüstenberg, 91–109. Frankfurt: Peter Lang, 2007.

McClain, Daniel Wade. "What (Not) to do with the Trinity: Doctrine, Discipline, and Doxology in Contemporary Trinitarian Discourse." *Anglican Theological Review* 100, no. 3 (2018): 606–12.

McCormack, Bruce L. *Karl Barth's Critically Realistic Dialectical Theology: Its Genesis and Development 1909–1936*. Oxford: Clarendon, 1995.

McDonnell, Kilian. *The Baptism of Jesus in the Jordan: The Trinitarian and Cosmic Order of Salvation*. Collegeville, MN: The Liturgical Press, 1996.

———. "A Response to D. Lyle Dabney." In *Advents of the Spirit: An Introduction to the Current Study of Pneumatology*, edited by Bradford E. Hinze and D. Lyle Dabney, 262–64. Milwaukee: Marquette University Press, 2001.

McGarry, Joseph. "Formed While Following: Dietrich Bonhoeffer's Asymmetrical View of Agency in Christian Formation." *Theology Today* 71, no. 1 (2014): 106–20.

Melanchthon, Philip. *Commonplaces: Loci Communes 1521*. Translated and edited by Christian Preus. Saint Louis: Concordia, 2014.

Milbank, John. "The Name of Jesus: Incarnation, Atonement, and Ecclesiology." *Modern Theology* 7, no. 4 (1991): 311–33.

———. *Theology and Social Theory: Beyond Secular Reason*. 2nd ed. Malden, MA: Blackwell, 2006.

Moltmann, Jürgen. *The Coming of God: Christian Eschatology*. Translated by Margaret Kohl. Minneapolis: Fortress, 1996.

Moser, J. David. "*Totus Christus*: A Proposal for Protestant Christology and Ecclesiology." *Pro Ecclesia* 29, no. 1 (2020): 3–30.

Moskowitz, Eva S. *In Therapy We Trust: America's Obsession with Self-Fulfillment*. Baltimore: Johns Hopkins University Press, 2001.

Moulaison, Jane Barter. *Thinking Christ: Christology and Contemporary Critics*. Minneapolis: Fortress, 2012.

Mulder, Mark T. *Congregations, Neighborhoods, Places*. Grand Rapids, MI: Calvin College Press, 2018.

Muller, Richard A. "A Note on 'Christocentrism' and the Imprudent Use of Such Terminology." *Westminster Theological Journal* 68 (2006): 253–60.

Nagel, Norman E. "*Martinus*: 'Heresy, Doctor Luther, Heresy!' The Person and Work of Christ." In *The Seven-Headed Luther: Essays in Commemoration of a Quincentenary, 1483–1983*, edited by Peter Newman Brooks, 25–49. Oxford: Clarendon, 1983.

Nation, Mark Thiessen. "Discipleship in a World Full of Nazis: Dietrich Bonhoeffer's Polyphonic Pacifism as Social Ethics." In *The Wisdom of the Cross: Essays in Honor of John Howard Yoder,* edited by Stanley Hauerwas, Chris K. Huebner, Harry J. Huebner, and Mark Thiessen Nation, 249–77. Eugene, OR: Wipf and Stock, 1999.

Nielsen, Kirsten Busch. "Community Turned Inside Out: Dietrich Bonhoeffer's Concept of the Church and of Humanity Reconsidered." In *Being Human, Becoming Human: Dietrich Bonhoeffer and Social Thought*, edited by Jens Zimmermann and Brian Gregor, 91–101. Eugene, OR: Pickwick, 2010.

Nikolajsen, Jeppe Bach. *The Distinctive Identity of the Church: A Constructive Study of the Post-Christendom Theologies of Lesslie Newbigin and John Howard Yoder*. Eugene, OR: Pickwick, 2015.

Nelson, Derek R. *What's Wrong with Sin: Sin in Individual and Social Perspective from Schleiermacher to Theologies of Liberation*. London: T&T Clark, 2009.

Nelson, E. Clifford, editor. *The Lutherans in North America*. Philadelphia: Fortress, 1975.

Nygren, Anders. *Christ and His Church*. Translated by Alan Carlsten. Philadelphia: Westminster, 1956.

Ochs, Peter. "Reparative Reasoning: From Peirce's Pragmatism to Augustine's Scriptural Semiotic." *Modern Theology* 25, no. 2 (2009): 187–215.

O'Donovan, Oliver. *The Desire of the Nations: Rediscovering the Roots of Political Theology*. Cambridge: Cambridge University Press, 1996.

Ozment, Steven. *The Age of Reform (1250–1550): An Intellectual and Religious History of Late Medieval and Reformation Europe*. New Haven: Yale University Press, 1980.

Pangritz, Andreas. "Dietrich Bonhoeffer: 'Within, Not Outside, the Barthian Movement.'" In *Bonhoeffer's Intellectual Formation*, edited by Peter Frick, 245–82. Tübingen: Mohr Siebeck, 2008.

———. *Karl Barth in the Theology of Dietrich Bonhoeffer*. Translated by Barbara and Martin Rumscheidt. Grand Rapids, MI: Eerdmans, 2000.

Pannenberg, Wolfhart. *Systematic Theology*. Vol. 3. Translated by Geoffrey W. Bromiley. Grand Rapids, MI: Eerdmans, 1997.

Pasquarello III, Michael. *Dietrich: Bonhoeffer and the Theology of a Preaching Life*. Waco, TX: Baylor University Press, 2017.

Paulson, Steven D. "Do Lutherans Need a New Ecclesiology?" *Lutheran Quarterly* 15 (2001): 217–34.

———. *Lutheran Theology*. London: T&T Clark, 2011.

———. "No Church of Christ without Christ." In *Seeking New Directions for Lutheranism: Biblical, Theological, and Churchly Perspectives*, edited by Carl E. Braaten, 171–94. Delphi, NY: ALPB Books, 2010.

———. "What Is Essential in Lutheran Worship?" *Word and World* 26 (2006): 149–61.

Pelikan, Jaroslav. "Bonhoeffer's *Christologie* of 1933." In *The Place of Bonhoeffer: Problems and Possibilities in his Thought*, edited by Martin E. Marty, 145–65. New York: Association Press, 1962.

———. *The Emergence of the Catholic Tradition*. Vol. 1 of *The Christian Tradition: A History of the Development of Doctrine*. Chicago: University of Chicago Press, 1971.

Peterson, Brian K. "Being the Church in Philippi." *Horizons in Biblical Theology* 30, no. 2 (2008): 163–78.

Peterson, Cheryl M. "The Church." *Lutheran Quarterly* 30, no. 1 (2016): 43–59.
———. "The Church as Confessing Koinonia of the Spirit." In *Being the Church in the Midst of Empire: Trinitarian Reflections*, edited by Karen L. Bloomquist, 71–90. Minneapolis: Lutheran University Press, 2007.
———. "An *Ecclesia* and *Missio Crucis*: Douglas John Hall's Contribution to the Missional Church Conversation." *Dialog* 54, no. 2 (2015): 162–70.
———. "Lutheran Principles for Ecclesiology." In *Critical Issues in Ecclesiology: Essays in Honor of Carl E. Braaten*, edited by Alberto L. García and Susan K. Wood, 148–71. Grand Rapids, MI: Eerdmans, 2011.
———. "The Question of the Church in North American Lutheranism: Toward an Ecclesiology of the Third Article." PhD diss., Marquette University, 2004.
———. *Who Is the Church? An Ecclesiology for the Twenty-first Century*. Minneapolis: Fortress, 2013.
Peterson, Daniel J. "Beyond Deep Incarnation: Rethinking Theology in Radical Lutheran Terms." *Dialog: A Journal of Theology* 53, no. 3 (2014): 240–49.
Pickard, Stephen. *Seeking the Church: An Introduction to Ecclesiology*. London: SCM Press, 2012.
Plant, Stephen. "'In the Sphere of the Familiar:' Heidegger and Bonhoeffer." In *Bonhoeffer's Intellectual Formation: Theology and Philosophy in His Thought*, edited by Peter Frick, 301–27. Tübingen: Mohr Siebeck, 2008.
———. *Taking Stock of Bonhoeffer: Studies in Biblical Hermeneutics and Ethics*. Surrey, Eng.: Ashgate, 2014.
———. "'We believe in one Lord, Jesus Christ': A Pro-Nicene Revision of Bonhoeffer's 1933 Christology Lectures." In *Christ, Church, and World: New Studies in Bonhoeffer's Theology and Ethics*, edited by Michael Mawson and Philip G. Ziegler, 45–60. London: T&T Clark, 2016.
Plant, Stephen and Ralf K. Wüstenberg, editors. *Religion, Religionlessness and Contemporary Western Culture: Explorations in Dietrich Bonhoeffer's Theology*. Frankfurt: Peter Lang, 2008.
Pless, John T. "Wayward Students of Harnack: Hermann Sasse and Dietrich Bonhoeffer on the Word of God." *Logia* 26, no. 3 (2017): 31–35.
Pribbenow, Brad. *Prayerbook of Christ: Dietrich Bonhoeffer's Christological Interpretation of the Psalms*. Lanham, MA: Lexington Books/Fortress Academic, 2018.
Radner, Ephraim. *A Brutal Unity: The Spiritual Politics of the Christian Church*. Waco, TX: Baylor University Press, 2012.
———. *The End of the Church: A Pneumatology of Christian Division in the West*. Grand Rapids, MI: Eerdmans, 1998.
Rauschenbusch, Walter. *Christianity and the Social Crisis*. 1907. Reprint, New York: Macmillan, 1916.
Rieff, Philip. *The Triumph of the Therapeutic: Uses of Faith After Freud*. 1966. 40th anniv. ed., Wilmington, DE: ISI Books, 2006.
Robinson, David S. *Christ and Revelatory Community in Bonhoeffer's Reception of Hegel*. Vol. 22 of *Dogmatik in der Moderne*. Tübingen: Mohr Siebeck, 2018.

Rochelle, Jay C. "Bonhoeffer and Biblical Interpretation: Reading Scripture in the Spirit." *Currents in Theology and Mission* 22, no. 2 (1995): 85–95.
Rowe, C. Kavin. *Early Narrative Christology: The Lord in the Gospel of Luke*. Berlin: de Gruyter, 2006.
Rumscheidt, Martin. "The Formation of Bonhoeffer's Theology." In *The Cambridge Companion to Dietrich Bonhoeffer*, edited by John W. de Gruchy, 50–70. Cambridge: Cambridge University Press, 1999.
Rutledge, Fleming. *The Crucifixion: Understanding the Death of Jesus Christ*. Grand Rapids, MI: Eerdmans, 2015.
Sánchez M., Leopoldo A. "More Promise Than Ambiguity: Pneumatological Christology as a Model for Ecumenical Engagement." In *Critical Issues in Ecclesiology: Essays in Honor of Carl. E Braaten*, edited by Alberto L. Garcia and Susan K. Wood, 189–214. Grand Rapids, MI: Eerdmans, 2011.
———. "Praying to God the Father in the Spirit: Reclaiming the Church's Participation in the Son's Prayer Life." *Concordia Journal* 32 (2006): 274–95.
———. *Receiver, Bearer, and Giver of God's Spirit: Jesus' Life in the Spirit as a Lens for Theology and Life*. Eugene, OR: Pickwick, 2015.
Sanneh, Lamin. *Translating the Message: The Missionary Impact on Culture*. 2nd ed. rev. Maryknoll, NY: Orbis, 2009.
Sasse, Hermann. *This Is My Body: Luther's Contention for the Real Presence in the Sacrament of the Altar*. Minneapolis: Augsburg, 1959.
Saucy, Mark. "Evangelicals, Catholics, and Orthodox Together: Is the Church an Extension of the Incarnation?" *JETS* 43, no. 2 (2000): 193–212.
Sayers, Mark. *Disappearing Church: From Cultural Relevance to Gospel Resilience*. Chicago: Moody Publishers, 2016.
Scaer, David P. "All Theology Is Christology: An Axiom in Search of Acceptance." *Concordia Theological Quarterly* 80, no. 1–2 (2016): 49–62.
Schliesser, Christine. *Everyone Who Acts Responsibly Becomes Guilty: Bonhoeffer's Concept of Accepting Guilt*. Louisville, KY: Westminster John Knox, 2008.
Schlink, Edmund. *Ökumenische Dogmatik: Grundzüge*. Göttingen: Vandenhoeck & Ruprecht, 1983.
Schmid, Heinrich. *The Doctrinal Theology of the Evangelical Lutheran Church*. 3rd ed. Translated by Charles A. Hay and Henry E. Jacobs. Minneapolis: Augsburg, 1899.
Schmitz, Florian. *"Nachfolge": Zur Theologie Dietrich Bonhoeffers*. Göttingen: Vandenhoeck & Ruprecht, 2013.
———. "'Only the believers obey, and only the obedient believe.' Notes on Dietrich Bonhoeffer's Biblical Hermeneutics with Respect to *Discipleship*." In *God Speaks to Us: Dietrich Bonhoeffer's Biblical Hermeneutics*, edited by Ralf K. Wüstenberg and Jens Zimmermann, 169–86. Frankfurt am Main: Peter Lang, 2013.
———. "Reading *Discipleship* and *Ethics* Together: Implications for Ethics and Public Life." In *Interpreting Bonhoeffer: Historical Perspectives, Emerging Issues*, edited by Clifford J. Green and Guy C. Carter, 147–53. Minneapolis: Fortress Press, 2013.

Schmitz, Florian and Christiane Tietz, editors. *Dietrich Bonhoeffers Christentum: Festschrift für Christian Gremmels*. Gütersloh: Gütersloher Verlaghaus, 2011.

Schwöbel, Christoph. "The Creature of the Word: Recovering the Ecclesiology of the Reformers." In *On Being the Church: Essays on the Christian Community*, edited by Colin E. Gunton and Daniel W. Hardy, 110–55. Edinburgh: T&T Clark, 1989.

Scott, Peter and William T. Cavanaugh, editors. *The Blackwell Companion to Political Theology*. Malden, MA: Blackwell, 2004.

Skydsgaard, K.E., *One in Christ*. Translated by Axel C. Kildegaard. Philadelphia: Muhlenberg Press, 1957.

Smith, Christian with Melinda Lundquist Denton. *Soul Searching: The Religious and Spiritual Lives of American Teenagers*. Oxford: Oxford University Press, 2005.

Smith, James K.A. *The Fall of Interpretation: Philosophical Foundations for a Creational Hermeneutics*. 2nd ed. Grand Rapids, MI: Baker Academic, 2012.

———. *How (Not) to Be Secular: Reading Charles Taylor*. Grand Rapids, MI: Eerdmans, 2014.

———. *Imagining the Kingdom: How Worship Works*. Vol. 2 of Cultural Liturgies. Grand Rapids, MI: Baker Academic, 2013.

———. *Introducing Radical Orthodoxy: Mapping a Post-Secular Theology*. Grand Rapids, MI: Baker Academic, 2004.

———. "The Logic of Incarnation: Towards a Catholic Postmodernism." In *The Logic of Incarnation: James K. A. Smith's Critique of Postmodern Religion*, edited by Neal DeRoo and Brian Lightbody, 3–37. Eugene, OR: Pickwick, 2009.

———. "A Principle of Incarnation in Derrida's (*theologische?*) *Jugendschriften*: Towards a Confessional Theology." *Modern Theology* 18, no. 2 (2002): 217–30.

———. *Speech and Theology: Language and the Logic of Incarnation*. London: Routledge, 2002.

———. *Who's Afraid of Postmodernism? Taking Derrida, Lyotard, and Foucault to Church*. Grand Rapids, MI: Baker Academic, 2006.

Sorum, Jonathan D. "Cheap Grace, Costly Grace, and Just Plain Grace: Bonhoeffer's Defense of Justification by Faith Alone." *Lutheran Forum* 21, no. 3 (1993): 20–23.

Sparks, Paul, Tim Soerens, and Dwight J. Friesen. *The New Parish: How Neighborhood Churches Are Transforming Mission, Discipleship and Community*. Downers Grove, IL: IVP Books, 2014.

Stackhouse, Ian. "The Text Has More Than Enough Thoughts: Bonhoeffer's Lectures on Preaching." In *Text Message: The Centrality of Scripture in Preaching*, edited by Ian Stackhouse and Oliver D. Crisp, 21–33. Eugene, OR: Pickwick, 2014.

Stayer, James M. *Martin Luther, German Saviour: German Evangelical Theological Factions and the Interpretation of Luther, 1917–1933*. Montreal: McGill-Queen's University Press, 2000.

Steiger, Johann Anselm. "The *Communicatio Idiomatum* as the Axle and Motor of Luther's Theology." *Lutheran Quarterly* 14, no. 2 (2000): 125–58.

Sumner, Darren O. "The Twofold Life of the Word: Karl Barth's Critical Reception of the Extra Calvinisticum." *International Journal of Systematic Theology* 15, no. 1 (2013): 42–57.

Tanner, Kathryn. *Christ the Key*. Cambridge: Cambridge University Press, 2010.

Taylor, Charles. *A Secular Age.* Cambridge, MA: Belknap Press of Harvard University Press, 2007.

———. *Sources of the Self: The Making of the Modern Identity.* Cambridge, MA: Harvard University Press, 1989.

Taylor, Derek W. *Reading Scripture as the Church: Dietrich Bonhoeffer's Hermeneutic of Discipleship.* Downers Grove, IL: IVP Academic, 2020.

Thompson, Richard P. "Gathered at the Table: Holiness and Ecclesiology in the Gospel of Luke." In *Holiness and Ecclesiology in the New Testament*, edited by Kent E. Brower and Andy Johnson, 76–94. Grand Rapids, MI: Eerdmans, 2007.

Tietz, Christiane. "Bonhoeffer on the Ontological Structure of the Church." In *Ontology and Ethics: Bonhoeffer and Contemporary Scholarship*, edited by Adam C. Clark and Michael Mawson, 32–46. Eugene, OR: Pickwick, 2013.

———. "'The Church Is the Limit of Politics:' Bonhoeffer on the Political Task of the Church." *Union Seminary Quarterly Review* 60 (2006): 23–36.

Tjørhom, Ola. *Visible Church—Visible Unity: Ecumenical Ecclesiology and "The Great Tradition of the Church."* Collegeville, MN: Liturgical Press, 2004.

Trowitzsch, Michael. "Luther und Bonhoeffer. Zugleich: Eine Meditation über das Mittleramt Jesu Christi." In *Luther—Zwischen den Zeiten*, edited by Christoph Markschies and Michael Trowitzsch, 185–206. Tübingen: Mohr Siebeck, 1999.

Trueman, Carl R. *The Rise and Triumph of the Modern Self: Cultural Amnesia, Expressive Individualism, and the Road to Sexual Revolution.* Wheaton, IL: Crossway, 2020.

Volf, Miroslav. *After Our Likeness: The Church as the Image of the Trinity.* Grand Rapids, MI: Eerdmans, 1998.

Volf, Miroslav and Maurice Lee. "The Spirit and the Church." In *Advents of the Spirit: An Introduction to the Current Study of Pneumatology*, edited by Bradford E. Hinze and D. Lyle Dabney, 382–409. Milwaukee: Marquette University Press, 2001.

Wannenwetsch, Bernd. *Political Worship: Ethics for Christian Citizens.* Translated by Margaret Kohl. Oxford: Oxford University Press, 2004.

———. "The Whole Christ and the Whole Human Being: Dietrich Bonhoeffer's Inspiration for the 'Christology and Ethics' Discourse." In *Christology and Ethics*, edited by F. LeRon Shults and Brent Waters, 75–98. Grand Rapids, MI: Eerdmans, 2010.

Ward, Graham. *The Politics of Discipleship: Becoming Postmaterial Citizens.* Grand Rapids, MI: Baker Academic, 2009.

Ward, Pete, editor. *Perspectives on Ecclesiology and Ethnography.* Grand Rapids, MI: Eerdmans, 2012.

Webster, John. "Ecclesiocentrism." Review of Nicholas M. Healy, *Hauerwas: A (Very) Critical Introduction. First Things* 246 (Oct. 2014): 54–55.

———. "'The Visible Attests the Invisible.'" In *The Community of the Word: Toward an Evangelical Ecclesiology*, edited by Mark Husbands and Daniel J. Treier, 96–113. Downers Grove, IL: Intervarsity, 2005.

———. *Word and Church: Essays in Christian Dogmatics.* Cornerstones series. London: Bloomsbury T&T Clark, 2016.

Wells, Samuel. *A Nazareth Manifesto: Being with God.* Malden, MA: Wiley Blackwell, 2015.

Wells, Samuel and Marcia A. Owens. *Living Without Enemies: Being Present in the Midst of Violence.* Downers Grove, IL: IVP, 2011.

Williams, Reggie L. "Dietrich Bonhoeffer, the Harlem Renaissance, and the Black Christ." In *Bonhoeffer, Christ and Culture,* edited by Keith L. Johnson and Timothy Larsen, 59–72. Downers Grove, IL: IVP Academic, 2013.

Wright, John W. *Telling God's Story: Narrative Preaching for Christian Formation.* Downers Grove, IL: Intervarsity, 2007.

Wright, N.T. *Creation, Power, and Truth: The Gospel in a World of Cultural Confusion.* London: SPCK, 2013.

———. *Jesus and the Victory of God.* Vol. 2 of Christian Origins and the Question of God. Minneapolis: Fortress, 1996.

———. *Paul and the Faithfulness of God.* Vol. 4 of Christian Origins and the Question of God. Book I. Minneapolis: Fortress, 2013.

———. *The Resurrection of the Son of God.* Vol. 3 of Christian Origins and the Question of God. Minneapolis: Fortress, 2003.

Wuthnow, Robert. *America and the Challenges of Religious Diversity.* Princeton, NJ: Princeton University Press, 2005.

Yakimow, Scott Edward. "Proclamatory Pragmatism: An Investigation into the Lutheran Logic of Law and Gospel." PhD diss., University of Virginia, 2014.

Yeago, David S. "'A Christian Holy People': Martin Luther on Salvation and the Church." *Modern Theology* 13, no. 1 (1997): 101–20.

———. "The Church as Polity? The Lutheran Context of Robert Jenson's Ecclesiology." In *Trinity, Time, and Church: A Response to the Theology of Robert W. Jenson,* edited by Colin E. Gunton, 201–37. Grand Rapids, MI: Eerdmans, 2000.

———. "Sacramental Lutheranism at the End of the Modern Age." *Lutheran Forum* 34, no. 4 (Christmass 2000): 6–16.

Yoder, John Howard. *The Politics of Jesus: Vicit Agnus Noster.* 2nd ed. Grand Rapids, MI: Eerdmans, 1994.

———. *The Priestly Kingdom: Social Ethics as Gospel.* 1984. Reprint, Notre Dame: Notre Dame University Press, 2011.

Ziegler, Philip. "Christ for Us Today—Promeity in the Christologies of Bonhoeffer and Kierkegaard." *International Journal of Systematic Theology* 15, no. 1 (2013): 25–41.

———. "'Completely Within God's Doing': Soteriology as Meta-Ethics in the Theology of Dietrich Bonhoeffer." In *Christ, Church, and World: New Studies in Bonhoeffer's Theology and Ethics,* edited by Michael Mawson and Philip G. Ziegler, 101–17. London: T&T Clark, 2016.

———. "Dietrich Bonhoeffer: A Theologian of the Word of God." In *Bonhoeffer, Christ and Culture,* edited by Keith L. Johnson and Timothy Larsen, 17–37. Downers Grove, IL: IVP Academic, 2013.

———. *Militant Grace: The Apocalyptic Turn and the Future of Christian Theology.* Grand Rapids, MI: Baker Academic, 2018.

Zimmermann, Jens. *Incarnational Humanism: A Philosophy of Culture for the Church in the World.* Downers Grove, IL: Intervarsity, 2012.

———. "Reading the Book of the Church: Bonhoeffer's Christological Hermeneutics." *Modern Theology* 28, no. 4 (2012): 764–80.

———. "Suffering with the World: The Continuing Relevance of Dietrich Bonhoeffer's Theology." In *Dietrich Bonhoeffer Jahrbuch 3: 2007/2008*, edited by Clifford J. Green, Kirsten Busch Nielsen, Hans Pfeifer, and Christiane Tietz, 311–37. Gütersloh: Gütersloher Verlagshaus, 2008.

Zimmermann, Jens and Brian Gregor, editors. *Being Human, Becoming Human: Dietrich Bonhoeffer and Social Thought.* Eugene, OR: Pickwick, 2010.

Zizioulas, John D. *Being as Communion: Studies in Personhood and the Church.* Crestwood, NY: St. Vladimir's Seminary Press, 1985.

Subject Index

Augustine, 1, 90n4

baptism, sacrament of, 19, 22, 68n140, 80–81, 111, 115–17, 136n37, 137n47, 147; of Jesus. *See also* Christ
Barth, Karl, 3, 28, 45–47, 54–57, 133n1
Bayer, Oswald, 5–7, 20–22, 27
Bethge, Eberhard, 75, 98n103, 114–15
Bible, ix, 1, 4, 7–9, 18, 19, 22, 24, 30, 31, 38n76, 44, 50, 55–57, 69, 74–79, 83, 86, 88, 105–6, 114–16, 118, 129, 132, 143n150, 147, 148, 150
Bonhoeffer, Dietrich: *Act and Being*, 43–46, 57, 90n10, 93n35, 94n56, 101n129, 152n7; biblical hermeneutics, 69–70, 74–79; Christology lectures, 8–9, 43, 46–57, 70–72, 82, 88–89, 92–93n35, 96n71, 99n112, 125–26, 151; Christology of, ix, 7–9, 43, 46, 57–58, 69, 70, 73, 75–76, 79–80; church-struggle, role in, 80, 114–15, 132; church-world relationship, tension in, ix, 80–82; "Contemporizing New Testament Texts," 59n5, 74–79, 140n100; dialectical thinking, ix, 9, 69–80, 151; *Discipleship*, 9, 64n87, 80–83, 92n35, 95n69, 106, 112, 114–19, 132, 151; ecclesiology of, 2, 114–18, 152n7; *Ethics*, 9, 72–73, 81–84, 87, 95n69, 107, 126, 130–32, 139n82, 140n95; formation into Christ, 71–73; *Letters and Papers from Prison*, 9, 67n128, 81–83, 85, 106–7, 121, 126, 128–30, 132, 143n149, 151; *Life Together*, 80–81, 83, 88, 92–93n35; pragmatism, 64n87, 151; preaching, 52, 78–79, 94n51, 134n5; quietism, 118–19; *Sanctorum Communio*, 57–58, 70–71, 101n129, 101n134, 124, 145n173, 152n7; world, understanding of, 80–84. *See also* marks of the church

Chalcedon, council of, 49–50
Christ: ascension of, 57, 87, 125–26; baptism of, 110, 121–24; centrality of Christology, 29–32; *communicatio idiomatum*, 49–51, 55–57; existing as church-community, 57–58, 71; *extra calvinisticum*, 55–56; *extra ecclesiam*, ix, 9, 19–20, 23, 25, 31–32, 69, 70, 73, 79, 87–88; humiliation of, 41n115, 43–44, 51–58, 73, 78, 87–88, 105–6, 119–20, 122–26, 131–32; incarnation of, 22, 32, 46, 51, 81, 83, 85, 87, 91n21,

104n160, 106, 117, 120, 123, 127; as Lord, 107–14; narrative of, 22, 30–32, 43–44, 48, 52–54, 56–57, 62n52, 74–76, 87–88, 105–7, 116; relationship with church, 54–58, 70–73, 105–7, 114–19, 125–33; relationship with world, 79–87, 105–7, 113–14, 119–20, 123, 125–27, 129–30, 133; resurrection of, 46, 48–49, 51, 54, 57–58, 83, 86, 87, 92n30, 125–26, 139n79, 148 as Servant, 112–13, 119–27, 129–31, 133. *See also* pneumatology; sin; spirit

Christendom, 2, 4, 6, 23, 37n62; post-, vii–viii, 4–7, 9, 24–27, 29–30, 106, 114, 128, 151–52

communion ecclesiology, 2–3, 7, 18, 28, 30

Dean, Robert John, 36n57, 50, 56, 76
DeJonge, Michael, 43–47, 55, 62n61, 97n78, 152n7
dialectic, as method, ix, 8–9, 69–70, 83–84, 86, 105–7, 147–48. *See also* Bonhoeffer, Dietrich

ecumenism, viii, 2–5, 26, 73, 103n159, 149
Eucharist. *See* Lord's Supper
extension of incarnation, church as, 58
extra nos. See justification

Feuerbach, Ludwig, 46–47, 56
Forde, Gerhard, 32n1, 33n13, 35n45, 67n129

Gorman, Michael, viii, 16n67, 120, 144n151

Hauerwas, Stanley, vii, 6, 24–25, 38n70, 84, 96n74, 97n78, 103n153, 139n87
Healy, Nicholas, 7, 11n15, 16n66, 29, 38n70, 89
Hegel, 56, 68n138

heresies, ecclesial, 26, 97n76; merged with world, 30, 133; overidentified with God, 30, 71–73
hermeneutics: biblical, 12n35, 149; ecclesial task, vii–ix, 5–8, 25, 69–70, 87–89, 148–50. *See also* Bonhoeffer, Dietrich
Hinlicky, Paul, 13n40, 49
Holl, Karl, 44–45
Horton, Michael, 24, 36n55, 36n60, 66n122, 73
Hunter, James Davison, 6, 102n147, 120–21
Hütter, Reinhard, 8, 13n38, 21–22, 26–31, 43, 45–46, 71

individualism, vii–ix, 5–6, 8, 18, 20–26, 43, 108–9, 118, 150

Jenson, Robert, 5, 7, 31, 64n96, 65n115, 73, 142n121
justification, 2, 65n101, 67n129, 93n35, 95n69, 103n154, 119, 138n56, 148; and Christology, 51–57, 150; and ecclesiology, 5, 16n62, 17–20, 23–26, 28, 32, 39n90, 45, 69, 114

Kolb, Robert, 18–19, 36n55

law and gospel, 22–24, 52, 71, 105, 147
Lindbeck, George, 3–5, 38n70
locality, 87–89, 118–19, 127–28, 130, 132, 133
Lord's Supper, 5, 7, 50, 52–55, 88–89
Luther, Martin, 122; Christology of, 41n115, 49–50, 55–57, 60n18, 64n93, 123, 125–26; ecclesiology of, 1, 18–19, 25, 26, 90n6, 91n17, 136n37. *See also* marks of the church

marks of the church: in Bonhoeffer, 37n62, 116–17; in Luther, 22, 116, 147; in Nicene Creed, 149–50
Mawson, Michael, 39n95, 83, 90n3, 152n7

McDonnell, Kilian, 40n110, 121–22
Melanchthon, Philip, 18–19, 25, 50, 138n67, 152n4
mission, vii–ix, 6–9, 18, 20, 21, 23–31, 44, 70, 71, 100n118; character of, 85–89, 107, 111, 113–14, 118–20, 121, 126–33, 138n75, 149–50; as Christ's, 25–26, 31, 51, 53, 58, 69–70, 72–76, 79–81, 84, 105–6, 108–9, 111, 116–17, 121, 147–48, 151–52;

narrative, 3, 103n151, 144n158; of God, ix, 7–8, 17, 26, 29, 83–85; identity of the church, 4–5, 7, 32, 57–58, 70, 72–75, 87–89, 108–9, 114–21, 126–33, 147–50; of individual conversion, 20–26; of the world, 83–85

Pannenberg, Wolfhart, 1–2
Paulson, Stephen, 20–23, 39n99
performative speech, 17, 20–22, 24–26, 32, 45, 78–79
Peterson, Cheryl, 5, 40n107, 40n109, 108–9
Pickard, Stephen, 38n69, 72–73, 79–80
Plant, Stephen, 61–62n52, 77
pneumatology, 67n136, 97n76; in Christology, 29–32, 41n116, 55–57; in ecclesiology, 13n39, 26–32, 43, 45–46; and the Word, 18–20, 22, 70–73
politics: ecclesial, necessity of, 17–18, 23–28, 31, 45–46, 102n142, 106, 114–15, 117–19, 126, 136n32; partisan, problem of, viii, 6, 23, 24, 26, 29–32, 71, 85, 120–21, 128, 130
preaching, 8, 10, 21–24, 54, 74, 76, 80, 86, 99–100n118, 128, 130, 133, 140n100, 150. See also word and sacrament, external

repentance, 7, 9, 18, 70–73, 76–79, 85, 89, 100n118, 105–8, 111, 113–15, 118–21, 130–33, 150–51. See also sin
ressentiment. See also politics

Rowe, C. Kavin, 107, 109–13

Sánchez M., Leopoldo A., 32
Schmitz, Florian, 95n69, 99n111, 115–16, 137n47
Scripture. See Bible
sin, 18–22, 24, 26, 54, 70, 80, 88, 98n103, 109–11, 113–15, 138n67, 148; in the church, 6–7, 29, 39n90, 74, 76–79, 83–87, 116, 118–19, 126–27, 129–33, 149; cor curvum in se, 44–45, 47–49; and holiness at the same time, 71–72, 89; and Jesus, 51–52, 56, 120–25, 133;
Smith, James K. A., 16n64, 89
solidarity, 9, 79–80, 83–87, 107, 119, 121, 123–28, 130–33, 148–49
speech act. See performative speech
Spirit. See also narrative; pneumatology; Trinity

Tanner, Kathryn, 30–32
theology of the cross, 76–78, 104n165
therapeutic, 6, 21, 24, 26, 32, 108–9, 114, 150
Trinity, 30–32, 66n119, 142n121

Volf, Miroslav, 11n14, 30–31

Webster, John, 36n56, 36n60, 95n57, 148
Wells, Samuel, 85–86, 125–26
word and sacrament, external, viii, 1, 5–7, 9, 17–20, 25–27, 29, 31, 43, 45, 52–53, 57–58, 59n13, 69–71, 73, 78–79, 81, 88–89, 115–17, 147, 149, 151
Word of God ecclesiology, 5–8, 17–28, 43, 45–46, 150
Wright, N.T., 107–10, 122–23

Yeago, David, 35n47, 115
Yoder, John Howard, 84, 96n74, 112

Zimmermann, Jens, ix, 55, 93–94n49, 97n77, 98n91

Scripture Index

Direct quotations of Scripture are italicized.

Gen. 12:3, 19

Deut. 7:7–8, 19, *33n18*

Is. 53:3–9, 125
Is. 61:1–2, 110

Matt. 2:15, 122
Matt. 3:13–17, *122–23*
Matt. 4:1–11, 123–24
Matt. 8:17, 129
Matt. 18:3, 144n156
Matt. 20:1–16, 142n130
Matt. 20:20–28

Mark 1:4, *121*
Mark 1:12–13, 124
Mark 4:30–32, 142n132
Mark 8:34–38, 142n132
Mark 9:32–37, 142n132
Mark 10:13–16, 143n132
Mark 10:31, *142n131*
Mark 10:35–45, 124
Mark 10:41, 124
Mark 10:42–45, 124–25
Mark 15:34, 125

Luke 1:5–2:52, 135n27
Luke 1:17, *109*
Luke 1:32–33, *109*
Luke 1:43, 109
Luke 1:68–72, *110*
Luke 1:74–79, *110*
Luke 4:18–19, *110*
Luke 5:1–11, *110–11*
Luke 9:20, *111*
Luke 9:23–24, *111*
Luke 9:23–27, 111
Luke 9:57–62, *111–12*
Luke 14:12–24, 142n130
Luke 15, 142–43n130
Luke 16:19–31, 142n130
Luke 18:9–14, 142n130
Luke 22:24–30, 112
Luke 22:27, *112*
Luke 22:47–53, 113

John 1:14, 104n160
John 1:18, *31*
John 13:15, *125*
John 14:9, *31*
John 15:16, *19*, *113*
John 18:6, 125

Rom. 1:17, 141n113
Rom. 8:3, *51*, *52*, *120*, *123*
Rom. 10:9, *107*
Rom. 13:1, 23
Rom. 13:9, 23
Rom. 15:1–4, 140n91

1 Cor. 1:23, 52, 53, 125

Gal. 4:4, *123*, 133
Gal. 4:19, 72

Gal. 6:2, 140n91

Eph. 1:23, 57
Eph. 5:23–32, 70

Phil. 2:5–11, 120
Phil. 2:6–7, *120*
Phil. 2:7, *52*, 73, *123*, 131

Col. 1:15, *31*
Col. 3:13, 140n91

About the Author

Theodore J. Hopkins is associate professor of theology, pre-seminary director, and family life ministry director at Concordia University, Ann Arbor. A systematic theologian by training (PhD Concordia Seminary, St. Louis, 2016), Hopkins' published work and presentations explore Dietrich Bonhoeffer's theology and the church-world relationship in North America as Christendom crumbles. Hopkins enjoys bird-watching, baseball, talking theology with anyone in his proximity, and spending time with his family outdoors. He resides, with his wife and two children, near Ann Arbor, Michigan.

www.ingramcontent.com/pod-product-compliance
Lightning Source LLC
Chambersburg PA
CBHW020121010526
44115CB00008B/923